MW00612065

Marketcraft

Marketcraft

How Governments Make Markets Work

STEVEN K. VOGEL

OXFORD
UNIVERSITY PRESS

OXFORD
UNIVERSITY PRESS

Oxford University Press is a department of the University of Oxford. It furthers
the University's objective of excellence in research, scholarship, and education
by publishing worldwide. Oxford is a registered trade mark of Oxford University
Press in the UK and certain other countries.

Published in the United States of America by Oxford University Press
198 Madison Avenue, New York, NY 10016, United States of America.

Library of Congress Cataloging-in-Publication Data
Names: Vogel, Steven Kent, author.
Title: Marketcraft : how governments make markets work / by Steven K. Vogel.
Description: New York, NY : Oxford University Press, [2018] |
Includes bibliographical references.
Identifiers: LCCN 2017035193 (print) | LCCN 2017044751 (ebook) |
ISBN 9780190699864 (updf) | ISBN 9780190699871 (epub) | ISBN 9780190699857 (hbk)
Subjects: LCSH: Free enterprise. | Capitalism. | Trade regulation. |
Economic policy. | Commercial policy.
Classification: LCC HB95 (ebook) | LCC HB95 .V646 2018 (print) |
DDC 381/.1—dc23
LC record available at https://lccn.loc.gov/2017035193

5 7 9 8 6 4

Printed by Sheridan Books, Inc., United States of America

To Justin, Ellie, and Juliette

May they live in a better governed world.

CONTENTS

ACKNOWLEDGMENTS

This project had a long gestation, and many generously assisted along the way. I sketched some of my initial thoughts in a chapter for a volume called *Creating Competitive Markets* edited by Mark Landy, Martin Levin, and Martin Shapiro, and the editors and author chapters provided valuable feedback. I am especially grateful to the many government officials, business people, and scholars in the United States, Japan, and Europe who agreed to be interviewed for this project. Many colleagues helped to arrange the interviews, including Tetsuya Kagaya, Mindy Kotler, Jun Kurihara, Manabu Nabeshima, Ichiya Nakamura, Peter J. Ryan, Masaaki Sakamaki, Pamela Samuelson, and Nicolas Véron.

Robert Fannion has been an incredible intellectual partner throughout this process, from early-stage brainstorming through brilliant feedback to intensive editing. I have been fortunate to work with an amazing group of doctoral students. In many instances, we reversed roles and they became my best dissertation advisers. Mark Huberty brought me up to speed on some of the key substantive issues at the early stages of research. Alex Roehrkasse educated me on some of the finer points of economic sociology, and provided critical feedback and editing on drafts. Kristi Govella meticulously researched Japanese policies, gathered critical data, and updated me on the latest research in my own field, political science. Brian Judge refined my understanding on theoretical issues and provided comments on the concluding chapter. Jay Varellas tutored me on the arcane details of the law, and offered valuable suggestions for further reading. Akasemi Newsome strengthened my grasp of key elements of the US case. Makoto Fukumoto helped me to find Japanese government documents and to update the sections on Japanese reforms. Maurice Ang, Jongwan Choi, Alex Duran, Trevor Incerti, Sae Kobayashi, Reina Sasaki, Taka Tanaka, Guillermo Tosca Díaz, and Amanda Zhao all provided superb research assistance.

Neil Fligstein, Ezra Vogel, and two anonymous reviewers for Oxford University Press read the entire manuscript and offered valuable comments.

Charles Duan, Kenji Kushida, David Makman, Elsa Massoc, Mari Miura, Manabu Nabeshima, Hiromitsu Ohtsuka, Karthik Ramanna, Daniel Rubinfeld, Toshiko Takenaka, Takakuni Yamane, Hidehiro Yokoo, and John Zysman kindly reviewed excerpts.

I presented papers related to this project at my home department's Comparative Politics Colloquium; a Japan Forum for Innovation and Technology (JFIT)/Stanford Project on Japanese Entrepreneurship (STAJE) Conference at the University of California, San Diego; and a Society for the Advancement of Socio-Economics (SASE) Annual Meeting in Berkeley. Participants offered valuable feedback, especially discussants Nathan Pippenger, Ulrike Schaede, and Yves Tiberghien. I also presented my work at a Center for Japanese Studies faculty luncheon on campus, and benefited from questions and discussion.

Robert Cooter, Barry Eichengreen, Marion Fourcade, Paul Pierson, and Zenichi Shishido—as well as the previously mentioned Fannion, Govella, Judge, and Roehrkasse—participated in a book manuscript workshop hosted by the Institute for International Studies at the University of California, Berkeley. All participants provided fabulous feedback and specific suggestions for improvement. Three Berkeley colleagues from other departments—George Lakoff, Daniel Rubinfeld, and Carl Shapiro—generously agreed to meet with me for some brainstorming and a bit of a tutorial in their respective areas of expertise.

I am grateful for a Japan-US Friendship Commission and National Endowment for Humanities Fellowship for Advanced Social Science Research on Japan. I also received generous financial support from the Committee on Research, the Center for Japanese Studies, and the Il Han New Chair at the University of California, Berkeley.

David McBride, Claire Sibley, and Emily Mackenzie at Oxford University Press masterfully guided the manuscript from review through publication; Prabhu Chinnasamy oversaw production; and Dorothy Bauhoff handled the copy editing.

Most of all, I thank my wife Giena for her love and support.

Marketcraft

The Marketcraft Thesis

Markets need rules not only to protect people and the environment from collateral damage, but also to function effectively in the first place. Our real-world choices therefore hinge not on whether markets should be governed, but on *how* they should be governed.[1] Consider the corporation, the institution at the heart of modern capitalism. There is nothing natural about it. The corporation is a construct that is granted legal identity, governing authority, and limited liability by the law. Or consider the stock market, the ultimate embodiment of the capitalist ethos. It is likewise neither free nor natural, but rather elaborately governed. Stock markets require trading rules not only to prevent abuses, but also simply to operate. And they need more extensive rules, such as corporate disclosure requirements and insider trading restrictions, to flourish and to grow. The following chapters review these and other examples in greater detail, demonstrating how and why governments make markets work. But first, this chapter outlines the core thesis of the book.

The argument begins with the basic recognition that real-world markets are *institutions*: humanly devised constraints that shape human interaction.[2] There is no controversy on this point in its most stripped-down form. Yet scholars differ fundamentally in how they understand market institutions. Market liberals acknowledge that markets require some minimal rules of the game: the government must create the basic infrastructure for a modern economy by enforcing the rule of law, protecting private property, and maintaining a monetary system.[3] Beyond that, however, they argue that the government should not "intervene" in market affairs. Other scholars have increasingly stressed that market systems are governed by a far more extensive web of institutions. Institutional economists, for example, view "transaction costs," such as the costs of obtaining information or enforcing contracts, as the friction in the market system, and property rights as the means to reduce these costs. They move beyond the basic legal and financial infrastructure to study institutions such as business groups and labor contracts.[4] Economic sociologists define market institutions even more broadly, including social networks and cultural norms.[5] They stress that markets are

always *embedded* in society.[6] In this book, I contend that a more expansive definition of market institutions is not simply more accurate, but that it is a prerequisite for informed policymaking and analysis of real-world markets.

I am certainly not the first one to pursue this line of argument. In fact, a
"market-institutional" perspective on political economy has emerged as a virtual consensus among policymakers and across social science disciplines when
applied to markets everywhere *except* in the advanced industrial countries.[7]
Scholars have come to recognize that modern market systems are not natural
phenomena that spontaneously arise, but rather complex institutions that must
be created and sustained by the visible hand of the government. They make this
same basic point with reference to three types of market transition: the historical transition from feudalism to market society in the West, the more recent
transition from communism to capitalism in Eastern Europe and East Asia, and
the ongoing struggle to create viable market systems in many developing countries.[8] Yet for the most part, scholars have failed to apply this same logic to the
subtler transition toward more competitive and more sophisticated market systems in the advanced industrial countries. If markets are institutions, however,
then market reform should be more a process of building institutions than one
of removing constraints, and this should be no less true for more developed market systems than for less developed ones. Ironically, this point is less obvious for
advanced industrial countries because they already have fairly well-developed
market institutions. This book explores why viewing markets as institutions—
complex combinations of laws, practices, and norms—is essential to understanding recent developments in advanced economies such as the United States
and Japan.

Moreover, while some scholars stress that modern markets require effective
governance, many policymakers, journalists, and pundits in the advanced economies continue to pretend that they do not. They speak and act as if there were
such a thing as a "free market" that thrives without governance. They frame economic debates in terms of the false dichotomy of government versus market.[9]
The very language of economic debates—such as the common juxtaposition
of "government intervention" versus "market freedom"—betrays these assumptions, and this conceptual confusion can beget some rather serious policy errors,
as demonstrated in the chapters to follow.

In this book I seek to advance the conversation in three ways. First, I specify
how conventional framing, such as the governments-versus-markets dichotomy,
hampers public debate, policy prescription, and scholarly analysis, and I offer
some modest suggestions for how to deploy more precise language, enhance
conceptual clarity, and refine analysis. Second, I push the logic of the argument further to show how the rather banal assertion that markets are institutions leads logically to some far less obvious propositions, as outlined in the

following section. Finally, in the concluding chapter I demonstrate how even the most sophisticated analysts of market institutions sometimes fail to appreciate the full ramifications of their own arguments. They fall into the same linguistic traps as their intellectual adversaries, for example, or they fail to capture the extent to which market behavior is learned, not natural, and market operations are constructed, not free. And I conclude by demonstrating how conceptual misunderstandings can beget policy errors, and by specifying some lessons for both progressives and market liberals.

This chapter presents the logical sequence of the argument, and the following three chapters explore real-world examples. The final chapter reviews the implications for various debates in the fields of rhetoric, economics, political science, sociology, political theory, and public policy.

The Core Propositions

1. *There is no such thing as a free or perfect market.* Conceptually, we can imagine the proverbial perfectly competitive market in which buyers and sellers would be seamlessly matched. Economists sometimes assume a perfect market for analytical purposes, and they have made important theoretical and empirical advances by building on such simplifying assumptions. But this perfect market does not exist, and it never has. Even primitive marketplaces were not "free" in that they required some basic rules, such as locations or hours of operation. And the institutions underpinning exchange grew more complex as societies introduced credit and money.[10] Douglass North illustrates this poignantly with his example of buying oranges from his favorite vendor. This simple exchange is governed by a personal relationship, market practices, and social norms, all underpinned by the rule of law.[11]

2. *Markets have to be created.* If markets are institutions, then that means that people have to create them. As Karl Polanyi famously quipped, "laissez-faire was planned."[12] The architects of these institutions might be governments, firms, or individuals. And they might create markets deliberately or spontaneously, at one moment in time or over decades or centuries. I am partial to the language of *crafting* markets, as evidenced in the title to this volume, because it highlights the artistry required for effective market governance; it recognizes this as a core government function comparable to statecraft; and it applies to both government and private-sector market governance. But this does not mean that governments always get it right: just as real-world statecraft can be masterful or clumsy, beneficent or disastrous—so it is with marketcraft.

3. *Market reform is primarily a constructive enterprise, not a destructive one.* Here we begin to shift from rather banal observations to less obvious implications.

Yet this proposition follows logically from the ones preceding it. If markets are institutions, then cultivating markets requires building institutions more than destroying them. In short, liberalizing the economy does not mean liberating it. This simple observation has profound implications for how we understand market reform, and fundamentally challenges some of the most common perspectives on the important issues of our day.[13] It demonstrates how a market-institutional perspective begets both scholarly analysis and policy prescriptions that diverge markedly from the market liberal view. Table 1.1 depicts contrasting analytical perspectives in italics, such as "privatization" versus market transition, and corresponding policy prescriptions below them, such as shock therapy versus gradualism. Market liberals have conceived of market reform as "liberalization" rather than institution building, and therefore they have advocated removing barriers ("privatization" and "liberalization") more than building capabilities (market transition and market development). Yet, as noted earlier, scholars have come to recognize that shifting from a planned economy to a market system requires building new institutions more than dismantling old ones, and promoting markets in developing countries requires cultivating the government's ability to sustain market institutions more than just getting overbearing governments out of the way. They have been slower to grasp the implications for the study of market reform in rich countries. Yet even for developed economies, making markets more competitive and expanding them into new realms requires not simply removing regulations that impede competition ("deregulation") but enhancing regulatory capacity and building market institutions, that is, *marketcraft*.

4. *There is no single market solution to a policy challenge.* If there is no such thing as a perfect market, then there is no single free-market solution. Any market solution constitutes a particular form of market governance. Real-world market governance varies across many dimensions: not just government versus market,

Table 1.1 **Market Reform: Removing Barriers or Building Institutions?**

	The Market-Liberal View: Removing Barriers	*The Market-Institutionalist View: Building Institutions*
Post-Communist Countries	*Privatization* Shock Therapy	*Market Transition* Gradualism
Developing Countries	*Liberalization* The Washington Consensus	*Market Development* Building Market Institutions
Advanced Industrial Countries	*Deregulation* Neoliberal Reform	*Market Reform* Marketcraft

but also public versus private governance, laissez-faire versus pro-competitive regulation, and so on. So this means that there are multiple market solutions to any given challenge, reflecting different combinations of points along these various dimensions.

Some market liberals might accept this proposition, yet insist that the crux of the issue still pits government intervention against market freedom. That is, the question is not whether markets have rules or not, but who sets them— the government or the market players. And the government imposes rules by force, whereas market players devise their rules voluntarily. Yet I would counter that in practice the government must play the leading role in market design, for reasons discussed further in the following section. Moreover, the market liberal perspective underestimates the scale and scope of regulation necessary to make modern markets work and overestimates the level of constraint imposed by government action and the degree of freedom allowed by the market. Reducing the government role would not necessarily unleash markets: in fact, it could just as well constrain market actors more, not less. For example, the government might compromise market freedom by failing to rein in private market power, or by withdrawing regulations that support markets. Chapter 5 returns to this issue of the relationship between government action and market freedom at greater length.

5. *There may not even be a more "free-market" or a more market-oriented alternative among policy options.* Even if there is no pure free market, market liberals might argue, we should still posit it as an ideal, a target for policy reform. That is, we should seek to move *toward* the free market, for this would enhance both economic efficiency and personal liberty. Yet most policy choices are not about government versus market, but rather about *how* to govern markets. And if we compare two market designs, it is often not obvious which is more market-like or closer to a free-market solution.

In some cases, it may be possible to judge one option as more market-oriented than another. For example, imposing a tariff implies more government control and less market competition, so removing it could reasonably be viewed as a move toward a hypothetical free market. We should not be surprised that the market liberal worldview fits international trade better than most domestic market governance issues, for it is precisely the issue that motivated Smith and subsequent liberal economists. In most contemporary debates, however, the relevant choices align along dimensions that defy characterization as more or less market oriented. For example, there are complex trade-offs between adversarial versus discretionary styles of government regulation, or open versus closed bidding models for auctions. More fundamentally, it is often not obvious what would constitute a move toward the market. If we shift antitrust policy from a more laissez-faire approach to a more pro-competitive approach, then which is the more market-oriented solution? If we tighten rules over the fair use of copyrighted material, is that a move toward the free market or away from it? The effort to describe these choices in terms of government versus the free market obscures the real choices involved. They involve real trade-offs, but not ones of government versus market. And many contemporary debates take precisely this form, as illustrated in Chapter 2.

6. *The government-versus-market dichotomy that animates most debates about economic policy is fundamentally misleading.* The assumption that there is a dichotomy between government and market impedes a more sophisticated understanding of this relationship. As we move from a thin definition of market institutions (the minimal rules of the game) to a thicker one (a broader range of laws, practices, and norms), the relationship between government and market becomes more complementary. Table 1.2 illustrates how the government-versus-market frame leads us to view economic debates in terms of a choice between government protection/regulation and free markets, rather than as a choice between underdeveloped and more developed markets. In practice, government regulation defines and enables markets, so market reform often entails more government (the arrow moving from less developed to more developed markets), not less (the arrow moving from protection/regulation to "free markets"). Moreover, the government-versus-market framing obscures the fact that the government plays a substantial role in the marketplace beyond that of a referee. The government is the largest consumer, employer, lender, borrower, insurer, and property owner in modern market economies.[14]

7. *The regulation-versus-competition dichotomy that animates most debates about economic regulation is fundamentally misleading.* The very language of "deregulation" belies this misperception. In conventional discourse, the term refers to less regulation and more competition, as if the two were naturally associated. In fact, generating more competition usually requires more regulation, not less. Thus the dominant trend in advanced industrial countries over the past 40 years has not been one of deregulation (less regulation), but rather one of market reform (more competition) through re-regulation (more regulation): that is, freer markets and more rules.[15]

Table 1.2 **Two Conceptions of Market Reform**

	Less Market	*More Market*
More Government	Protected/ Regulated Markets	More Developed Markets
Less Government	Less Developed Markets	"Free Markets"

Deregulation in the literal sense of less regulation and more competition is possible, of course: reducing or eliminating price and entry regulation, for example, should foster more competition. In practice, however, the relationship between regulation and competition tends to be more positive than negative (Figure 1.1). We can refine this point by noting that the relationship between regulation and competition varies across time and across sectors and subsectors. It may be more positive at an early stage of market development, when the government has to create the basic infrastructure to support market competition, and more negative at a later stage, when an incremental increase in the government's role may be more likely to impede than to enhance competition. And it may be more positive in sectors that are conducive to monopoly, such as network industries, and more negative in sectors where barriers to entry are low, such as retail.

Several distinct mechanisms underlie the overall trend toward more regulation with more competition. First, as governments introduce competition in sectors characterized by natural monopoly, such as public utility sectors, they have to deploy pro-competitive regulation to create and sustain competition. Second, as financial markets become more competitive and more sophisticated, governments have to enhance regulation to support these markets, with stricter disclosure requirements, more elaborate trading rules, and more intensive supervision. Third, as product and service markets become more competitive, with a greater number of players, then regulation tends to become more codified and legalistic. Fourth, as transport and product markets become more competitive, governments need to strengthen environmental, health, and safety regulations. If truckers compete more fiercely, for example, governments have to strengthen safety regulation, such as limits on driving hours. In practice, market reform means increasing regulations that enhance competition, such as antitrust rules, and removing regulations that impede it, such as price and entry restrictions.

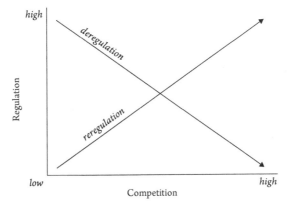

Figure 1.1 Deregulation versus reregulation.

And understanding this process requires carefully differentiating between the two. Despite the overall trend toward greater regulatory complexity, it may be possible to devise simpler regulatory solutions that are equally or more effective in some cases. In finance, for example, higher capital reserve requirements, the structural separation of commercial and investment banks, and a financial transaction tax represent simpler regulatory mechanisms that might reduce the need for some detailed behavioral rules and intensive supervision.

8. *A liberal market economy (LME) like the United States is just as governed as a coordinated market economy (CME) like Japan, possibly more.* LMEs feature more competitive labor, financial, and product markets, whereas CMEs favor greater coordination among firms, banks, and other firms. Scholars of comparative capitalism tend to view LMEs as less institutionalized or less embedded than CMEs.[16] But if markets are institutions, then all markets are governed by distinct combinations of laws, practices, and norms, so LMEs and CMEs are equally governed. Chapter 3 examines this proposition via a detailed case study of the United States, demonstrating how this "freest" of market economies relies on a massive infrastructure of market governance.

One could even argue that a more liberal market system would actually require a *more* elaborate institutional apparatus. Chapters 3 and 5 return to this proposition in greater detail, but one possible synthesis would hinge on differentiating between two different meanings of "more governed." LMEs may require more governance in the limited sense of more laws and regulations to support markets. But with respect to the private side of governance, such as business practices or social norms, it may make more sense simply to conclude that all markets are governed, and to leave it at that.

9. *A coordinated market economy like Japan requires more governance, not less, to shift toward the liberal market model.* This proposition follows logically from propositions 3 and 8. Chapter 4 examines this proposition at length, demonstrating that Japanese leaders publicly vowed to shift in the direction of a more liberal market system beginning in the 1990s, but to do so they had to enact a daunting array of legal and regulatory reforms and to launch campaigns to alter business practices and embrace market values. And despite all of this effort, Japan still did not converge on the liberal market model.

10. *The information revolution requires more market governance, not less.* Advances in information technology (IT) have dramatically reduced the cost and increased the speed of many market transactions. Yet technology has also created new challenges of market design that defy the government-versus-market dichotomy. The information economy requires more governance because the core commodity—information—is itself the product of rules, such as patent and copyright protection. So governance becomes more essential to economic performance, and also more complex. IT markets also rely heavily on

sectors where regulation is essential, such as telecommunications and finance. The information revolution enables the fabrication of sophisticated markets, such as complex auctions or financial derivatives markets, which in turn rely on more intricate market governance. And the information economy poses new challenges for antitrust enforcement, discussed further in Chapters 2 and 3.

Some of these propositions (1–7) follow logically, whereas others (8–10) will require more empirical evidence for support. The next three chapters review the evidence, but first let us address the critical question of whether governments must govern markets, and define a few key terms.

Market Governance

We have established that markets require governance, but does that mean that governments have to do the governing? Governments have been the central actors in the three transformations noted in the preceding sections: the historical evolution of the market system in the West, the transition from command to market economies in Eastern Europe and East Asia, and the construction of market institutions in developing countries today. Governments play the central role in market governance because they have the unique ability to create and enforce laws and regulations over a given territory.[17] Ronald Coase argues, in his seminal article on "The Problem of Social Cost," that private actors could resolve problems of market governance on their own via private settlements *if* there were no transaction costs.[18] This essay motivated some market liberals to deploy the "Coase theorem" to argue that private contracts could replace government regulation in various arenas.[19] In practical terms, however, governments have to establish the property rights system that undergirds private settlements. Governments also have greater administrative and financial capabilities than private-sector actors, and they tend to be more neutral, legitimate, and accountable. David Moss argues that governments have several critical attributes when it comes to risk-management: for example, the ability to compel participation; a near-perfect credit rating, based on the power to tax and print money; and unparalleled monitoring capabilities, rooted in regulatory and enforcement powers.[20]

Yet governments certainly do not govern markets alone. They sometimes delegate regulation to private-sector "self-regulatory organizations" and standard-setting bodies. A wide range of private-sector organizations contribute to market governance, from industry associations to trade unions. The relationships among private-sector actors—such as management-labor relations, bank-industry relations, supply chains, and distribution networks—also structure markets. Private-sector practices govern markets, from vocational training systems to research and development consortia. And of course societal norms powerfully condition market behavior.

In order to study market governance, therefore, we have to examine both government and private-sector governance, and the interaction between the two. Thus I favor the term *governance* rather than *regulation* because the latter tends to refer more exclusively to government regulation. I define *governance* as follows, following Mark Bevir:

> Governance refers to all processes of governing, whether undertaken by a government, market, or network; whether over a family, tribe, corporation, or territory; and whether by laws, norms, power, or language. Governance is a broader term than government because it focuses not only on the state and its institutions but also on the creation of rule and order in social practices.[21]

Bringing private governance into the analysis is critical for making sense of several of the key propositions in the preceding section. For example, there is no free market (Proposition 1) and the government-versus-markets dichotomy is misleading (Proposition 6) in part because even if we were able to eliminate the laws and regulations that govern markets, this would still leave the private governance of markets in place. And the regulation-versus-competition dichotomy is misleading (Proposition 7) because even if we were able to eliminate anti-competitive laws and regulations, this would leave private anti-competitive practices intact.

Market liberals would contend that government regulation is nonetheless more problematic than private governance not only because it is more threatening to personal liberty (as noted earlier), but also because it is more vulnerable to capture by special interests seeking to game the system for their own benefit. These interests may seek to influence regulation to earn "rents," in the terminology of political economy, meaning unearned income or returns above market value. But if markets are always governed, and market governance includes both government regulation and private-sector practices, then it follows that private firms can seek rents whether or not the government acts. Private firms may seek monopoly profits by anti-competitive behavior in the marketplace as well as by lobbying the government to favor them.[22] In fact, they may be freer to seek rents in the absence of government regulation. To be clear, I am not arguing that government regulation is not vulnerable to capture. Chapters 2–4 will provide many examples of regulatory capture. But I contend that capture is a variable and not a constant; that public sector governance is no more conducive to rent-seeking than private governance; that government failure to act can foster rent-seeking just as much as government action; and that effective government regulation can limit it.

Let me now turn to defining market and market development, before presenting a simple typology of market governance. The *market* can refer to an abstraction, the proverbial perfect market, or to a concrete real-world market: a place of exchange such as a farmers' market, or a product market such as the automobile market. A perfect market would have many buyers and sellers, comparable products, complete information, no enforcement costs, and supply and demand would determine prices. This volume focuses on real-world markets, not perfect markets, so it defines *markets* simply as arenas in which buyers and sellers come together to exchange goods and/or services.[23]

To move beyond the perfect market ideal to study real-world market institutions, we need to conceive of *market development* in a way that does not rely exclusively on that ideal. Of course the perfectly competitive market provides a valuable metric: more buyers and sellers, better information, and better enforcement of contracts represent elements of market development. The most critical piece is competition, which can be defined by the number of firms in a given product market and the market shares of those firms (market structure), the ability of new entrants to challenge incumbents (contestability), and the ability of challengers to redefine the market. But market development also includes the expansion of the scale of the market (whether measured by trading volume or geographical territory), the expansion of the scope of the market (to more products and services), the creation of new markets (including new marketplaces, such as stock exchanges, as well as the "fabricated" markets discussed in the following chapter), and the increase in the sophistication of markets (including greater speed and accuracy in the transmission and storage of data, more developed financial markets, and more elaborate market design).[24] Chapter 2 explores the myriad ways in which market governance can foster or impede market development broadly defined in this way. It identifies institutional prerequisites for certain types of market development, but it also stresses the diversity of governance arrangements. I do not assume that market development necessarily promotes societal welfare. I set aside for the conclusion a fuller discussion of the normative question of the ultimate goals that markets serve, such as growth, innovation, equity, health, safety, and environmental protection. For present purposes, however, I can simply note that I view markets as means, not ends. We can craft them to achieve whatever purposes we want—and we should.

We can usefully divide market governance into three broad clusters: laws and regulations, practices and standards, and norms and beliefs. Table 1.3 divides these clusters into subcategories with selected examples. *Laws* refer to any legislation passed by the government, from corporate law to labor law. *Regulations* include more detailed rules derived from laws; directives issued by government agencies, courts, or self-regulatory organizations; and enforcement by these agencies, courts, and organizations. *Practices* comprise a wide range of

Table 1.3 **Market Governance by Category (With Selected Examples)**

Laws and Regulations	Practices and Standards	Norms and Beliefs
• Laws enacted by national or state legislatures • Regulations issued by government agencies, courts, or private-sector organizations • Enforcement of regulations by government agencies, courts, or private-sector organizations • Litigation, such as shareholder or private antitrust suits	• Private-sector monitoring, such as credit agencies or professional guilds • Private-sector market design, such as the mortgage-backed security market • Business collusion, such as cartels • Business coordination, such as industry associations or R&D consortia • Interfirm networks, such as bank groups or supply chains • Business customs, such as recruiting practices • Conventions, such as technical or accounting standards • Codes of conduct, such as corporate governance codes	• Social norms, such as company loyalty • Moral codes, such as minimizing harm or maximizing personal liberty • Legal doctrines, such as the rule of reason for antitrust cases • Ideologies, such as market liberalism or Marxism • Regulatory doctrines, such as fair-value accounting • Policy paradigms, such as the Chicago School of antitrust • Theories, such as the efficient markets hypothesis

private-sector behavior, including monitoring, such as credit agencies or professional guilds; market design, such as the creation of the mortgage-backed security market; collusion, such as cartels; coordination, such as industry associations or research and development (R&D) consortia; interfirm networks, such as bank groups or supply chains; and business customs, such as employment or corporate governance systems. *Standards* refer to conventions, such as technical or accounting standards, and codes of conduct, such as corporate governance codes. Laws and regulations differ from practices and standards in that they are binding and enforceable. Laws and regulations also tend to be public and formal, while practices and standards are private and informal—but there are exceptions and hybrid cases that preclude a clear demarcation. For example, private self-regulatory bodies sometimes issue binding and enforceable rules, and public agencies sometimes issue non-binding guidance. *Norms* encompass values, such as company loyalty or shareholder value, and moral codes, such as minimizing harm or maximizing personal liberty. *Beliefs* subsume broad political ideologies, such as market liberalism; legal doctrines, such as the rule of reason; regulatory doctrines, such as fair-value accounting; policy paradigms, such as the Chicago School of antitrust; and theories, such as the efficient markets thesis.

We can also break down market governance by substantive issue area. The examples in Table 1.4 are merely illustrative; they do not represent a comprehensive list, nor do they depict a particular national model. Many analysts of

Table 1.4 **Market Governance by Substantive Issue-Area (Selected Examples)**

	Laws and Regulations	*Practices and Standards*	*Norms and Beliefs*
Corporate Governance	Limited liability	Committee-system corporate boards	Companies should maximize returns to their shareholders.
Accounting	Corporate financial disclosure rules	Accounting standards	Companies should disclose information to investors thoroughly and honestly.
Banking	Capital reserve requirements	Private lending pools	Banks should base lending on the borrower's ability to pay.
Capital Markets	Insider-trading regulation	Stock exchange trading practices	Brokers should act in the best interests of their clients.
Labor Markets	Dismissal rules	Private mediation	Employers should hire on the basis of merit, not relationships.
Antitrust	Merger rules	Price competition strategies	Firms should not be allowed to dominate an industry.
Sector-Specific Regulation	Price and entry regulation	Electricity trading practices	Firms should compete, not collude.
Intellectual Property Rights	Fair-use rules	Cross-licensing	Firms should only receive patents for substantial innovations.

political economy focus on particular types of regulations that constrain markets, such as tariffs and quotas or price and entry controls. This volume shifts attention to the broader range of governance mechanisms that create, define, and empower markets. It focuses primarily on market governance (financial, labor, and industry regulation) and not social regulation (such as health, safety, and environmental regulation) because it seeks to explore the degree to which markets require governance to function and/or to flourish in the first place— not why they require regulation to limit harm to people and to nature. It is far more obvious that markets require regulation to limit collateral damage (social regulation) than that markets require regulation for their own sake to function and to flourish (market governance). Market governance and social regulation are interrelated, of course, and the concluding chapter explores this relationship further. For present purposes, however, this remains a useful analytical distinction that allows us to focus on market governance per se.

2

The Elements of Marketcraft

How do you craft a market? This chapter reviews some of the key institutions necessary to make markets function and flourish (summarized in Table 2.1). These institutions structure markets by defining market actors, such as corporations; constructing goods, such as intellectual property rights; establishing market arenas, such as stock exchanges; setting the rules of exchange, such as trading practices; and promoting competition via antitrust enforcement. In all of the substantive issue cases reviewed in this chapter, government regulation and private-sector coordination are not impediments to markets, but rather preconditions to their creation, expansion, and dynamism. There is no free-market solution to the governance challenges they pose. It is even difficult to imagine what it would mean to move *toward* the free-market ideal because attempts to reduce government or private-sector regulation would be more likely to undermine markets than to liberate them. There is not a single market solution, but rather a multitude of possible market arrangements. Some countries may achieve equally effective solutions to these governance challenges in different ways; some may develop better or worse solutions; and some may fail to resolve them altogether. The policy options do not align along a spectrum from government to market, or from regulated to competitive markets. Rather, the critical debates involve practical questions of market design and political choices about whom to favor in that design.

Table 2.2 presents some of the key trade-offs involved in the substantive choices over market design, and some of the interest cleavages that characterize political debates. Some of these interest cleavages align along familiar divides of right versus left, capital versus labor, or producer versus consumer, but many split along different axes, such as managers versus shareholders, rights holders versus users, or incumbents versus challengers. In some cases, the interest cleavages follow the market design trade-offs in a relatively straightforward manner. Copyright holders will prefer stronger copyright protection, for example, and users will favor more generous fair use provisions. In many cases, however, the interest cleavages are more complex. Financial institutions will favor some

Table 2.1 Market Governance Challenges and Possible Solutions (Selected Examples)

	Challenge	Possible Solution(s)
The Corporation	Firms need a legal status distinct from the individuals involved.	Incorporation
	Owners in a partnership can force the liquidation of assets.	Asset "lock in"
	Investors are reluctant to purchase shares due to liability risk.	Limited liability
Accounting	Market actors need comparable measures.	Accounting standards
	Investors need access to information about firms to buy and sell shares.	Disclosure requirements
Banking	Banks are vulnerable to bank runs.	Deposit insurance
	Deposits insurance may allow banks to take more risks (moral hazard).	Monitoring and supervision, restrictions on the use of assets, reserve requirements
Capital Markets	Investors need assurance that they will not be defrauded by insiders.	Insider trading rules
	Investors need third-party evaluations of credit risk in bond markets.	Credit-rating agencies
Corporate Governance	Managers may serve their own interests over the interests of the firm or shareholders.	Stakeholder representation on boards, independent directors
	Managers may serve other stakeholders over shareholders.	Shareholder representation on boards, shareholder voting rights
Labor Markets	Employers may take advantage of workers.	Labor market regulation
	Workers may halt economic activity via strikes in essential sectors.	Prohibitions on strikes in certain sectors, government mediation of labor disputes

Table 2.1 **Continued**

	Challenge	Possible Solution(s)
Antitrust	Firms may collude.	Antitrust enforcement
	Dominant firms may abuse market power.	Regulate mergers, break up larger firms
Sector-Specific Regulation	Companies in network industries may exercise monopoly power.	Price regulation
	Incumbents may continue to exercise market power, even with competition.	Pro-competitive regulation (favoring challengers over incumbents)
Intellectual Property Rights	Firms or individuals may not have sufficient incentive to innovate.	Patents and copyrights
Fabricating Markets	Some markets may require such elaborate coordination that they will not spontaneously appear.	Deliberate market design by the government and/or private firms
	Markets may be so complex that they require some shared knowledge to function.	Training for market participants

financial regulations some of the time, for example, because sound regulation can stabilize markets and foster more financial activity, but they will oppose regulations they view as too costly or constraining. And the cleavages across sub-segments of the financial industry—such as investment banks versus commercial banks—will reflect the specific nature of regulation and competition among these segments in that particular country at that particular time.

The Corporation

The visible hand of the government created the corporation. Governments had to assume this responsibility because the corporation is a legal entity. And yet governments did not have to craft corporations in the particular ways that they did. Political and business leaders struggled over how to govern the corporation, and they continue to do so today. There is no single market solution to the question of how to structure a corporation. Different countries have devised different ways to hold managers accountable, to limit the legal liability of investors, and to define the rights and obligations of shareholders. In practice, those

Table 2.2 **Market Governance Trade-offs and Political Cleavages**
(Selected Examples)

	Market Design Trade-offs	*Political Interest Cleavages*
The Corporation	Limited liability versus corporate accountability	Shareholders versus claimants
Accounting	Relevance versus reliability versus comparability Fair value versus historical value Rules-based versus principle-based	Industrial firms versus financial institutions versus accountants Managers versus shareholders
Banking	Efficiency versus stability Deposit insurance versus moral hazard	Banks versus corporate clients versus retail customers versus taxpayers
Capital Markets	Efficiency versus stability Innovation versus fraud prevention	Investment banks versus commercial banks Wall Street versus Main Street
Corporate Governance	Managerial discretion versus shareholder control Shareholder versus stakeholder sovereignty	Managers versus shareholders versus workers versus other stakeholders (customers, the community)
Labor Markets	Employer flexibility versus worker security Managerial authority versus worker participation	Employers versus workers
Antitrust	Economies of scale versus benefits of competition Laissez-faire versus aggressive enforcement	Large firms versus small firms Dominant firms versus challengers Producers versus consumers
Sector-Specific Regulation	Economies of scale versus benefits of competition Laissez-faire versus pro-competitive regulation	Incumbents versus challengers Service providers versus consumers
Intellectual Property Rights	Innovation versus technology diffusion Strong protection versus fair use	Rights holders versus users Producers versus patent trolls
Fabricating Markets	Public interest versus private profit	Taxpayers/citizens versus private firms Health insurance companies versus care providers versus patients

governments that have cultivated the most dynamic markets have also devised the most elaborate rules.

In late medieval Italy, merchants began to form "companies" to share risks and profits. Over time, governments sanctioned these companies as legal identities distinct from their partners.[1] In the seventeenth century, the English government directly chartered companies such as Hudson's Bay Company and the East India Company to run state monopolies.[2] Governments granted companies a legal monopoly over a line of business in exchange for the companies' commitment to serve certain public functions. The government typically took an ownership share alongside private investors.

At the beginning of the nineteenth century, most enterprises beyond individual or family firms were still organized as partnerships. Several wealthy individuals might invest in an enterprise. Typically these individuals knew each other, and their personal relationships established the trust to share risk. They would reap rewards according to their levels of investment, and share liability for losses and claims for damages. Partnerships had several critical drawbacks relative to the limited liability corporations that emerged in the nineteenth century. All of the partners could sign contracts binding the whole firm, meaning that a single rogue partner could bring down the firm. Partnerships were generally required to dissolve upon the death of a partner.[3] And partners bore unlimited liability for the firm's debts and damages.

New York State enacted the world's first incorporation law for manufacturing companies in 1811, with a provision that limited shareholder liability to the amount invested, and other states gradually followed suit.[4] In England, partisans fought a protracted battle over the legal basis for the modern corporation that culminated in victory for the proponents of limited liability with the Joint Stock Companies Act of 1856. The limited liability corporation subsequently emerged as the dominant form of firm organization. Limited liability was transformative because it allowed larger numbers of smaller shareholders to invest in a corporation without the fear of losses that could far exceed the initial investment. Hence the limited liability corporation facilitated portfolio investment and diversification, and set the stage for modern financial markets and capitalism as we know it today.[5]

The irony of the rise of the corporation—and the critical point for our purposes—is that the government had to actively intervene in the economy to "liberate" modern financial markets. It had to create and to define an artificial commodity: an ownership share in the form of a stock certificate. And it had to offer shareholders a particular form of protection—limited liability—for corporations to thrive. Adam Smith, among others, was highly critical of the joint stock corporation, stressing that it would undermine the principle of individual responsibility:

> This total exemption from trouble and from risk, beyond a limited sum, encourages many people to become adventurers in joint stock

companies, who would, upon no account, hazard their fortunes in any private copartnery. Such companies, therefore, commonly draw to themselves much greater stocks than any private copartnery can boast of. . . . The directors of such companies, however, being the managers rather of other people's money than of their own, it cannot well be expected that they should watch over it with the same anxious vigilance with which the partners in a private copartnery frequently watch over their own.[6]

In other words, the community would bear part of the risk of the company's losses, so managers would be more likely to take excessive risks or otherwise shirk their duty.

Modern capitalism developed on the foundation of this particular institutional innovation. One could argue about which would be a more natural or "free-market" solution: unlimited or limited liability for shareholders. One might contend that unlimited liability would be the "liberal" solution because it preserves individual responsibility: individuals are liable for their full share of the liabilities of the corporation. They do not rely on the government for protection from their own follies. And yet limited liability represents the "market" solution in the sense that it does the most to expand and invigorate markets. The government has an interest in reducing investors' risk, which it does by limiting liability, because this promotes risk-taking that provides a public good in the form of investment capital.

Corporations thus defy the libertarian dichotomy between government constraint and market freedom. They are government-crafted institutions that enable and empower markets. David Ciepley stresses that corporations differ from partnerships because they have contractual individuality—the right to own property, to make contracts, and to sue and be sued as an individual—and governing rights—the ability to set and enforce rules within their jurisdiction. In this sense, the government allows corporations to violate the standard rules of property, contract, and liability. In a partnership, the partners own the property, make contracts, and take legal action. And if partners want to leave the enterprise, they take their equity with them. This either dissolves the partnership, or forces the remaining partners to liquidate assets to cover the cost. With a corporation, however, investors cannot directly pull out their contributions, but must find someone to buy their shares. Thus the corporation's assets are "locked in" because they are corporate property. This contributes to market development because it allows corporations to commit their assets to production more fully, since they are not vulnerable to investors who may want to sell their stake, requiring the liquidation of assets.[7]

While the political battle over limited liability has been resolved, the struggle over how corporations should be governed—discussed further under the section "Corporate Governance" later in the chapter—continues to this day. But first we turn to three other realms that also constitute elements of corporate governance: accounting, banking regulation, and capital market regulation.

Accounting

If corporations give modern capitalism its organizational form, then accounting gives it a common language. Accounting began as a way to record transactions, and for participants in economic exchange to communicate information. Common accounting standards support markets because they allow actors to evaluate and to compare. They enhance trust in impersonal market exchanges because they provide a means of verification. And they are essential to modern financial markets because investors require reliable information as a basis for buying and selling shares. Over time, more sophisticated market systems have naturally required more elaborate accounting systems.

As in the case of the corporation, there is no free-market solution to the accounting challenge: markets need common accounting rules to function, and they need a coordinating authority to set standards. Accounting is a public good: accounting rules are both non-rival (use by one person does not exclude use by another) and non-excludable (one person cannot prevent use by others).[8] Accounting differs from corporate law, however, in that it is more amenable to private governance. It does not necessarily require the force of law, and private actors have a strong interest in common standards to facilitate commerce and to enable financial markets, so they may be able to coordinate on their own. In fact, accounting originally evolved as a set of common practices, and modern accounting continues to be based more on private-sector coordination (self-regulation) than other facets of market governance.

Accounting may be a technical exercise, but there is no objectively true and fair, or even neutral, accounting. There are certainly better and worse accounting techniques, but there are also inevitable trade-offs and value judgments. For example, accounting rules should be *relevant*, providing the information that market actors require; and they should be *reliable*, not susceptible to fraud or manipulation to the extent possible. Yet these attributes may conflict: the information that is most relevant for assessing a company's performance may not be the most reliable.[9]

Ideally, accounting systems should constrain fraudulent behavior by articulating clear principles and should limit firms' ability to manipulate their accounts by enforcing specific rules. Yet, in practice, accounting involves complex judgments about market design. For example, the US Generally Accepted Accounting Principles (GAAP) are based more on rules than principles, but a rule-based regime can lead firms to comply with the letter but not the spirit of the rules. The GAAP system was originally meant to reflect the actual financial status of a company rather than formal measures, but the authorities gradually shifted toward more detailed codes over time as companies grew more ingenious at getting around the existing rules.[10] Meanwhile, the International Financial Reporting Standards (IFRS) favored in Europe are based more on principles, and this can leave firms with greater leeway in practice. A more flexible accounting regime may give managers more freedom to structure reporting so that reasonable decisions do not unduly alarm investors, but it can also leave more room for deception or outright fraud. Meanwhile, the professional accountants who serve as corporate auditors face a dilemma over whether to support their clients by tolerating overstatements of performance and other manipulation of accounts, or to adhere strictly to professional standards of accurate reporting.

The accounting of stock options (discussed further later in the chapter) illustrates the tension between form and substance. In form, they are not a cost at the time of issuance because they are options that have not been exercised. In practice, however, they impose a cost because they are likely to be exercised. Yet assessing the cost of stock options requires a calculation model that estimates the anticipated volatility of the share price.[11] In the United States, the Financial Accounting Standards Board (FASB) issued a proposal in 1993 to require options to be expensed at their current value on the grant date, but business interests, particularly technology companies in Silicon Valley, strongly resisted, and the FASB backed down in 1995. It subsequently imposed the requirement in 2004, however, in the wake of the Enron and WorldCom scandals.[12]

Accounting systems have faced increasing challenges as shareholders have demanded more detailed financial information, and financial institutions have devised more complex financial instruments. For example, accountants have difficulty assigning fair value to derivatives because this requires an assessment of risk. Meanwhile, the IT revolution has made it more difficult to assign revenue to a particular location, has increased the scale of non-cash transactions (such as exchanges of web advertising space), and has proliferated intangible assets that are difficult to value.[13]

The seemingly arcane realm of accounting turns out to be riddled by politics precisely because the rules affect market outcomes—such as business strategies and corporate profits—so powerfully. The different interested parties—such as financial institutions, accounting firms, managers, shareholders, and the government—have distinct preferences. For example, one of the critical debates in accounting is how far to shift toward "fair-value" accounting. Financial service firms tend to assert that a corporation's financial assets should be assessed at market value, the actual market value if that is available (mark-to-market), or the best approximation of that, as opposed to a simpler alternative, such as "historical" cost, the price at which the assets were purchased. They prefer fair value accounting because it gives them a more realistic picture of a company's finances. But managers are less keen on it since it makes a company's accounts vulnerable to stock market fluctuations. It can actually run counter to accurate disclosure by forcing the reporting of temporary blips in values that can spook investors. Meanwhile, workers may be hurt by fair-value accounting because it can press managers to be more sensitive to short-term fluctuations in share prices, and therefore more aggressive in cutting labor costs.[14]

Karthik Ramanna argues that the shift toward fair-value accounting in the United States since the 1990s made accounting systems more vulnerable to manipulation; exacerbated the propensity for firms to overpay for mergers and acquisitions; distorted the allocation of financial resources; and contributed to the Enron and global financial crises. Moreover, the financial services firms that were most likely to benefit from the greater ability to manipulate accounts played a central role in shifting FASB standards in this direction. The shift to fair-value-added accounting has led GAAP earnings reports to become more volatile, less consistent, and—ironically—less informative of stock-market values. The accounting literature suggests that this may be because GAAP rules have degenerated and/or because investors have become more fixated on pro forma metrics fabricated by managers than on the official GAAP numbers. [15] SEC guidelines allow managers to publish their own (pro forma) accounting numbers so long as they report the official GAAP numbers as well, and studies suggest that share prices follow the pro forma numbers more than the GAAP ones.[16]

The Banking System

The government provides the core infrastructure for the financial system by creating a currency, conducting monetary policy, channeling funds through the banking system, operating public banks, supervising private banks, and enforcing financial contracts. Banking regulation vividly illustrates how regulation can support markets. Depositors require trust to put their money in a bank, and a bank requires trust to lend those funds out. This can take the form of the personal trust of one person for another, or it can build on forms of collateral and/or legal structures to ensure responsible behavior. An effective regulatory regime enhances trust and thereby allows more financial transactions to take place at a lower cost. Banks are particularly vulnerable because their assets, such as commercial and home mortgage loans, are illiquid and opaque, while their liabilities, such as checking accounts and certificates of deposit, are liquid and transparent. They suffer a mismatch in the terms of these assets and liabilities because they accept short-term deposits to make long-term loans.[17] And they back only a small percentage (typically about 10 percent) of their deposits with cash on hand that is available for withdrawal. In essence, banks make their money by lending out funds from their deposits, so they want to lend out as much as possible, retaining only minimal reserves. Yet this makes them vulnerable to bank runs, because if many depositors demanded their money back at the same time, they would not have those funds.

Bank failures are particularly devastating because they harm other financial firms, corporate clients, and retail customers, and they undermine confidence in the economy more broadly. A bank failure may cut off lines of credit to viable firms, wreaking havoc on the real economy. By preventing bank failures, governments enable banking activity at higher leverage and a larger scale than would be otherwise possible. Governments can achieve this through ex ante deposit insurance and/or post hoc bailouts. The beauty of deposit insurance is that it can prevent runs in the first place, because depositors will not rush to the bank to withdraw funds if they are confident that their deposits are secure. This solution has been quite effective, but it generates its own problems. Since the deposits are insured, banks may be susceptible to "moral hazard": they may take greater risks due to this insurance. And regulatory competition among jurisdictions—such as states within the United States or national governments at the international level—can exacerbate the moral hazard problem, as financial institutions seek to locate their activity in more permissive jurisdictions.[18] Governments address the moral hazard problem in various ways: they set reserve requirements that force banks to keep a certain share of total assets in a liquid form; they specify the kinds of investments banks can make, limiting risk exposure; and they supervise the banks to make sure they are acting prudently.

Banking regulation posits multiple challenges of market design. Regulators have to calibrate the balance between allowing banks to engage in activities that will earn higher returns and limiting their exposure to risk. Some proponents of financial "deregulation" have misunderstood the relationship between regulation and financial market development, arguing that less regulation would beget freer markets. In practice, however, reducing regulation could undermine markets by compromising market design.

The United States and Japan both enjoyed relatively stable banking systems in the postwar era, yet they accomplished this in very different ways. The United States had a formal system of deposit insurance, whereas the Japanese Ministry of Finance offered a more tacit guarantee that it would organize a bailout if one were ever necessary. US regulators relied more on detailed formal rules, inspections, and sanctions, whereas Japanese authorities deployed more informal "administrative guidance" (non-binding directives) and ongoing close communication with financial institutions. US regulators were fragmented across many agencies, whereas Japanese regulatory authority was centralized in the Ministry of Finance plus the Bank of Japan. The US banking system had remarkably few failures until the Savings & Loan crisis of the 1980s (see Chapter 3), and the Japanese system had no failures at all until crisis hit in the 1990s (Chapter 4).

Capital Markets

The limited liability corporation and accounting represent two elements of the governance of financial markets: investors need to know that their liability is limited, and that they can get accurate information about companies' finances. Beyond this, modern financial markets require an elaborate legal and institutional foundation. After all, robust securities markets require investors to transfer funds to strangers for intangible rights, whose value depends on the quality of the information that the investors receive and on the honesty of the sellers.[19] Katharina Pistor drives home this point with her legal theory of finance:

> Financial markets do not exist outside rules but are constituted by them. It is possible to distinguish different rules and rule makers, such as private and public ones. This has led some to argue that actors can opt out of the legal system and constitute their own system. . . . This system, however, is also rule-bound. The more a financial system moves from relational finance to entities and ultimately markets, the more it depends on a formal legal system with the capacity to authoritatively vindicate the rights and obligations of contractual parties or to lend its coercive powers to the enforcement of such claims.[20]

In other words, the law provides the foundation for financial markets; it may be complemented by private governance, but private governance is still bound by rules and ultimately grounded in law.

The key requirements for strong securities markets boil down to two main things: shareholders need good information about the value of a company's business, and they need to have confidence that the company's managers and controlling shareholders will not cheat them out of the value of their investment. Yet to achieve these two goals, contemporary financial markets require a daunting array of laws and regulations. Bernard Black's list of critical institutions for vibrant securities markets includes an effective securities regulatory agency; a strong court system; a prohibition on market manipulation; strong rules to restrict insiders from engaging in transactions that benefit themselves at the expense of shareholders more broadly and to ban insider trading of shares altogether; civil liability for insiders, accountants, investment bankers, and independent directors; criminal liability for insiders who intentionally violate disclosure and self-dealing rules; rules to ensure market transparency (such as the disclosure of trading prices); good discovery rules; an effective organization to write accounting rules; good accounting and auditing rules; a stock exchange with rigorous listing standards and monitoring of insider trading; and the inclusion of independent directors on company boards.[21]

Black thus definitively dispenses with the notion that the financial markets at the heart of modern capitalism are the product of free exchange, or that the rules that enable these markets can be reduced to the protection of private property. In fact, he stresses that the institutional infrastructure that supports vibrant capital markets goes beyond government regulation to include the broader social context in which financial markets operate, such as professional norms, training programs, and an active financial press. Intermediaries such as accounting firms, investment banking firms, law firms, credit rating agencies, and stock exchanges play a critical role by providing financial information and constraining managers from self-dealing. Regulations are most effective in a context in which financial professionals share a strong ethic of professionalism and a culture of compliance that motivates them to adhere to standards, even when a narrow cost-benefit analysis might tempt them to do otherwise.[22]

Of course, even the United States does not meet Black's standards for capital market governance (see Chapter 3). And other countries, such as Japan, have achieved strong economic performance despite diverging widely from this ideal (Chapter 4). In fact, postwar Japan had no independent securities regulator, weak disclosure requirements, lax insider trading rules, lenient courts, and illiquid securities markets. Corporate managers guarded their autonomy from shareholders and favored flexibility in accounting. They deployed cross-shareholding as a deliberate strategy to insulate themselves from shareholder pressures. Stock traders did not have strong professional norms against insider trading practices, and major brokerage firms were engaged in manipulation of share prices. Postwar Japan had less robust capital markets than the United States, yet it succeeded economically via a financial model by which the government deliberately promoted savings and investment and allocated credit via government financial institutions and private banks.

Corporate Governance

Corporations require rules to define who runs the entity and to establish procedures for effective management. They need to ensure that managers fulfill their responsibilities and do not elevate their own interests above those of shareholders or other stakeholders, or engage in outright fraud. Corporate law and securities law (discussed earlier) shape corporate governance, but corporate practices and social norms condition them as well.

Scholars, policymakers, and business leaders have debated extensively over whether corporations should exclusively represent the interests of their shareholders or serve a broader range of stakeholders, including workers, banks, affiliated companies, customers, and their communities.[23] Liberal market economies such as the United States and Britain tend toward a shareholder model, whereas coordinated market economies such as Germany and Japan favor a stakeholder model.[24] In the United States, the law facilitates court cases in which shareholders can sue companies for taking actions that do not serve their interests, even if the companies do so to reward workers or customers. The United States has more diffuse share ownership, whereas Germany has more concentrated ownership by financial institutions, and Japan has more cross-holding of shares among related companies. German and Japanese blockholding enables banks to play a larger role in monitoring corporate management.[25] The United States gives managers substantial leeway in appointing directors, whereas large German corporations are required to have both finance and labor interests represented on supervisory boards ("co-determination"), and Japanese boards are dominated by the corporation's own executives. The United States has shifted considerably toward a shareholder model over the past 40 years (as discussed further in Chapter 3).[26] Meanwhile, Japanese leaders have embraced the rhetoric of shareholder value, and the government and corporations have enacted substantial reforms, yet Japan has not converged upon the shareholder model in practice (Chapter 4).

Activist institutional shareholders, primarily based in the United States, have contributed to the shift toward the shareholder model in many countries. They have pressed governments to improve shareholder protections and corporations to increase shareholder returns. They have lobbied to strengthen requirements for independent directors, to permit stock options, to loosen restrictions on share buybacks, and to raise standards for shareholder representation via proxy votes and participation in annual general meetings. They have asked corporations for a greater voice in corporate governance, and they have filed class-action lawsuits, especially in the United States, winning increasingly sizable settlements.[27]

Many governments have passed laws to allow or promote stock options, ostensibly to align manager incentives with shareholders by linking compensation to the company's share price.[28] Yet stock options lost some of their luster after the 2002 Enron scandal and the 2008 global financial crisis. Critics contend that they do not align incentives because they reward good performance but do not punish bad performance or even fraud. They encourage executives to maximize short-term returns (targeting the point in time when the executives can exercise their options) rather than long-term value, and to manipulate accounts to maximize nominal share prices. They also contribute to soaring executive compensation that can undermine shareholder returns.[29]

Advocates of the shareholder value model also favor more independent board directors—meaning directors without strong prior ties to the company or its management. They view these directors as an important check on management, for independent directors are less likely to blindly follow management's lead. Some managers feel that outside directors are less competent than insiders, and are more likely to waste time or to propose inappropriate actions. Academic research has not found a strong positive correlation between outside directors and corporate performance.[30]

In theory, an active market for corporate control would support the shareholder model. Managers who failed to maximize shareholder value would be vulnerable to a hostile takeover. An outside entity could make a hostile offer to shareholders, or the aggrieved shareholders could forge an alliance to oust management. Even short of a successful takeover, the threat of one would discipline managers, motivating them to better serve shareholder interests. Yet only the United States and perhaps a few other economies, such as Britain and Hong Kong, have active markets for corporate control, and even US corporations have mobilized a considerable array of "poison pills" to fend off takeover attempts.[31]

In the realm of corporate governance, as in other cases in this chapter, one ostensibly "liberal" vision contradicts another. One might argue that a shareholder model with an active market for corporate control would be the ultimate embodiment of capitalism or the free-market system. After all, how could we have real capitalism without managers serving shareholders? And wouldn't that mean firms themselves being subject to the market mechanism, with shareholders able to challenge incumbent managers who are failing to maximize returns? And yet fostering a shareholder model—much less producing an active market for corporate control—requires a massive legal and regulatory structure, plus the cultivation of particular practices and norms.

Labor Markets

Labor market governance is a tricky case for the argument presented here because the distinction between market governance and social regulation advanced in the previous chapter becomes particularly fuzzy—that is, it is difficult to tease out how much governance is *necessary* for labor markets to function and flourish, and how much governance is simply *desirable* to protect workers from exploitation. While recognizing that much labor regulation is designed to protect workers rather than to empower markets, I contend nonetheless that labor markets *require* adequate governance to function properly.

At a minimum, labor markets require governance to prevent the two extreme outcomes that would undermine them altogether: employer exploitation going so far as to destroy the labor force via death, disease, exhaustion, or injury; and labor resistance going so far as to end work via strikes of extreme length or scope, or outright rebellion. These outcomes may be unlikely, but effective labor market governance also precludes movement too far in one direction—that is, a labor market regime should not give managers too much freedom to demand that employees take personal risks, or too little liability for negligence that results in worker accidents. And it should not give managers too little prerogative to give orders to workers or to demand loyalty, thereby compromising the normal conduct of business. Beyond this, labor markets require institutions to ensure that they function well, just like other markets. They need mechanisms to train workers, to match employers with employees, and to resolve disputes.

As with other issues covered in this chapter, there is no free-market solution to the governance of labor markets. Governments set the basic legal framework for labor contracts. They can do so to favor employers or to favor workers, but neither of these represents the obvious or natural market solution. If the government allows public-sector workers in vital roles, such as air traffic controllers, to strike, is that a market solution or not? What if it allows employers to engage in union-busting strategies? Or if it mediates in protracted disputes? And who should be liable for workplace injuries, the employer or the worker? Labor law and regulation involve judgments that often defy characterization as more or less market-oriented. Employers and employees are locked into a relationship that is insulated from the market for a certain time and space, so they require effective governance mechanisms to mediate that relationship.[32] Labor laws set the terms for labor disputes, establishing guidelines for what constitutes good faith bargaining or justifiable dismissal.

The government can also enact active labor market policies, such as retraining, job matching, or mediation, which entail more government but strengthen markets. It can set minimum wage laws or provide unemployment insurance, directly affecting labor market outcomes. It can promote labor mobility by shifting from defined benefit to defined contribution pension plans. Or it can promote job security by subsidizing corporate benefit plans, such as company housing and health plans.

Scholars in the Law and Economics school, often associated with a libertarian worldview, have traditionally advocated minimal labor regulation, arguing that any regulation imposes an efficiency cost.[33] More recently, however, scholars have argued that regulation can enhance the performance of labor markets. Deakin and Wilkinson conclude,

> The theory of labor law and the labor market which we have offered here, then, turns orthodoxy on its head by suggesting that in a "free" labor market, wages are unable to perform the allocative and incentive functions which are traditionally ascribed to them, and that labor market regulation is necessary in order to restore both equity and efficiency. Our understanding of "efficiency" refers not just to allocative efficiency in the static sense, but rather to efficiency in the sense of a dynamic process of economic growth, carried on under conditions conducive to innovation and economic sustainability.[34]

Specifically, they argue that unregulated markets tend to mismatch effort and reward and to misallocate liability for workplace accidents or violations of contract. Moreover, "free" markets may be inefficient in dynamic as well as static terms because they may not foster labor-management cooperation, organizational learning, and technological innovation over the long term. Consistent with the argument in this volume, Deakin and Wilkinson are not suggesting that regulation necessarily makes markets more efficient, but they are contending that regulatory action must not be judged against an idealized free market, but rather should be informed by a sober assessment of how labor markets really work.[35]

Different countries approach these issues in very different ways. LMEs like the United States and Britain favor competitive labor markets, with bargaining rules that favor employers, looser dismissal rules, weaker active labor market policies, and fewer worker protections. Germany has a powerful collective bargaining system (albeit it one that is slowly eroding), tougher dismissal rules, stronger active labor market policies, and stronger worker protections. Japan's long-term employment system has been based less on hard law than that of Germany, and more on business practices and social norms. The Japanese courts have tended to defer to societal norms on appropriate justifications for dismissal. Japan has stronger active labor policies and worker protections than the United States, but weaker than those in Germany.

Private-sector practices also powerfully shape labor markets. Private institutes offer more vocational training in the United States; industry associations coordinate training programs in key sectors in Germany; and private manufacturing firms provide more on-the-job training in Japan. Private employment agencies, temp agencies, and labor attorneys all play a bigger role in the United States; whereas public employment agencies and government mediation are more prominent in Japan.

The corporate governance regimes discussed in the preceding section also affect labor markets. US firms are more likely to lay off workers in a downturn due to pressure to maximize shareholder returns. Japanese firms are less likely to lay off workers, because they rely on a loyal workforce to enable them to invest in training in company-specific skills and to foster management-labor collaboration for quality control. US unions are more likely to have an adversarial relationship with management, and are less likely to have a say in management decisions. Japanese company-based unions tend to have a more collaborative relationship with management, with well-developed channels of communication.

Antitrust

Competition is at the heart of the market economy—yet it is anything but natural. As Adam Smith recognized, businessmen would prefer to collude than to compete, given the choice.[36] They might engage in outright collusion, such as fixing prices, or subtler anti-competitive practices, such as exclusive dealing arrangements with business partners. In practice, therefore, governments sometimes have to encourage or even to compel businesses to compete, or they have to fabricate competition where it does not naturally arise. The contradiction between limiting government and fostering markets may be most obvious in the cases of antitrust and sector-specific regulation. In these cases, more competitive markets require more government action.

In practice, antitrust policy addresses three broad groupings of anticompetitive practices. Two or more competitors may devise "horizontal" restraints, such as agreements to fix prices or limit supply. A manufacturer may engage in "vertical" restraints with a dealer or supplier: it might restrict sales to certain dealers, for example, or develop alliances with suppliers that exclude competitors. Or dominant firms may engage in unilateral exclusionary practices, such as predatory pricing or bundling products to impede market entry.[37] Antitrust authorities issue and enforce rules prohibiting or restricting these practices, and they monitor mergers to prevent firms from acquiring too much market power. In some cases, they may require dominant firms to break up or divest.

In the postwar era, many countries outside the United States, especially Germany and Japan, designed antitrust policies to permit valued forms of coordination among private firms, including block shareholding, collaborative vocational training systems, and R&D consortia. They also differed markedly from the United States in that private antitrust suits were extremely rare.[38] The Japanese government gradually strengthened its antitrust regime beginning in the late 1980s, but it remains more tolerant of industry coordination and collusion than its US counterpart. The European Union has grown more sophisticated and more aggressive since the 1980s; it has even taken a more aggressive stance than US authorities on dominant firm practices and merger cases.[39] Japan and the European Union have substantially augmented their capabilities, but the United States still has a larger administrative apparatus and employs more extensive and more intricate economic analysis.[40]

In the United States, the antitrust debate juxtaposes two different market visions: a laissez-faire approach that advocates government restraint, even if this means less competition, and a pro-competitive stance that favors activist government to sustain and promote competition. This debate has taken the form of a rivalry between the "Chicago School" and its critics, including the "Harvard" and "Post-Chicago" schools. Scholars in the Chicago School contend that monopolies tend to be fragile and competition robust because firms that attempt to charge monopoly prices are likely to be challenged by new competitors over time. They assert that most practices that might be deemed "exclusionary" are in fact pro-competitive because they reflect firms' efforts to lower prices or to innovate. In any case, the government may be incapable of devising an appropriate remedy, or it may be captured by political interests, such as small businesses. Hence these scholars are reluctant to prescribe government action even where they find that a firm dominates a market or engages in anti-competitive practices.[41]

In contrast, Harvard School scholars focus more on the structural attributes of a market, such as firm size and product differentiation. They tend to view anti-competitive practices as more durable than their Chicago School counterparts, and to support more government action to reign in these practices. They would be inclined to rule against mergers at lower market shares and in less concentrated markets. The Harvard School shifted partway toward the Chicago School in the 1970s, however, relaxing its concern with entry barriers and vertical integration, and favoring a detailed examination of firm conduct prior to advocating government action.[42]

The Post-Chicago School approach that has dominated US practice since the 1980s grew out of the Harvard School concern that Chicago School models miss the complexity of real-world markets. Post-Chicago scholars prefer careful assessment of market specifics to simple dismissal of antitrust action, often building on game theory to devise models of strategic interaction between firms.[43] They contend that certain market structures and firm practices can be more harmful to consumers, and government action more beneficial than Chicago School writers imagine. For example, post-Chicago scholars argue that even firms without a dominant position can raise prices by "locking in" consumers to aftermarket parts or services.[44]

The information technology revolution has posed new challenges for antitrust enforcement that have reshaped both theory and practice. Although some of the underlying dynamics—such as network effects and interdependencies among products—are not unique to high technology, they have appeared in novel and sometimes more extreme forms. IT markets bestow major benefits to first movers due to a particular kind of network effect that tends to produce a dominant standard. Consumers want goods and services that other users already have, and will pay more for those. So powerful companies can eliminate competitors that have superior products by leveraging these effects, as market leaders such as Microsoft and Google have done in the United States (see Chapter 3). The digital platform economy is particularly conducive to monopoly, with platform operators—such as Google, Amazon, Apple, eBay, and Airbnb—establishing dominant positions and setting the terms of competition on their platforms.[45] Daniel Rubinfeld argues that the stakes are particularly high for antitrust policy in the dynamic network industries characteristic of the IT sector because the path of innovation at one moment can have huge effects on product quality and price in the future. The authorities have to move quickly in these cases, because once a market locks in to a particular technical standard, it can be difficult or even undesirable to undo the anticompetitive effects of one firm's behavior.[46]

Sector-Specific Regulation

In some sectors, governments have regulated price and entry directly. Network sectors such as telecommunications and electricity sectors are characterized by natural monopoly conditions, meaning that a private monopoly is likely to prevail in the absence of government regulation to create competition. In the traditional landline telephone sector, for example, once a provider had built up a network, it had an overwhelming advantage over potential competitors. It would not be cost-efficient for another company to build a second network, and customers would not want to switch because they could not connect to the customers of the incumbent company. Network sectors exhibit increasing returns to scale, like the IT sectors discussed in the preceding section, meaning that the network becomes more valuable as the number of subscribers increases.

In these sectors, most governments historically provided services directly through public agencies. Alternatively, the government could allow a private corporation a monopoly in a particular sector and/or region in exchange for performing public interest functions, such as providing universal access. The government would then regulate rates so that the company would not abuse its market power. Some regulators, for example, employed a rate of return formula whereby they estimated the company's operating costs to assess a reasonable rate of return. This did not give the service provider much incentive to lower costs, so other regulators preferred a price-cap formula whereby they fixed rates at a particular level indexed to inflation.

Governments struggled with the challenges of market design as they introduced competition into network sectors. As stressed in the previous chapter, the common usage of the term *deregulation* does not accurately capture the essence of these reforms. In telecommunications, governments had to confront the monopoly power of the incumbent service provider.[47] The incumbents held an overwhelming advantage because they owned and operated the infrastructure, maintained access to the customers, controlled technical standards, and commanded the technical expertise. So the government could not simply allow competition—it had to *create* it. It usually did so with some form of "asymmetric" regulation: imposing restraints on the incumbent and giving advantages to the competitors. It could break up the incumbent into multiple companies (divided along functional and/or regional lines); force the incumbent to reduce charges in non-competitive areas (such as local service); prohibit the incumbent from lowering charges in competitive areas (such as long distance); restrain the incumbent from introducing new services; and/or require the incumbent to lease its lines to the competitors. This last measure was critical, because the incumbent carrier controlled the phone lines, so creating viable competition meant forcing the incumbent to lease lines to its competitors. The regulatory battle then hinged on the rate of the interconnection charge the incumbent would levy on its competitors. In many cases, the incumbent and the competitors devised complex rationales to justify their respective positions. Incumbents naturally favored "historic" cost calculations (including past investment in the infrastructure), whereas challengers preferred "incremental" costs (only the added cost of allowing more traffic on the lines). Yet these debates essentially boiled down to political judgments about how much to favor the incumbent versus the challengers.

When British authorities launched a bold telecommunications reform program in the early 1980s, the reform advocates recognized that they would need to increase regulation to generate competition, but they believed that this would be a temporary phenomenon. As competition took hold, the government could allow regulation to wither away.[48] Yet these reformers misread the relationship between regulation and competition in the sector. The process of regulatory adjustment has not ended because the incumbent never completely lost its structural advantage, and technological and market changes have required constant recalibration of the regulatory balance. And given the growing complexity of the telecommunications sector, and the interrelationships between different lines of business (such as land-based telephony, mobile communications, satellite communications, cable television, and Internet services), the overall level of regulation has increased, rather than decreased over time.

In electricity, government agencies traditionally dominated both generation and distribution, or the government franchised private monopolies, subject to price, quality, and safety regulation. Electricity is distinctive in that it cannot be efficiently stored, so the system operator must instantly match supply and demand. The transmission network, or grid, connects electricity generators to consumers. Large generation plants (usually nuclear or coal) run continuously and supply the base load, while smaller plants run discontinuously and supply the peak load. Hence regulatory reform has taken the form of allowing independent generators to supply some of the peak load, thereby allowing competition in wholesale markets but not in retail markets. The authorities have confronted daunting technical challenges in designing markets. They have to reconcile the operation of the power system, which requires centralization, with competitive power markets that allow trading in electricity capacity. They have to create independent system operators, so that neither the government nor the market players control the grid. They have to design a sophisticated auction system, combining auctions at different time points, such as day-before and hour-before. They have to adjust for the peculiarities of electricity markets, such as the limited number of bidders on the demand side and the relative inelasticity of supply. And they have to carefully balance the benefits of competition against the risk that generators and/or traders might exercise market power.[49]

In transport sectors, market reform also takes the form of fabricating competition over a common infrastructure, but the technical challenges of market design are less complex. These cases come the closest to "deregulation" in the literal sense because they require less regulation to generate and sustain competition. In trucking, for example, the government could simply run the infrastructure (the highway system) and allow trucking companies to compete using that infrastructure. There was no functional necessity for market regulation, and thus regulatory reform was relatively straightforward. Crafting competition was somewhat more challenging in the railway sector given the need to coordinate routes and technical interfaces. The British government adapted a highway model for railways in 1992, creating a single public rail track authority and auctioning franchises to service providers, with problematic results. Rail workers promptly went on strike, and the new independent companies wreaked havoc on railway service—raising prices, canceling services and refusing to invest in new railway cars.[50] In aviation, competitors have to share the common infrastructure of airports and airspace plus the limited capacity for routes, yet the market design challenges have been more manageable than for telecommunications or electricity.

In an earlier work, I compared the British and Japanese experiences with the "deregulation" movement. Both countries initiated reforms in a wide range of sectors during the same period of time (the 1980s), and political leaders presented them in similar terms as efforts to reduce government intervention in the economy. Yet the two countries enacted starkly contrasting policies. Across a range of sectors, British authorities aggressively promoted competition, devolved authority to independent regulatory agencies, codified and legalized regulation, and enacted regulatory change in a disjointed and adversarial manner. Across these same sectors, Japanese authorities carefully orchestrated the introduction of competition, maintained regulatory authority within the central ministries, protected ministerial discretion, and enacted change in a smooth and coordinated fashion. During this period, the US approach to regulatory reform resembled that of Britain, whereas the French and German patterns more closely resembled that of Japan. [51] Chapters 3 and 4 update this story by examining more recent regulatory reforms in the United States and Japan.

Intellectual Property Rights

Intellectual property rights (IPR) drive home the core argument of this book especially starkly, for IPR markets literally would not exist if not created and sustained by political choices. A patent system allocates ownership rights to inventions, including manufactured products, designs, or processes. It creates a particular type of artificial property right. As Scott Morton and Shapiro put it,

> a patent is by definition a right to exclude, or more precisely a right to go to court to try to either exclude a party alleged to infringe that patent or to extract royalties from that party. Transferring probabilistic "exclusion rights" is fundamentally different from transferring more conventional assets, such as production facilities, or other intangible assets, such as trade secrets, brand names, or skilled personnel. [52]

One could imagine a market economy without patents, but that would mean that inventors would not be rewarded adequately and society would yield a far less than optimal level of invention. Inventors are motivated by many things beyond material rewards, such as personal curiosity or a desire to contribute to society, but patents offer a powerful and consistent incentive that induces a higher level of innovation. So a dynamic market economy has to offer some kind of subsidy to induce more innovation. [53] As Douglass North has argued, societies achieve greater technological development and economic growth when the ratio of the private return from innovation (the inventor's reward) to the social rate of return (society's benefit) rises, and patents are prime mechanisms to achieve this shift. [54]

Almost every innovation builds on earlier ones, so US patent law requires applicants to demonstrate that the innovation is novel, non-obvious, and useful. If applicants meet these requirements, they gain the right to prevent others from using their inventions for 20 years. Yet patents bear a substantial downside: they confer a monopoly, so they tend to raise prices and restrict output, transferring wealth from consumers to patent holders. Patents can impede other inventors, who must avoid violating the exclusionary privileges of existing patent holders. This can make things particularly difficult for producers of complex devices that build on multiple patents.[55] As in the other issue cases in this chapter, there is no unambiguous market liberal position on intellectual property rights. A market liberal might support a strong patent regime as essential protection of private property, or oppose it as government intrusion that impedes entrepreneurial freedom. In practice, patent policy confronts complex issues of market design, as government officials weigh the benefits of promoting innovation against the costs of limiting competition.

The pharmaceutical sector starkly illustrates the challenges of patent protection, because patents are so critical to fostering innovation, and yet the inability to access a patented medication can be deadly, literally. In 1984, the US Congress passed the Hatch-Waxman Law to streamline the process for regulatory approval for low-cost generic drugs, while preserving a sufficient reward for brand-name pharmaceutical companies to continue to innovate. This led to a boom in the generic sector, but brand-name companies then exploited a loophole in the law to initiate patent infringement actions against the generic companies and negotiate blatantly anticompetitive settlements. In these "exclusion payment" deals, the brand-name company pays the generic company to stop producing the drug. In effect, it divides the profits from high prices with its generic competitor, which gets paid for doing nothing. The courts have issued judgments against these exclusion payments, but some brand-name companies have managed to continue the practice, perpetuating high prices for consumers.[56]

Patent protection is not the only mechanism to spur innovation. The government can conduct research and development directly, or offer subsidies or tax breaks to promote it. Or the government could buy out innovations, putting them into the public domain and allowing free use. This would provide an incentive for innovation without raising prices or restricting further use of the invention. For this to work, however, the promise to pay would have to be credible and the buyout price would have to be appropriate—that is, high enough to provide an incentive, but not so high that it would give inventors windfall profits at taxpayer expense. Or the government could sponsor research tournaments, providing a cash prize on a specified date whether or not an invention was complete. The prize would go to the company making the most progress on a new drug, for example. But the government would confront the difficulty of judging innovation in progress, as well as setting the right price.[57]

While patents promote the "useful arts" like technology, copyrights are directed at "writings," including music and movies, to encourage culture, the arts, and the development of general knowledge. As with patents, copyrights are designed to provide an incentive for creative activity. Copyright protection is generally easier to get and lasts longer than patent protection. Copyright holders can prohibit others from making copies and producing derivative works, but not from using similar themes and concepts. And independent creation of work constitutes a defense against claims of copyright infringement.[58] In addition, the doctrine of fair use allows people to use a certain amount of copyrighted material without payment for scholarly or creative purposes.[59]

Fabricated Markets

All markets are governed, so all markets must be crafted in a sense. But some markets require more conscious fabrication. We might imagine a spectrum from more "organic" to more "fabricated" markets, with the latter being characterized by the deliberate planning of market design, a specific moment of market launch, and/or the creation of a product and a market that would not exist in the absence of conscious design. Laissez-faire in these cases would mean no market at all: the opposite of the conventional presumption. As we shift toward more complex and sophisticated markets, the need and the potential for conscious design increase. We have already seen one example of market design: the creation of markets for electricity.[60]

Auctions represent an important subset of fabricated markets, and computer technology plus advances in the field of market design, including game theory modeling and simulation experiments, have empowered more sophisticated auction models.[61] The US government conducted the first electronic auction in 1994 for licenses for electromagnetic spectrum for paging services, raising $617 million for 10 licenses covering a small sliver of spectrum. The government had originally allocated spectrum by administrative decision, reviewing applications on their merits. It then shifted to a lottery system, literally giving away licenses. In one case, a group of dentists won a lottery and immediately sold their license to a telephone company for a $41 million windfall profit. In 1993, Congress gave the Federal Communications Commission (FCC) the authority to auction licenses. The FCC wanted to achieve multiple goals: generate revenue; use the spectrum productively; upgrade technology; promote competition; and ensure that some licenses go to minority-owned, female-owned companies, small businesses, and rural telephone companies. The FCC eventually opted for a simultaneous ascending auction. Multiple licenses are open for bidding at one time, and bidding remains open so long as there is bidding on any of the licenses. Bidding occurs over rounds, with the results of each round announced before the start of the next one. The FCC devised more than 130 pages of rules to govern the auction. For example, the rules specified requirements for staying active in bidding, the size of bid increments, and penalties for withdrawing a bid. The designers favored this approach over simple sequential auctions of each license because many of the licenses are interdependent. That is, the licenses can be more valuable if a company holds two in contiguous regions, for example; or some companies might need multiple licenses to meet their business goals. The government had raised $42 billion by 2001. Mexico, Canada, Italy, Brazil, the Netherlands, and other countries have followed suit with spectrum auctions of their own.[62]

Governments have also designed markets in pollution rights. Under the Clean Air Act of 1990, the US Environmental Protection Agency (EPA) issued licenses that allowed the holder to emit one ton of sulfur dioxide in a year. The firms could trade these rights freely. The government determined the allowable level of pollution and enforced compliance. It devised a "double auction" system whereby potential buyers would submit bids and potential sellers would submit price offers. The EPA ordered the bids from highest to lowest and the offers from lowest to highest. It then matched the highest bidder with the lowest offer, and continued in that order until it completed the last match for which the bid exceeded the offer. This market design was flawed because it gave sellers an incentive to offer low prices. But the market participants compensated for this flaw by creating their own private market in pollution rights complementary to the EPA auction. Those plants that were able to reduce emissions most economically would exceed the reduction targets and sell rights to plants that incurred higher costs in reducing emissions. This market gave companies an incentive to develop cleaner fuels and better cleanup chemicals and procedures. The program reduced emissions 30 percent below the ceiling the government had set at a cost lower than alternative approaches.[63]

The European Union designed a "cap-and-trade" system to control carbon emissions and thereby help meet its commitments for reducing carbon emissions under the 1998 Kyoto Protocol on climate change. It set an overall cap on the amount of emissions, issued rights to the major emitters, and then allowed countries to trade. Many economists consider a carbon tax to be a more efficient mechanism because it provides the most direct incentive to reduce emissions, but this option was rejected for political reasons. EU member states were reluctant to allow the increased revenues from a tax to go to Brussels. Furthermore, the cap-and-trade approach was easier to pass because it was classified as an environmental policy, subject to qualified majority voting, rather than a tax that falls under a unanimity rule.[64] The Emissions Trading Scheme (ETS) began with an initial trial period in 2005–2007, followed by four-year trading periods. In the trial period, it became apparent that the initial estimate for the number of permits was too high, and a lack of transparency on supply and demand for permits led to extreme price volatility. The market price collapsed to near zero in 2006. In the second phase, emission permit prices remained relatively low, suggesting faulty market design. In the United States, nine northeastern states created the Regional Greenhouse Gas Initiative in 2008, and California launched its own cap-and-trade system in 2012. The Obama administration announced a Clean Power Plan in 2015 that would set uniform national emission targets for greenhouse gas emissions, but would allow states considerable flexibility in how they meet the targets, including emissions trading schemes. The Supreme Court issued a stay in 2016 blocking the plan, pending legal challenges. In March 2017 President Donald Trump announced a review of the Clean Power Plan, and in June the United States officially withdrew from the Paris Climate Change Accord of 2015, under which signatory countries pledged substantial long-term efforts to mitigate global warming.

Local governments and nonprofit organizations have also devised a remarkable variety of markets to promote public goods. Peterborough, England, launched its celebrated social-impact bond program in 2010 to support prisoner rehabilitation. Investors would fund social programs for male prisoners released after short sentences, and they would be repaid with a return if they hit a target for reducing repeat convictions within one year of release. If the program were successful, this would reduce government expenditures, and the government could pay off investors at no net cost and improve public welfare at the same time. Social-impact bond markets have since proliferated around the world, targeted at a wide range of social issues: health, education, training, homelessness, and veterans services.[65] Local currencies such as BerkShares represent another type of fabricated market. BerkShares are a form of currency pegged to the dollar that are only valid at certain businesses in the Berkshire region of Massachusetts. Consumers can purchase them at 95 cents per share and then redeem them at a value of one dollar at these businesses. Local leaders devised this system in cooperation with the Schumacher Center for a New Economics to promote the local economy. And of course bitcoins constitute the ultimate fabricated currency, a decentralized digital currency that relies on a particular software protocol invented in 2008.

The US state health insurance marketplaces under the Affordable Care Act of 2010 ("Obamacare") represent a hybrid case in that they meet only two of the three criteria for "fabrication" as defined at the beginning of this section—that is, they were deliberately planned and launched at a specific moment, but they did not really create a product or a market that would not exist otherwise. Yet they illustrate nicely a key point about fabricated markets: that the finer details of market design can have enormous welfare implications. One study found that California was more successful than New York because it selected a limited number of insurers to sell coverage, and this allowed it to leverage its ability to select plans to keep initial premiums low. Covered California, the state's official health insurance marketplace, estimated what premium rates should cover the patient population's risks while allowing a 2% profit for the insurers, and it used these estimates to select the first round of insurers. But it also guaranteed that that it would not open the market to additional insurers for three years. California also went further than New York in standardizing coverage, making it easier for consumers to shop on the basis of price. As a result, the study's authors found that competition was more effective in California, especially in areas with few insurers.[66] Overall, the law reduced the proportion of US citizens without health insurance from 16 percent in 2010 to 9 percent in 2015 and improved the quality of insurance for many, but it also suffered from insurance company defections and high premium increases, as too few healthy people signed up and the government and the insurers were not able to control health-care provision and drug prices rapidly enough. These flaws could have been addressed with market design adjustments, but they undermined political support for the program. Presidential candidate Donald Trump and Republican candidates for Congress targeted Obamacare's market design flaws in the 2016 election campaign. Yet they faced their own market design challenges as they sought to eliminate the universal coverage mandate and other core features of the program without provoking a broader failure in health insurance markets. [67] The House passed a bill to repeal and replace the Affordable Care Act in May 2017, but the Senate failed to pass legislation through three highly publicized attempts.

The government does not necessarily have to serve as the master architect of a fabricated market. Private-sector actors have taken the lead in designing many financial markets, such as those for mortgage-backed securities (discussed further in Chapter 3). The information revolution has allowed the creation of markets that eliminate many of the standard transaction costs, matching buyers and sellers almost seamlessly. EBay, the popular Internet marketplace, disseminates information easily, and buyers and sellers are almost instantly matched. EBay has a fairly sophisticated set of formal rules and informal guidelines that govern transactions. In the place of face-to-face trust gleaned over a long period of time, participants in the market rely on reputational scores from third parties. And eBay transactions ultimately rely on the larger property rights regime as a fallback option in the case of disputes. In other words, eBay has a market culture and an institutional structure, even if the culture and the structure are different from those of previous marketplaces. And eBay is still linked to the broader market governance system. Thus the IT revolution affects the form of market institutions, but it does not challenge the basic logic of the argument presented thus far. Even Internet markets require rules to govern property, exchange, and market structure, and governments have actively shaped these rules.[68]

The examples presented in this chapter definitively refute the "free-market" view that governments should simply provide the basic rule of law, including the protection of private property, and markets will flourish. They demonstrate the myriad ways in which government action is required to create, nurture, and empower markets. They leave room, however, for a more sophisticated market liberal perspective (discussed further in Chapter 5) that would maintain that governments should build those institutions that empower markets most effectively.

To be clear, I am not arguing that governments never impede markets. In fact, we have already seen examples where the government-versus-markets image captures the essence of the story. In the paradigmatic substantive issue in the field of political economy, international trade, tariffs represent government actions that constrain markets. And in the case of regulatory reform in trucking and aviation, government regulation undermined competition, so its removal enhanced competition. This implied *deregulation* in the literal sense, with a net decrease in regulation coupled with an increase in competition. Yet the dominant logic is nonetheless one in which market governance empowers markets rather than constrains them, as argued in Chapter 1. The scope of the issue areas and industrial sectors in which governments create and sustain markets is considerable, as illustrated in this chapter. And the realm of marketcraft is growing, not contracting, over time, as markets become more sophisticated and require more elaborate governance, and as information technology poses new challenges for antitrust and intellectual property rights and creates new possibilities for market design.

3

Marketcraft American Style

Why the World's "Freest" Market Economy
Is the Most Governed

The United States not only regulates markets, like other countries, but the very market-like features of its liberal market model are themselves products of laws, practices, and norms. The US market system cannot be understood in negative terms, as the absence of Japanese-style government intervention or private-sector coordination, for example, but only in positive terms, as the product of specific institutions of market governance. In fact, the United States, the "freest" of market economies, is arguably the most governed. The United States leads the world in the quantity and complexity of government regulation.[1] In fact, US regulation has continued to boom throughout the era of "deregulation" since the mid-1970s.[2] This may seem paradoxical, yet it follows naturally from the argument presented thus far: that is, if markets require governance, then the economy with the most developed capital markets, the most fluid labor markets, and the most competitive product markets should require the most elaborate governance. Of course, laws and regulations can constrain markets as well, but a vibrant market economy requires more of certain kinds of laws and regulations, such as corporate law, financial regulation, and pro-competitive regulation.[3]

This chapter first establishes that the US economy relies on a massive infra-structure of market governance (Proposition 8 from Chapter 1) by surveying the core features of the postwar model. It then illustrates how market reform ("deregulation") is less a process of removing constraints than one of enhancing market governance (Proposition 3) by reviewing reforms since 1980 in specific substantive realms. And finally, it concludes with two case studies of American-style market governance with global impact, the information revolution and the financial crisis, one that spurred innovation and growth and another that destroyed value and undermined growth.

The Postwar Model

The US postwar model was not a "free" market, but rather a particular constellation of political and market institutions linked together into a distinctive system of market governance. The US model is certainly not monolithic: it varies over time, across regions, industrial sectors, and firms.[4] This chapter focuses on broad national patterns that differentiate it from the Japanese case that follows, but also addresses sectoral and regional variants, especially in the last two sections of the chapter.

This section reviews the core features of the postwar model from the 1950s through the 1970s, focusing on political institutions, the financial system, labor markets, and the competition regime. Table 3.1 presents selected examples of these features, but it is not intended to imply that these features applied uniformly across time and space. In fact, these features have been contested continuously in one way or another. It is important to situate the US model in time since some of the features commonly associated with it, such as a pro-competitive antitrust regime, have come under challenge since 1980, while others, such as

Table 3.1 **US Market Governance, 1945–1980 (Selected Examples)**

	Laws and Regulations	Practices and Standards	Norms and Beliefs
Accounting	Substantial disclosure requirements; some standardization	Private-sector standards bodies	Managers should have some discretion in reporting.
Banking	Fragmented regulatory system; fixed deposit interest rates; deposit insurance system	Arms-length bank-industry relations	Bankers should cultivate strong relationships with their business clients.
Capital Markets	Fixed commissions	Professional codes for brokers	Brokers should represent their clients' interests.
Corporate Governance	Low threshold for incorporation in Delaware	From managerial to financial model	Managers should have autonomy in running the business (managerialism).

Table 3.1 **Continued**

	Laws and Regulations	*Practices and Standards*	*Norms and Beliefs*
Antitrust	Activist policy under the Warren Court 1953–1969	Some collusion, anti-competitive practices, less industry coordination than Japan	Big is bad, economically and politically; companies should compete, not collaborate.
Labor	Union certification rules; National Labor Relations Board quasi-judicial review	Golden age for unions, labor-management relations	Employers should pay fair wages.
Electricity	Price and entry regulation	Coordinated transmission, independent generators, some electricity trading	Access should be universal; utilities should prioritize safety over low cost.
Airlines	Price and entry regulation	Competition in service quality over price	Carriers should prioritize safety and service over low cost.
Tele-communications	Price and entry regulation	Dominant carrier obstruction	Access should be universal; AT&T should perform public-interest R&D.
Patents	Relatively lax protection, government support for R&D	Building patent portfolios	Patents promote innovation.
Copyrights	Relatively strong protection, government support for R&D	Litigation	Copyrights promote creative work.

the shareholder value model of corporate governance, have only really taken hold since 1980.

In the golden age of the postwar era, the 1950s through the 1970s, the US government was more active in reshaping the economy, spurring innovation, strengthening regulation, and promoting welfare than it was before or has been since; and labor unions were more influential at the corporate, sectoral, and national levels. The New Deal reforms had given the federal government greater powers, and war mobilization had consolidated central authority. Postwar leaders emerged with confidence in the ability of government to steer the economy, to support industrial growth, and to promote economic welfare. In comparative terms, however, the political system remained more fragmented, the government less inclined to guide the economy, and unions weaker than in Western Europe and Japan.

Political institutions in the United States were fragmented in at least three ways. Authority was shared between the federal and state levels; power was divided among the three branches of government, with an unusually strong judicial branch; and the executive branch itself was split into multiple departments and regulatory agencies with overlapping jurisdiction. The federal structure made authorities vulnerable to regulatory arbitrage, whereby firms could shift business activity to states with more favorable regulatory environments. The fragmentation of regulatory authority made it more difficult for the federal government to unify policies, to coordinate across issue-areas, and to maintain consistency over time. And the prominent role of the courts in regulatory affairs, compounded by an adversarial and legalistic approach to regulation, gave bureaucrats less discretion and firms greater ability to challenge rules in the marketplace or the courts.[5] The United States was not characterized by the stable corporatist bargaining patterns of Western European countries or the strong government-industry ties prevalent in Japan.[6] Businesses certainly wielded political influence, but they were more likely to lobby on their own, to form new associations and disband others, or to put together ad hoc coalitions to promote specific policies.[7]

The United States had a more modest welfare state than most Western European countries, a less progressive tax system, and a higher tolerance for economic inequality.[8] American leaders favored free trade in principle, although not always in practice, and generally eschewed a proactive industrial policy that would favor a particular sector or technology. The government nonetheless diverged from market liberal ideals in many sectors of the economy, including defense, agriculture, and regulated sectors such as communications, transport, and finance.[9]

The postwar United States has been described as a liberal market economy (LME), with competitive labor, financial, and product markets. Firms had weaker ties with their workers, banks, and suppliers than their counterparts in coordinated market economies (CMEs) such as Germany and Japan. Firms had less capacity and less inclination to coordinate wage bargaining, vocational training, technical standards, or research and development (R&D). Hall and Soskice depict this as a stable equilibrium, with complementarities among the labor, training, financial, and competition systems. LME firms derive their comparative institutional advantage from flexible labor markets, dynamic financial markets, and competitive product markets, whereas CME firms rely more on long-term partnerships with workers, banks, and other firms.[10]

The financial system that emerged after the New Deal was characterized by a decentralized banking sector with a fragmented regulatory structure. Regulatory authority was divided among the Federal Reserve Bank, the Treasury Department, the Comptroller of the Currency, the Securities and Exchange Commission (SEC), and the stock exchanges, among others. The government designed the financial system to serve local communities and to promote home ownership. It created a separate tier of savings and loan (S&L) institutions, requiring them to invest in long-term housing loans rather than short-term commercial loans in exchange for certain privileges, including the right to offer slightly better deposit interest rates. By the postwar era, the United States had become an ownership society with substantially higher levels of home and stock ownership than other rich countries, but also higher mortgage and consumer debt.[11] The financial system was more "equity based," as opposed to "credit based" in Japan, meaning that large firms were more inclined to finance themselves through stock and bond markets plus retained earnings than via bank loans.[12] The firms preserved a more arms-length relationship with banks, in contrast to the relationship-based "main bank" system in Japan.

In the early postwar years, the diffuse ownership of most US corporations allowed managers to control the nomination and election of board directors, impeding shareholders from monitoring management.[13] Neil Fligstein argues, however, that in the late 1950s a financial model of the firm, in which the firm was viewed as a bundle of assets to be deployed to maximize short-term earnings, began to displace a sales-and-marketing model, in which the firm maximized sales through marketing, product differentiation, and the diversification of product lines. Aggressive antitrust policy during the Truman and Eisenhower administrations impeded firms' abilities to grow through vertical mergers (with suppliers, for example) or horizontal mergers (with competitors), so the increasingly finance-oriented managers shifted toward diversification through mergers with firms in different lines of business as a strategy for growth.[14]

The United States had more competitive labor markets than most industrial countries, with weaker unions and fewer collective bargaining arrangements. The government provided more modest social safety net provisions for marginal workers and the unemployed, and weaker active labor market policies, such as job creation, vocational training, and job placement programs.[15] American workers had greater job mobility, both across firms and across regions, and less job security.[16] These features of the US labor market were embedded in law, as well as in business practices and social norms. Labor law in the United States made it harder for unions to gain certification than in most other industrial countries, gave firms more leeway to impede union organization, and allowed firms to replace striking workers.[17] The United States did not have the more developed mediation institutions of Germany or Japan, and relied primarily on the courts to adjudicate labor disputes. Nonetheless, the postwar years featured relatively cooperative industrial relations, with substantial wage growth, more multiyear labor contracts, and lower strike activity.[18] Management-labor ties during this period were not as strong as they were in Germany and Japan, but substantially more collaborative than they became after 1980. Western and Rosenfeld contend that unions during this period contributed to a moral economy that institutionalized norms for fair pay, including equitable wages and flatter wage dispersion, even for non-union workers.[19]

Antitrust policy in the United States was more pro-competitive than in Germany or Japan, and this shaped the industrial structure by limiting coordination among firms. Thus Hall and Soskice are correct to view a strong antitrust regime and weak interfirm networks in the United States as opposite sides of the same coin.[20] American antitrust policy would not permit many of the types of industry coordination common in Japan, such as R&D consortia, recession cartels, general trading companies, and certain forms of exclusive dealership arrangements or industrial groups. For precisely this reason, as we shall see in Chapter 4, Japanese authorities systematically undercut the antitrust regime they adopted from the United States after World War II through a combination of legislated exceptions and lax enforcement. In the United States, interfirm coordination was relatively weak, even in those areas where it was legally permissible, such as vocational training or setting technical standards, due to the private sector's lack of ability and propensity to collaborate. Antitrust enforcement strengthened under the Warren Court (1953–1969), when the courts were suspicious of dominant firms, skeptical of intellectual property laws, and convinced that aggressive antitrust remedies would enhance public welfare.

The postwar innovation regime was characterized by strong investment in R&D by the federal government and private companies, and a relatively lax intellectual property rights (IPR) system conducive to technological diffusion. More than half of federal R&D focused on the defense sector, but this R&D, plus defense procurement, produced substantial commercial "spin-offs." Federal government R&D funding was distinctive in that much of it flowed through private companies, such as AT&T, IBM, and DuPont, that boasted major research capabilities. Smaller firms played a key role in innovation in certain sectors, such as biotechnology and information technology, and this role increased markedly in the 1970s. The United States also had the world's strongest network of research universities.[21] The government imposed compulsory licensing in some cases, and aggressive antitrust enforcement favored the diffusion of technology by promoting liberal licensing and cross-licensing.[22]

The following sections of this chapter review how the US model has evolved since the 1980s in finance, corporate governance, labor relations, antitrust, regulatory reform, and intellectual property rights (Table 3.2).[23] These cases

Table 3.2 **Reforms of US Market Governance, 1980–Present (Selected Examples)**

	Laws and Regulations	*Practices and Standards*	*Norms and Beliefs*
Accounting	Sarbanes-Oxley 2002	Increase in consolidated accounting	Fair-value accounting norms emerge.
Banking	Depository Institutions Deregulation and Monetary Control Act 1980; Garn–St. Germain Act 1982; interstate banking permitted 1994	Shift to fee-based model, consolidation	Banks shift from relationship-based to price-based banking norms.
Capital Markets	Gramm-Leach-Bliley Act 1999; Commodity Futures Modernization Act 2000	Financial innovation, investment banks shift from partnerships to public companies	Banks shift from relationship model to profit maximization; public turns on Wall Street after the 2008 crisis.
Corporate Governance	Buybacks allowed; stock options encouraged; Sarbanes-Oxley 2002	Increase in executive compensation, especially stock options; also buybacks, outside directors, takeovers	Norms shift toward shareholder value model.

(continued)

Table 3.2 **Continued**

	Laws and Regulations	Practices and Standards	Norms and Beliefs
Labor	Business-friendly appointments to National Labor Relations Board; reform attempts fail 1993 and 2007	Union-avoidance tactics, downsizing	The moral economy of fair pay erodes.
Antitrust	Enforcement eased 1980s; Microsoft settlements 1994 and 2001	Increase in mergers, anti-competitive practices in information technology	Dominant stream shifts to Chicago School and then Post-Chicago School.
Electricity	Deregulation laws 1978 and 1992	Market manipulation in the 1990s	Public support for competition erodes after California crisis 2000–2001, then gradually rebounds.
Airlines	Airline Deregulation Act 1978; Civil Aeronautics Board eliminated 1984	Solidification of hub-and-spoke model, rise of price discrimination	Status hierarchy among carriers emerges with consolidation.
Telecommunications	AT&T breakup 1982; Telecommunications Act 1996; net neutrality affirmed 2015 then challenged 2017	New competitors challenge rules; dominant-carrier obstruction	Competition norms adjust with intermodal competition 1990s; net neutrality norm emerges 2000s.
Patents	Bayh-Dole Act 1980; Court of Appeals for the Federal Circuit established 1982; America Invents Act 2011	Emergence of patent trolling	The open-source movement spreads.
Copyrights	Sonny Bono Act 1998; Digital Millennium Copyright Act 1998	File-sharing; copyright holder takedown notices	The fair-use doctrine emerges.

demonstrate in some detail how movements described as "deregulation" actually entailed the reconstruction of market governance, not the withdrawal of regulation. The United States and Britain began to experiment with regulatory reforms in the 1970s, but the global neoliberal reform movement—aimed at controlling taxing and spending, rolling back government regulation, and unleashing "free markets"—took hold fully with the rise of Prime Minister Margaret Thatcher (1979–1990) and President Ronald Reagan (1981–1988).[24]

American and British corporations were more supportive of the neoliberal turn than were their counterparts in Germany and Japan. Firms in liberal market economies like the United States competed more on the basis of cost and less on quality, so they were more likely to advocate market reform and other policies designed to lower costs. And because they relied less on coordination with other firms or the government, they were less inclined to advocate policies to cultivate, preserve, or strengthen institutions that foster such coordination.[25] Furthermore, the US political system enabled more rapid and extensive market reform because corporations took advantage of the fragmentation of the regulatory structure and the legalistic regulatory style to aggressively challenge regulation in the marketplace, in the courts, and through political channels. Industry associations did not forge delicate compromises with reform opponents, as they did in Germany and Japan.[26] The American political structure facilitated pro-competitive reforms because firms wishing to challenge the status quo had multiple avenues for appeal, whereas opponents could not easily reverse the process once competition had been introduced in a given market.

Financial Reform

The overhaul of market governance in the United States since the 1970s has been particularly dramatic in the realm of finance. Financial reforms produced a financial sector that was more competitive and less stable, facilitated financial innovation, fueled a sustained increase in the financial sector's share of national income, exacerbated economic inequality, permitted a major consolidation of the sector, and contributed to the shift toward a shareholder value model of corporate governance (discussed further in the next section).[27] They also set the stage for the S&L crisis of the 1980s and the global financial crisis examined at the end of this chapter.

Financial reforms in the United States began earlier and proceeded further than in other industrial countries, notably Japan.[28] American financial institutions drove financial reforms through marketplace challenges to the existing regulatory regime, combined with political appeals for legal and regulatory changes. Several investment firms challenged the New York Stock Exchange's system of fixed brokerage commissions in the 1960s by offering discounts on commissions for certain listed stocks, and institutional investors began to complain that commission rates subsidized individual investors at the expense of institutions. The SEC eventually forced the stock exchange to liberalize commissions in 1975.

In the 1970s, inflation soared to the point where it exceeded deposit interest rate ceilings, meaning that savers were losing money in real terms by leaving their funds in the bank. Investment banks contested the regulatory divide between commercial and investment banking by creating money market funds, and commercial banks responded with interest-bearing checking accounts known as negotiable order of withdrawal (NOW) accounts. The savings and loan (S&L) institutions were hit particularly hard as depositors shifted funds from savings accounts to money market funds. Congress phased out deposit interest ceilings under the Depository Institutions Deregulatory and Monetary Control Act of 1980, and then sought to strengthen the competitive position of S&Ls and other banks under the Garn–St. Germain Depository Institutions Act of 1982. The latter liberalized the banks' use of funds, which helped them to achieve higher returns with their investments; permitted adjustable-rate mortgage loans, which moderated their risk exposure; and authorized money market deposit and "super" NOW accounts, which helped them hold on to more of their depositors. But by allowing the S&Ls to take more risks without strengthening regulation and supervision, the government set the stage for a massive crisis in the sector by the late 1980s.

Meanwhile, Bankers Trust tested the accepted interpretation of the Glass-Steagall Act—that banks could not underwrite or distribute commercial paper (short-term unsecured promissory notes) by placing it with investors for corporate customers in 1978. This led to a protest to the Federal Reserve Board, which denied the petition; an appeal to the Supreme Court, which reversed this denial in 1984; subsequent clarifications by the Board; and a 1987 decision by the Board to permit three major commercial banks, including Bankers Trust, to set up securities subsidiaries. Meanwhile, in 1994, the Clinton administration permitted interstate banking, fueling consolidation in the financial sector. Then the large commercial banks and investment banks aggressively lobbied Congress to repeal the Glass-Steagall Act outright, prevailing in 1999 with the Financial Services Modernization (Gramm-Leach-Bliley) Act, which allowed banks, securities firms, and insurance companies to forge financial conglomerates.

The financial reforms of the 1980s and 1990s not only set the stage for the global financial crisis, but they also fueled the financialization of the US economy.[29] The financial sector has taken up a growing share of the economy in recent decades, without delivering greater benefits to investors. The cost of finance—in stark contrast to the cost of wholesale or retail trade, for example—has increased despite advances in information technology.[30] Thomas Philippon argues that the high cost of finance is due in part to increased trading activity, yet increased trading has not led to more informative stock prices or to improved risk sharing. Thus he estimates that the financial sector's share of gross domestic product (GDP) is about two percentage points higher than it needs to be.[31]

Corporate Governance Reform

The United States has shifted markedly toward a shareholder model of corporate governance since the 1980s as a result of substantial changes in regulation and business practices. In the 1980s, the Reagan administration eased antitrust rules, thereby facilitating mergers and acquisitions, and reduced corporate income taxes, thereby providing more capital for the merger movement.[32] Managers waged an extraordinary series of battles in the courts and state legislatures with shareholder advocates and corporate raiders to preserve their autonomy and contain the market for corporate control. Meanwhile, the federal government vacillated between defending managers and strengthening shareholder protections. Congress passed tort reform in 1995 and 1998 to reduce managers' vulnerability to securities litigation, while the SEC promoted shareholder interests by enacting reforms to enhance managerial accountability and financial transparency.

The US government also moved earlier than other industrialized countries to transfer the burden of pensions from employers to employees, thereby broadening and expanding share ownership. The government promoted a shift from defined-benefit pension plans to defined-contribution plans—such as individual retirement accounts (IRAs) and 401(k) plans—by providing tax deductions for contributions. In 1974, Congress passed the Employment Retirement Income Security Act (ERISA), which introduced IRAs and increased corporations' liability for paying out benefits from underfunded defined-benefit plans, thus encouraging employers to switch to defined-contribution plans. A 1978 amendment to the law then created 401(k) plans, allowing pension funds and insurance companies to invest large proportions of their portfolios in the stock market and thereby fueling the rise of large and powerful institutional investors.[33]

Institutional investors used their market power plus direct appeals to press companies to deliver higher returns. They recognized that some companies had valuable assets despite low share prices, so they sought to buy the companies out, break them up, and sell off the assets. Corporate managers who wanted to retain control would deploy strategies to boost the share price, including buying back shares, divesting divisions, and laying off workers.[34]

Neil Fligstein stresses that the embrace of the shareholder value model constituted a shift in cognitive frame, a new conception of the firm. Prominent economists built on agency theory, viewing shareholders as principals and managers as agents, to argue that managers had too much discretion to stray from their core task of serving shareholders. They charged that the sole legitimate purpose of a firm is to maximize shareholder value, that good managers should raise the firm's share price, and that unsuccessful managers deserve to be ousted by the board.[35]

Proponents of the shareholder value model believed that managers would more faithfully represent shareholder interests if their compensation were more closely tied to stock performance through stock options, for example, and their companies were more vulnerable to takeover.[36] Government regulation and tax policy encouraged companies to issue stock options: companies did not have to deduct the value of the options from their income statement (until 2004, as noted in the previous chapter), and executives did not have to report the options as income until they exercised them. Executive compensation via stock options soared as the stock market boomed, most dramatically in the 1990s and 2000s.[37]

The United States had generated a market for corporate control by the 1980s.[38] Investment banks were facing more competition and tighter margins in their traditional business lines in the wake of financial reform, so they sought activities that could generate higher fees, especially mergers and acquisitions. In the process, they cultivated new techniques for transferring corporate control, such as the leveraged buyout (LBO), which enabled investors to purchase a company by borrowing against the company's own assets. Investment bankers at Drexel Burnham Lambert and elsewhere developed the junk bond market as a source for investments in LBOs, fueling the expansion of the takeover market.[39]

Policymakers recognized structural flaws in the US corporate governance model, but they were only pressed to act after a stock market collapse in 2000, combined with the spectacular failure of Enron and other corporate scandals in 2001–2002. Congress responded with the Sarbanes-Oxley Act of 2002, the most comprehensive corporate governance reform since the 1930s. The Act created a new regulatory body, the Public Company Accounting Oversight Board, to enforce tougher accounting standards, and made corporate boards more independent and strengthened their auditing function.[40] Reform advocates remained dissatisfied because the Act did not address some of the key flaws in the US corporate governance system, such as managers' effective control over the nomination of directors. Meanwhile, corporate managers were alarmed by the enormous costs of compliance with the new regime.[41]

Effective corporate governance can contribute to productivity, growth, and innovation.[42] Yet in recent years the US shareholder model has eroded business performance and economic equality. Compensation via stock options has given executives incentives to engage in both speculation and manipulation, at the expense of investments to foster innovation, boost employment, and promote long-term growth. Executives speculate by overstating the company's performance and then exercising their options, and they manipulate the share price with stock repurchase programs.[43] Over the long run, these management practices have impaired corporate performance and have weakened the US economy overall.[44] One study even found that the shareholder model compromised product safety: companies with more generous stock option programs were more likely to have serious product recalls.[45]

Reforms of financial regulation and corporate governance have also contributed to growing economic inequality, especially the enormous rise in the fortunes of the top 1% and the very top 0.1% of the most wealthy. Financial executives have enjoyed extraordinary increases in compensation, and executives at non-financial firms have benefited from financial gains through stock options. And the move from defined-benefit to defined-contribution pension plans has boosted the financial services market and has shifted market risk from the government and employers to individuals.[46]

Labor Market Reform

The US government has not enacted major reforms of labor law since the 1950s, yet labor market governance has transformed considerably in practice. Congress failed to pass measures to preserve union strength; national leaders took other steps to undermine it; state governments passed laws hostile to labor; and employers increasingly deployed practices to discourage union organization.[47] Union density decreased, labor's political power waned, and firms grew more willing to lay off workers. Golden, Wallerstein, and Lange find that only the United States and Britain—among a sample of twelve industrialized countries, including Japan—experienced a dramatic decline in union influence in the 1980s and 1990s, and they suggest that government policy played an important role in this decline.[48]

The Reagan administration attacked union power by confronting public sector unions, facilitating corporate restructuring, and paring back labor protections. And it undermined working-class living standards by cutting taxes, reducing welfare benefits, and combatting inflation. Reagan set the tone in 1981 by firing workers from the Professional Air Traffic Controllers Organization who went on strike. Bruce Western argues that this helped to establish the union-free environment as a legitimate goal for employers, and demonstrated the feasibility of hiring replacement workers to break strikes.[49] Western and Rosenfeld contend that union decline also eroded the moral economy of fair pay, contributing to greater inequality in wages and higher compensation for managers and professionals.[50] The administration appointed more business-friendly representatives to the National Labor Relations Board, and enacted rule changes that made it easier for companies to decertify unions and harder for unions to win elections.[51] Employers grew increasingly combative in fighting union organization, and a growing corps of specialized consultants actively promoted anti-union philosophy and strategies.[52] Union-avoidance tactics increased, reported violations of the National Labor Relations Act surged, and strike rates plummeted.[53] Unions and their allies faltered in two key efforts to pass labor reform due to Senate filibusters, despite solid Democratic Congressional majorities. In 1993, they failed to pass the Workplace Fairness Act, which would have outlawed the permanent replacement of strikers; and in 2007 they fell short with the Employer Free Choice Act, which would have facilitated union organizing and collective bargaining and cracked down on unfair labor practices.[54]

The shift to the shareholder value model affected US corporations' approach to restructuring, fueling a shift toward selling assets and shrinking the workforce.[55] American companies began large-scale downsizing of their workforce in the late 1970s, accelerating in the 1980s and 1990s. They initiated the trend during an economic downturn but continued through upturns to the point where better economic conditions in the 1990s actually correlated with *more* downsizing. Gregory Jackson calculates that US firms were three to four times as likely as Japanese firms to have workforce reductions greater than 10% in the 1991 and 2001 periods.[56] While Japanese job tenure was increasing during hard times, US job tenure was decreasing in good times.[57]

Studies of downsizing in the United States find that it had no positive effect on corporate financial performance—as defined by profits, productivity, or stock price—and a negative impact on organizational performance, especially employee morale.[58] Major downsizing can increase errors, accidents, and shutdowns; strain relations with suppliers; undermine organizational memory; and require expensive compensation, legal, and/or outsourcing services.[59] Art Budros contends that downsizing in the United States is not economically rational but is *socially* rational. Managers downsize in pursuit of non-economic rewards such as favorable reputations, rather than economic rewards such as better financial performance.[60] McKinley, Zhao, and Rust take a more cognitive approach, stressing that managers take for granted the proposition that downsizing is effective.[61] Thus US firms are not biased against downsizing due to concerns about dislocating workers, but rather are biased *toward* it due to social norms that attach value to it and/or preconceptions about its efficacy.

The decline of union power, combined with the rise of the shareholder model, has fueled a long-term decline in labor compensation as a share of national income, from 62.6% in 1990 to 57.2% in 2016.[62] The unions' loss of leverage vis-à-vis employers has been compounded by declining political power, and that has contributed to policies that are less friendly to labor and more supportive of employers.[63] The Trump administration has moved further to reduce worker protections: removing Obama-era guidance on employment law, proposing cuts in research on workplace hazards, and seeking to eliminate a program that supports unions and nonprofit organizations.[64]

Antitrust Reform

The proactive approach of US antitrust policy in the 1950s and 1960s was increasingly challenged by the Chicago School in the 1970s and 1980s, as noted in the previous chapter.[65] This transition in policy allowed a gradual consolidation of market power in many sectors by the first decade of the 2000s, with some particularly dominant players in information technology sectors characterized by strong network effects. William Baxter, the head of the Antitrust Division under Reagan, shared the Chicago School's conservative outlook but favored more detailed case-specific analysis. The authorities shifted from defining competition by the number of competitors to economic analysis centered on consumer welfare: low prices, high output, and potential for innovation.[66] Baxter dropped a major antitrust case against IBM, and issued guidelines that reduced the scope for merger case action. He resisted cases against manufacturers for distribution practices, arguing that most of these agreements were designed to lower costs and few impeded competition.[67] The number of attorneys in the Antitrust Division dropped from 456 in 1981 to 229 in 1988.[68] The courts placed more procedural constraints on plaintiffs, and the number of antitrust cases dropped dramatically.[69] Mergers boomed in the 1980s, including strategic acquisitions to strengthen core competencies, in contrast to the diversification of the earlier postwar era, and hostile takeovers designed to boost shareholder returns.[70]

The Supreme Court review of antitrust cases declined under Chief Justice William Rehnquist (1986–2005), leaving conflicts among lower federal courts unresolved and errant or outdated judgments uncorrected.[71] During this period the government gradually shifted toward the Post-Chicago School, which preserved some of the Chicago School's skepticism toward activist antitrust policy but recognized that anticompetitive practices could impose substantial consumer welfare costs in specific cases. Yet the government did not return to the aggressive pro-competitive stance of the 1960s.

The antitrust regime faced particular challenges in information technology given the powerful network effects in that sector, most prominently in the Microsoft case. Microsoft negotiated a contract with IBM that allowed it to license its MS-DOS operating system to IBM's competitors, thus breaking IBM's control over the value chain. Microsoft then deployed elaborate strategies to consolidate a dominant position. It leveraged its dominance in operating systems, for example, to enter the market for applications. Competitors claimed that Microsoft gave its internal application teams proprietary information on new operating system specifications, providing them a head start on the competition for Windows applications. The Federal Trade Commission (FTC) launched an investigation in 1990; the FTC commissioners deadlocked twice on whether to bring an antitrust case; and the case was transferred to the Justice Department in 1993. Microsoft agreed to a consent decree in 1994 that prohibited it from certain licensing practices, such as requiring computer manufacturers to sign long-term contracts.[72] Microsoft deployed similarly anticompetitive tactics in confronting Netscape, the leading browser at the time. Under a 2001 settlement, Microsoft agreed to give computer manufacturers more freedom to install competing browsers and to share its application interface information, but it admitted no liability and retained the right to add other software features to its operating system.[73] But by that time, Netscape was no longer a competitive threat to Microsoft.

The FTC took on another giant, Google, in 2011. Critics contended that Google leveraged its dominant position as a search engine, giving favorable treatment to its businesses and business partners in displaying Internet search results.[74] But the FTC found that Google's practices had benefited consumers and that any negative impact on competitors was incidental to that goal. Google made some minor concessions, agreeing to not include third-party content in specialized Google search results, and to license cellphone patents for critical standardized technology to competitors for devices such as smartphones, laptop computers, and game consoles.[75] The European Commission took a much tougher position, imposing a $2.7 billion fine on Google in June 2017 for favoring its own shopping service in search results.[76]

A Council for Economic Advisors study found that market concentration increased in many core sectors from 1997 through 2012, with the largest increases in transportation, retail trade, finance and insurance, wholesale trade, real estate, and utilities.[77] John Kwoka attempts to quantify the impact of one element of US antitrust policy: merger decisions. He concludes that most mergers have resulted in competitive harm, usually via higher prices. In many cases the harm is substantial, with post-merger price increases greater than 10%. And nonprice effects tend to follow price effects: mergers that result in higher prices also wind up with reductions in quantity, quality, and research and development. He also finds that policies intended to remedy mergers, such as divestiture and conduct remedies, have not restrained price increases. And he concludes that the antitrust authorities have been much more likely to approve mergers that they should not have allowed than to disallow mergers they should have approved.[78]

Regulatory Reform

The US government launched the global "deregulation" movement in the mid-1970s, when Senator Edward Kennedy and others began to herald the cause in congressional hearings. The movement brought competition to monopoly and oligopolistic sectors, propelled a leap in the scope and complexity of economic regulation, and contributed to both the information revolution and the global financial crisis (discussed in the final two sections of this chapter). Three key cases discussed here—the creation of electricity markets, telecommunications reform, and the net neutrality debate—vividly demonstrate a core argument of this volume: that promoting competition can require proactive, aggressive, and extensive government action.

An unusual bipartisan coalition supported the regulatory reform movement, including academics, government officials, and business and consumer groups. Economists challenged the public interest rationale for regulation, arguing that policymakers should not assume that a market failure justifies government action, but rather should carefully weigh the costs and benefits of regulation. And they charged that technological change and market dynamics had undermined the original rationale for regulation in many sectors.

The government began with the airlines, but quickly moved on to other areas, including trucking and electricity. In the airline sector, the Civil Aeronautics Board began to approve substantial discounts and to lower barriers to entry in the mid-1970s. Congress passed the Airline Deregulation Act in 1978, producing the closest thing to "deregulation" in the literal sense as it abandoned price and entry regulation, and this eventually led to the elimination of the Civil Aeronautics Board in 1984. The government continued to manage congestion by coordinating investment in airport capacity and controlling air traffic.[79] Airline reform was followed by reductions in prices, but it is tricky to sort out the impact because prices were already coming down prior to reform. And the reforms have brought lower service quality and reduced service for some smaller airports.[80] Moreover, the benefits from competition have waxed and waned over the years as the industry structure has evolved, from intense competition in the 1980s to oligopoly in the 2010s. Fifty-eight new carriers entered between 1978 and 1990, but only one of these remained by 2005. Carriers reorganized into a hub-and-spoke routing model, with the dominant carrier controlling more than half of traffic at many major hubs. By 2014, the sector was dominated by four carriers.[81]

In electricity, the authorities began to explore options for market reform in the wake of the energy crises of the 1970s. The government opened the generation market to independent suppliers in 1978, but retained restrictions on access to the transmission network. The Federal Energy Regulatory Commission

(FERC) tried to open access through various regulatory levers. For example, it approved several mergers on the condition that the merged utility would provide access to its grid. And under the Energy Policy Act of 1992, the government created a new class of wholesale generators exempt from certain regulations and promoted access to transmission.

In California, a flawed market design resulted in a major crisis in 2000–2001, with extensive brownouts and blackouts, huge losses for taxpayers, and the bankruptcy of a major utility company. Progressives blamed the crisis on market reform, while market liberals decried insufficient reform. Yet the crux of the problem was the market design. The California regulatory scheme froze the retail prices they charged consumers but not the wholesale prices they paid to generators, leaving the electric companies vulnerable to wholesale price increases. The market was particularly vulnerable to manipulation because it was fragmented into geographical zones and it lacked efficient procedures to manage congestion. These features combined with a supply shortage to produce a full-fledged crisis. The California case is particularly galling because Enron and other trading firms pressed for a market design that would favor them in a supply shortage, and then shamelessly gamed the market after the reforms.[82]

Other US regional markets developed more successful market designs for electricity markets. The FERC introduced "capacity" markets that allow utilities to pay for reserves as a hedge against supply changes, but these markets require even more intensive administrative management, and they are politically contentious due to the enormous stakes involved.[83]

In telecommunications, private companies challenged AT&T's monopoly, leading the Federal Communications Commission (FCC) to review the regulatory regime more broadly.[84] The Justice Department filed an antitrust case against AT&T that came to trial in 1981. The Defense Department charged that the proposed breakup would undermine national security by segmenting the communications network; the Commerce Department contended that it would undermine US technological leadership by undercutting AT&T's R&D capability; and many political leaders rallied to defend AT&T. In 1982, however, Baxter announced a consent decree whereby AT&T would spin off all of its local phone companies in exchange for permission to enter the computer business. While it was difficult to assess the economic benefits of the judgment at the time, it set the stage for the dynamism of the telecommunications market and the information revolution to follow.[85]

The 1996 Telecommunications Bill allowed regional bell operating companies, long-distance carriers, and cable television companies to enter each other's lines of business. Proponents of the bill argued that it would promote "intermodal" competition (between telephone and cable companies, for example) and foster stable competition in the sector. In practice, however, the cable companies and telephone companies entrenched their dominance on their own turf, and two companies (the dominant cable company and the dominant telephone carrier) came to control the market for broadband Internet services in most local markets. The United States wound up with higher prices and inferior service relative to most advanced countries.[86]

Meanwhile, government authorities faced the question of whether to maintain open internet rules, also known as net neutrality, that prohibit Internet service providers (ISPs) from giving preferential access to some users over others, or privileging their own content over that of others. The net neutrality issue nicely illustrates the argument presented in the previous chapter, for openness in this case is the product of the imposition of a rule, not the lack of one. Net neutrality rules comprise restrictions that preserve freedom in the sense that they constrain ISPs from acting as gatekeepers to the flow of content on the Internet; and they facilitate competition in Internet services by guaranteeing that new entrants are not subject to inferior service or demands for premium payments. As Marvin Ammori notes, opposition to net neutrality could be viewed as contradicting the market liberal values of entrepreneurship, market competition, and free speech.[87] Moreover, in the US context the most straightforward path to greater openness and more dynamic competition lay with a relatively heavy hand of regulation via classification of the Internet as a public utility. The American version of the net neutrality saga also demonstrates how the political cleavages on key regulatory issues defy standard categories, such as government versus market, and can entangle both Republicans and Democrats in webs of contradiction.

In 2002, Michael Powell, then FCC chairman, classified Internet communications as an "information service" rather than as "common carriage" such as telephone service under Title II of the Federal Communications Act, thereby circumscribing the FCC's authority to regulate it. Powell judged that the Internet was distinct from the traditional communications infrastructure and that competition could protect consumers from abuses by access providers.[88] The FCC nonetheless issued net neutrality rules in 2010, prohibiting ISPs from favoring their own content or paid content. The ISPs vehemently opposed these rules, defending their right to differentiate prices and services among users, and lobbied members of Congress from both parties for support. Verizon challenged the FCC rules in court, prevailing in a January 2014 federal appeals ruling. This left the FCC with the choice of modifying the net neutrality rules to comply with the court ruling, or reclassifying Internet service as a utility. In April 2014, the FCC circulated a proposal to amend the rules to allow broadband carriers to charge content providers for faster service. Major corporations, including Netflix and Twitter, a broad range of technology companies, and public interest groups promptly protested. While Republicans tended to side with the ISPs and Democrats favored net neutrality, both sides experienced breaks in their ranks. One group of 74 Democratic members of Congress wrote a letter to the FCC opposing the net neutrality rules in May 2010, while several prominent Republicans publicly supported it. Pro-neutrality lobbyists credit John Oliver's parody on HBO in June 2014, which poked fun at FCC Chair Wheeler and the ISPs, as a turning point that garnered national attention for the issue. [89] The FCC reportedly received 4 million comments supporting net neutrality, and President Barack Obama himself declared support for reclassification in November 2014. The FCC voted 3 to 2 along party lines for reclassification in February 2015, and followed with a 313-page document specifying and justifying the rules in March. The rules banned the blocking of content, the slowing of transmissions, and the creation of fast lanes on the Internet.[90]

In 2016, the FCC proposed to break cable and satellite companies' control over the set-top boxes that most consumers lease by forcing them to provide their shows on alternative devices. This would allow consumers to access streaming content and paid content from the same platform. As in the net neutrality case, therefore, an open platform and increased competition would be the product of the imposition of a rule. With Trump's victory in the presidential election, however, incoming FCC Chair Ajit Pai abandoned plans to open the cable-box market and set about to roll back net neutrality rules.[91]

Thus US "deregulation" has entailed a major expansion in the level and complexity of regulation, especially in the electricity and telecommunications sectors. Tony Freyer notes one less obvious way in which American-style regulatory reform has produced an expansion of governance. As government command and control regulation declined, private antitrust litigation increased. This not only implied a substitution effect, whereby private litigation replaced government regulation, but the scale of the litigation suggests that many private businesses found it worthwhile to test the competition rules.[92] In contrast, as explored in the following chapter, Japan sometimes replaced government price and entry regulation with private-sector coordination or even collusion.[93]

Intellectual Property Rights

The US intellectual property rights regime has fundamentally transformed since 1980 as the government has extended patent protection to new actors, such as universities, and new products, such as software and business methods. This has created a booming secondary market for patents, yet it has in turn created problems that have undermined patent protection's core goal of promoting innovation, including the patent "thicket" and "troll" phenomena discussed in this section. Coriat and Weinstein argue that US policy changes have combined to produce a "commodification of knowledge": that is, a market in patents and the proliferation of firms that hold intellectual property rights but do not earn a profit by the sale of goods and services other than these rights. And this has forged a complementarity between the IPR regime and US financial markets, as the commodification of knowledge has offered financial institutions new opportunities to invest in high-risk ventures and to participate in the expanding IPR markets.[94]

The Bayh-Dole Act of 1980 authorized the granting of patents for the results of publicly funded research and permitted universities and public laboratories to sell exclusive licenses to private firms or to set up joint ventures with these firms to exploit their intellectual property. Many universities soon mobilized technology transfer offices to sell patents to third parties.[95] In the 1980s the US Patent Office began to issue patents for computer software, which had been considered unpatentable as mathematical algorithms that do not qualify as human inventions. In 1982, Congress established a Court of Appeals for the Federal Circuit (CAFC) for patent cases, and in 1998 the CAFC ruled that methods of doing business would be patentable as well. The Patent Office was subsequently inundated with applications for patents for computer software and business methods.

Over this period the costs of the patenting system have grown while the benefits in terms of encouraging innovation have declined.[96] As patents proliferated, they began to produce a "patent thicket": a dense web of patent rights that companies must hack through to commercialize new technology.[97] Companies stockpile patents for strategic purposes, including generating litigation revenues, defending against litigation threats, and trading patents. And non-practicing entities—companies that do not have their own inventions but make a business in patents, commonly referred to as "trolls"—buy up huge numbers of patents (largely for software), search for possible infringements, and demand financial settlements or seek judgments through litigation.[98] In the process, they impede the development of new products, increase costs for businesses and consumers, and clog the judicial system.[99] Japan and Europe have not experienced the patent troll phenomenon, partly because they are more restrictive in issuing patents for software and business methods.

The US government has introduced reforms but it has not fundamentally resolved these problems. In 2011, Congress passed the America Invents Act, which shifted from a first-to-invent to a first-to-file system, as is common in most countries; broadened the definition of "prior art," meaning practical knowledge that precedes an invention; and created an administrative board within the Patent Office with the power to invalidate patents before disputes go to court.[100] In 2013, President Obama directed the Patent Office to require companies to be more specific about what their patents cover, to tighten scrutiny of overly broad patent claims, and to curb patent-infringement suits against consumers or small businesses that are simply using off-the-shelf technology.[101] The Supreme Court also made several judgments with the potential to restrain abusive patent litigation between 2010 and 2015. It restricted patent eligibility to abstract ideas, natural phenomena, and laws of nature; it clarified standards for defendants to recover attorney's fees; and it strengthened pleading standards such that plaintiff lawsuits must be supported by factual allegations.[102]

The information revolution has also fundamentally transformed copyright policy, prompting new battles between copyright holders and users. Under the 1976 Copyright Act, the US Congress specifically excluded ideas, processes, procedures, systems, and methods of operation from copyright protection. Meanwhile, a special commission took up the thorny question of whether computer programs should be protected. It recommended giving copyright protection to the text of a computer program but not to the processes embodied in the program, and this approach was adopted in an amendment to the 1976 law that passed in 1980.[103] Software presents distinctive challenges to copyright law because software programs can easily combine industry standards, such as menu commands, with more proprietary content, and this leaves the courts with the delicate task of determining what constitutes reasonable use of industry standards.[104] Some software developers believe that software should be non-proprietary, and they have forged a powerful open-source movement.[105] Politically, copyright debates pose the copyright holders, including the powerful movie and recording industries, against the users, including high-technology firms and the general public. But the dynamics can be complex, as some business conglomerates include both sides of the divide, and some technology companies have shifted positions over time. The Republican and Democratic parties are divided, with advocates for stronger and weaker enforcement on both sides of the aisle.

The United States extended copyright protection from 50 to 70 years after an author's death under the Sonny Bono Copyright Term Extension Act of 1998, and it even applied this extension retroactively. Proponents argued that artists were living longer and deserved to benefit from the sale of their works during their lifetimes, and that longer protection would give copyright owners an incentive to restore, update, and improve legacy works. Opponents charged that the extension was little more than corporate welfare, and that it would have a corrosive effect on culture in the public domain. The extension defies justification in terms of the core rationale of copyright protection, because authors are not likely to be motivated by the extra 20 years, and certainly not by retroactive extension.[106]

The cost of producing works served as a major impediment to copyright infringement in the past, but digital technology has made reproduction much easier and less costly, essentially costless in the case of copying computer files. This generated political conflicts between content producers that sought maximum copyright protection and content users and Internet firms that wanted the freedom to copy and share content. The media industry lobbied for higher penalties for copyright protection and longer terms of protection. The 1998 Digital Millennium Copyright Act (DMCA) gave copyright holders new remedies for potential violations, such as the right to issue "take-down" notices that order violators to remove content from the Internet without resorting to costly and time-consuming lawsuits. It also allowed for statutory damages of up to $150,000 per infringing act, including the circumvention of technical copyright protection such as encryption. The law made it illegal to break a copy protection algorithm or other electronic lock on a protected good, or even (with a few exceptions) to build a software tool that would enable such circumvention.[107] Critics contend that this went too far because it allowed content producers to limit dissemination by technological fiat through encryption rather than relying on legal standards, such as the fair use doctrine.[108]

The Recording Industry Association of America (RIAA) aggressively deployed take-down notices to pursue peer file-sharing services like Napster that enabled widespread distribution of digital content, and filed lawsuits against individuals to recover damages and to deter copying. The RIAA subsequently backed off from mass lawsuits on file sharing due to public backlash, and targeted providers of file-sharing software such as Limewire and Megaupload instead. RIAA forged agreements for compensating copyright holders with streaming service companies, such as Spotify, while challenging others, such as Pandora, in court. In 2014, the RIAA proposed fundamental reforms to licensing procedures that would better suit the streaming age: simplifying licensing by aggregating works under a blanket license, covering all the rights necessary to bring music releases to market; and ensuring that all parties in the value chain receive fair market value for their contribution.

The following sections turn to case studies that demonstrate how the distinctive institutions of US markets have driven two of the most important developments in recent history: the information revolution and the global financial crisis. One showcases the power of US institutions to generate new wealth; the other reveals the vulnerability of these institutions to market risk.

The Marketcraft of the Information Revolution

The information revolution poses a double paradox: it is a global phenomenon, yet it has distinctively American roots; and it enables the closest thing possible to perfect markets, yet these "seamless" markets require more governance, not less. It illustrates the core argument of this chapter: that the US market is heavily governed, and that it is governed in a distinctive way. But it also demonstrates the welfare implications of market governance, a theme we return to in the concluding chapter. Let us attempt to unravel the two paradoxes one at a time.

The information revolution is characterized by the dramatic expansion in the ability to process and distribute digital data, which has transformed products, production processes, and markets.[109] The US military, university, and corporate research systems fostered an exponential increase in computing power from semiconductors, plus key technical advances in transmission, networking, and applications.[110] Intel Co-Founder Gordon Moore predicted in the 1960s that the density of transistors on a silicon chip, and thus computing power, would double every 18 months—and his "Moore's Law" has held roughly ever since.[111] This propelled the digital revolution, whereby information became a commodity that could be expressed in binary form and transmitted at virtually no cost.

American government policy and market institutions gave this revolution its distinctive form. The government's role in this case contrasts with that in the financial crisis case to follow, as the government exhibited administrative capacity, a long-term perspective, and relative insulation from interest group pressures. Antitrust policy shaped the information revolution by preventing vertically integrated firms like IBM and AT&T from dominating the electronics sector. The antitrust authorities forced IBM to publish technical information so independent maintenance companies could service IBM machines. Other manufacturers used these specifications to produce computers that would run software and connect to devices made for these machines. IBM unleashed the independent software sector by unbundling software from hardware sales to reduce its vulnerability to an antitrust suit.[112] The authorities allowed IBM and AT&T to make semiconductors for use in their own computers and communications systems, but not for sale on the market. They feared that otherwise IBM and AT&T could drive out competition by cross-subsidizing their semiconductor business, incorporating some of the cost of developing semiconductors into their computer sales. As a result, the US semiconductor industry was composed of specialist firms like AMD and Intel, not vertically integrated electronics firms like Japan's NEC and Hitachi. During the US–Japan semiconductor wars of the 1980s, analysts argued that this put US firms at a disadvantage.[113] Yet US antitrust policy also set the stage for the decomposition of the value chain under the "Wintelist" paradigm, named for Microsoft Windows plus Intel, as software firms like Microsoft and component manufacturers like Intel gradually seized more control over their own link within the value chain. They were no longer simply subcontractors to assembly firms, but they were driving market developments, setting technological standards, and shaping technological interfaces.[114] By constraining system integrators like IBM and AT&T, the US authorities left more room for new entrants into the emerging IT sector than their counterparts in Japan or Europe.

The shift to a Wintelist production paradigm also contributed to the broader decomposition of production into global supply chains. Technical interfaces become more open and universal, allowing a shift from an integral production model, in which the assembly firm controlled the production process, to a modular model, in which manufacturers in one country could produce a standard subsystem, such as a hard-disk drive, for installation in a final product anywhere in the world.[115] The assembly firm could outsource production, focusing more on research, design, and marketing. Meanwhile, upstream suppliers could capture more of the production value.

The breakup of AT&T and subsequent regulation also fostered competition in telecommunications.[116] This divided the system into distinct market segments: terminal equipment, long-distance, local, and value-added services. The Baby Bells still enjoyed a monopoly in local service, but they faced competition in other business lines. This motivated them to devise new ways to apply information technology to increase efficiency and provide innovative services. They emerged as one class of corporate users of information technology that propelled user-driven innovation. Moreover, regulatory reform brought lower communications costs, including flat-rate local service, which enabled venture firms to offer value-added services and household consumers to experiment with new applications at a reasonable cost. Regulatory reform also created a more competitive environment in the financial sector, driving financial services firms to marshal information technology for competitive advantage.[117]

The US government "created" the Internet in the sense that the Defense Department's Advanced Research Projects Agency (DARPA) funded the development of the ARPANET, which provided the underlying architecture. The ARPANET transmitted data through packet switching, breaking down information into its components and then recombining them before their destination.[118] It linked various military research institutes and university laboratories, permitting electronic communication (such as email) and sharing of data and analysis. In 1985, DARPA transferred the ARPANET to the National Science Foundation (NSF), and decreed that all NSF-related sites would use the TCP/IP protocol, establishing it as the dominant data-transmission protocol. The government loosened restrictions on the commercial use of the network in 1991, and the first private commercial Internet service began in 1992. In 1991, a researcher at the European Organization for Nuclear Research (CERN) in Switzerland developed the software and specifications that came to support the World Wide Web. And in 1993, researchers at the University of Illinois created the Mosaic web browser for the Microsoft Windows platform.[119] This demonstrated the benefits of linking networks to networks, making every personal computer a window into a global store of data, thereby propelling the Internet boom.[120] As applications proliferated and became more sophisticated, they required a broadband infrastructure. Governments supported this rollout in different ways. The US government relied on a combination of cable companies and telephone companies to build up the network, resulting in less overall coverage and more variation in network forms, whereas the Japanese government invested more directly.[121]

American market institutions, and the Silicon Valley model in particular, fostered the innovative start-ups that played a key role in commercializing the Internet, with innovations in devices, computing, transmission, and services. The US government funded the research that produced much of the relevant technology, and provided early-stage capital for many of the most successful high-tech firms.[122] US research universities served as incubators and partners for venture firms. Immigration provided an important source of technical skill, plus research connections with other countries, especially India and greater China. Fluid labor markets generated a supply of talent, and made entrepreneurs more willing to take risks, knowing that they could probably find new opportunities if a particular venture failed. The Silicon Valley area offered links to major research universities; deep human resource networks; strong support service sectors, such as specialist legal, accounting, and human resource firms; and a vibrant venture capital industry.[123] Venture capital firms enabled start-ups to grow more quickly because the start-ups did not have to build up retained earnings over time or to rely on bank loans. The venture capital firms also worked closely with the start-ups, providing managerial advice and business contacts.[124] Financial markets offered avenues for start-ups to go public or to be acquired. And government policy facilitated the issuance of stock options that could boost the potential compensation for managers while limiting immediate outlays. The next chapter recounts how the Japanese government tried to emulate the Silicon Valley model over several decades, with little success.

The US-led information revolution yielded several distinctive features: a breakdown of the hierarchical value chain; greater value creation and technological leadership from upstream industries, such as component and software firms; dynamic innovation by start-ups in data communications, software, and e-commerce; new IT strategies from large corporate users; and mass experimentation by consumers. While the model of innovation operated primarily from the bottom up—from users to producers, and component producers to assembly firms—the US government nonetheless fostered the institutional environment that supported it. American firms enjoyed a first mover advantage in this emerging sector, and benefited from the fact that their business models meshed well with a new production paradigm that emerged from US institutions. American firms seized dominant positions in operating systems, business software, and search engines.[125]

Let us turn now to our second paradox: how Internet markets are more governed, not less. At one level, the Internet appears to offer the closest thing to perfect markets, with transaction costs lowered dramatically toward zero.[126] Consumers can locate counterparts and execute transactions seamlessly on eBay, and businesses can source products and services electronically via virtual marketplaces such as Perfect Commerce. But even these marketplaces operate with an elaborate set of rules, both formal and informal; and they rest on the foundation of the broader legal system that defines and enforces property rights.

If we consider some of the key issues addressed in this chapter and the previous one—antitrust, telecommunications regulation, and intellectual property rights—we can now flesh out Proposition 10 from Chapter 1: that the information economy demands more governance, not less. The information revolution challenges antitrust policy because it makes it easier for dominant firms to lock in an advantage over challengers. Antitrust authorities that want to preserve competition have to be more aggressive in combatting abuses, both in terms of researching business practices and moving quickly when needed. They also must assess the distinctive nature of competition in the information economy when passing judgment on merger plans. Likewise, the electronic marketplace is defined by the architecture of network configuration software. As Alvin Roth puts it, "Internet marketplaces have very precise rules, because when a market is on the Web, its rules have to be formalized in software."[127] And whoever controls the network can decide who can participate and sets the rules for that marketplace. They can choose open or restricted access, offer equal or differentiated access, and structure the bidding or buying process.[128] So that leaves the government to decide whether to allow private firms to set the specifications as they like, or to impose restrictions to enhance competition. Moreover, information is non-excludable, so the core commodity of the information economy is an artifact of a rule: intellectual property rights. With digital technology, the cost of reproducing and redistributing content falls virtually to zero, making copyright rules essential for content producers to earn a return.[129] As US patents were extended to business models, processes expressed in digital form—such as the eBay auction protocol or the Amazon checkout strategy—transformed shared knowledge into a commodity under law.[130] Government authorities must strive continually to strike a balance between content creators and users that fosters market competition, promotes innovation, and protects personal privacy.

The Marketcraft of the Global Financial Crisis

In 2008, the failure of Lehman Brothers triggered a stock market plunge in the United States that rapidly escalated into a global crisis. What caused this crisis? And how did distinctive features of the American political economy affect its form? Scholars and practitioners have compiled a long list of factors that contributed to the crisis, and offered judgments about how the various factors shaped specific developments.[131] We can begin by separating out the macroeconomic factors that drove the US housing market bubble from the microinstitutional factors that shaped the financial crisis. The US financial system is not uniquely vulnerable: countries with many different types of financial systems have experienced financial crises.[132] Japan, with a fundamentally different set of institutions, suffered a particularly debilitating crisis in the 1990s. Yet I contend here that the institutions of American capitalism contributed to the scale of the housing bubble, the fury of the crash, and the impact of the crisis on ordinary homeowners.

Easy money certainly fueled the housing bubble.[133] Defenders of the Federal Reserve Bank, including Chairman Alan Greenspan himself, argue that the Bank's primary mission is to combat price inflation, not asset inflation; that it is particularly difficult to distinguish an asset bubble from legitimate appreciation of the underlying value of assets; that it is tricky to deflate a bubble by raising interest rates; and that any move to offset a bubble would be unpopular politically.[134] Yet the Fed's mission is to oversee the overall health of the US economy and the global economy more broadly, and as such it has a duty to watch for asset bubbles. It had other tools in addition to interest rates, including limiting banks' exposure to risky mortgages or raising capital requirements. Evidence available at the time indicated that the US housing and stock markets were dangerously inflated, and some experts warned of a looming financial crisis.[135]

Global imbalances in capital flows also inflated the housing bubble. High savings in China and other Asian and Middle Eastern countries generated a glut of assets searching the globe for attractive investments, yet not finding ample opportunities due to surplus funds in many markets. Global savings poured into the United States, and targeted the housing market for investment. This drove global interest rates lower, pressing investors to seek riskier assets and greater leverage to maximize returns.

A short list of the specific developments that contributed to the crisis—all shaped by the institutional contours of American capitalism—would include financial reforms (outlined earlier in this chapter); the failure to regulate derivatives; lax supervision by the regulatory authorities; reliance on private-sector self-regulation; the development of a market for mortgage-backed securities that broke the direct link between borrower and lender and enabled lenders to issue riskier mortgages and financial professionals to deploy them for speculation; failures by private-sector monitors, including credit agencies, accountants, and financial analysts; and irresponsible behavior by investment banks, lenders, and borrowers.

Some analysts blame policies to promote home ownership, especially measures to encourage lending to low-income borrowers, for fueling the housing bubble. In particular, they charge that Fannie Mae and Freddie Mac distorted the mortgage market because they operated with implicit government guarantees, artificially increasing the demand for mortgages and for homes.[136] Yet Fannie Mae and Freddie Mac provided mostly prime mortgages, not the subprime ones that drove the crisis, and Community Reinvestment Act loans targeted at low-income borrowers actually had a default rate below average.[137] In the late stages of the housing boom, it was not Fannie and Freddie but other financial institutions that were driving developments in the mortgage market, especially the subprime segment.[138]

The US government moved the earliest and the furthest among major industrial countries to promote competition in financial services, as detailed earlier, and it was relatively permissive with new financial instruments. In contrast to the information revolution case, financial regulation revealed clear signs of regulatory capture. The financial sector enjoyed a combination of financial resources, organizational power, and network ties to the government that enabled it to shape a favorable regulatory regime. Government and financial sector elites were interpenetrated, with top Wall Street executives playing key roles in the Treasury Department and financial regulatory agencies. Furthermore, political leaders relied on a strong economy, and the financial sector played a critical role in providing credit and fueling the stock market. So any administration would be wary of taking measures that would undermine the financial sector's ability to play these roles.[139] The large US investment banks lobbied to maximize their freedom to innovate by lowering the barriers between banking and securities or permitting derivative products, for example. In contrast, Japanese financial institutions were more inclined to lobby to preserve regulations, such as fixed brokerage commissions and deposit interest rates, that moderated competition and stabilized revenues.

The fragmentation of the US financial regulatory regime not only required a high level of coordination among agencies, but also made the system vulnerable to regulatory lapses, such as abuses falling between the cracks. It gave financial institutions the ability to engage in regulatory arbitrage: taking advantage of differences in regulation across different markets or jurisdictions to increase profits.[140] Given the fragmentation of authority plus the more legalistic regulatory style, the US approach to financial regulation is more post hoc than ex ante—that is, financial institutions test the limits, and then the regulators judge whether the institutions have violated a rule.[141] American-style private-sector innovation in derivative instruments would be impossible in Japan, because financial institutions would not introduce new instruments without consulting the authorities in advance. In fact, the Japanese authorities' operating principle was precisely the opposite: they prohibited everything not expressly permitted (the "positive list" approach), rather than allowing everything not expressly forbidden ("negative list").

It is difficult to separate out the ideological from the institutional elements of the US model since the two reinforce each other in practice, yet certain prevalent strains of thought certainly influenced financial regulation. Many scholars and practitioners were convinced that more sophisticated financial markets enhance the efficiency of markets and the performance of the economy of the whole, and elaborate hedging strategies could deliver a combination of efficiency and stability. Many abided by the "efficient markets" hypothesis that financial markets are rational in that they take into account all available information about the value of shares. Moreover, political figures and opinion leaders tended to believe in the effectiveness of private-sector self-regulation. They figured that private-sector actors would be motivated to self-regulate effectively to preserve their reputations, since these reputations are so critical in finance.[142]

These distinctive features of the US political economy shaped specific government regulatory policies, including the non-regulation of over-the-counter (OTC) derivative securities markets. Derivatives—such as futures, options, and warrants—are financial instruments whose price is derived from the value of underlying assets, such as bonds, stocks, or real estate. In a futures contract, for example, one party agrees to sell a given asset to another party at a given price at some future date. Derivatives were originally designed to hedge risk, but they can also be used for speculation. They were often traded over the counter, meaning that there was no central market that governed the transactions, with less regulation of the transactions and the assets that underpinned them. The Commodity Futures Trading Commission (CFTC) had exempted derivative securities from regulation based on the statutory authority given by Congress under the Futures Trading Practices Act of 1992.

Under Brooksley Born, who ran the CFTC from 1996 to 2000, the commission questioned whether the derivatives exemption was justified given the risks they posed and the rapid growth of the market after 1992.[143] Treasury Secretary Robert Rubin, Deputy Treasury Secretary Larry Summers, SEC Chairman Arthur Levitt, and Federal Reserve Chairman Alan Greenspan all opposed regulation. They contended that the Futures Trading Practices Act had only granted authority to the CFTC to grant exemptions, not to pursue additional regulation. Moreover, CFTC action would create uncertainty in the derivative markets, which by this time were very large, and could thus destabilize financial markets.[144]

The authorities left hedge funds and similar operations intended to mitigate investment risk through complex trading strategies largely unregulated because these funds targeted high-worth individuals and institutions with professional advisors, not ordinary consumers. They judged that the government had no business keeping sophisticated investors from gambling with their own money. Yet these funds created systemic risk through opaque derivatives, interlocking portfolios, and a lack of market transparency. They relied on trading strategies based on statistical prediction techniques that were extremely sensitive to outlier events. And as the funds exploded, the buy-in thresholds declined, exposing more individuals to risky investment strategies, and the hedge funds had more trouble achieving high returns, thus encouraging greater risk-taking.

In the 1980s, most major US investment banks shifted from partnerships to publicly listed corporations. This meant that managers had less stake in the long-term health of the firm and more interest in the short-term maximization of profits, and this encouraged riskier behavior. It also opened up the possibility of compensating executives via stock options, which further promoted risk-taking.

The SEC also revised capital requirements for investment banks in 2004, essentially allowing them to rely on their own internal models to assess risk and thereby set their own capital requirements.[145] This revision did not relax leverage restrictions per se, but it did encourage investment banks to favor mortgage-backed securities over other assets, thereby contributing to the rapid rise in exposure to these instruments.[146]

These various regulatory decisions and non-decisions set the stage for the drama to follow, with the market for mortgage-backed securities taking center stage. By collecting many mortgages into large pools, securitizing them, and then selling them off to investors, these instruments broke the direct link between the lender and the borrower. The investment banks divided the mortgages into tiers, with the lowest-rated tranches (the subprime mortgages) earning the highest returns. This gave them an incentive to favor subprime loans, because it allowed them to expand the mortgage market and earn higher returns.[147] To make matters worse, the investment banks were increasing their leverage ratios to maximize their ability to profit from high volume with small trading margins—in essence, they were using their ability to borrow more funds to make bigger bets. But this higher leverage left them vulnerable to even a small drop in housing prices.

Meanwhile, the investment banks deployed elaborate hedging strategies to insure themselves against default risk. Companies like AIG used credit-default swaps (CDSs) to help investors, such as banks, hedge their risk exposure to mortgage-backed securities. In essence, a CDS contract would specify that an investor would pay a periodic fee to another party, which in turn would promise to pay out a given sum if the party liable for the loan asset were to default. In theory this should have reduced risk, but in practice the hedging strategies enabled the financial institutions to take greater risks and to overwhelm the capacity of the insurers in the case of a systemic crisis.

The credit agencies continued to give mortgage-backed securities AAA ratings, judging that these were relatively safe investments that pooled risk. The government granted preferential authority to private rating agencies to provide ratings for creditworthiness and credit risk. The credit agencies wielded enormous power in the financial markets because their ratings determined the ability of firms and other institutions to raise capital. The agencies charged fees for assessing the creditworthiness of specific firms or assets. This generated a conflict of interest, since the firms paying those fees desired high ratings.

The financial crisis was also affected by fair-value accounting on both sides of the boom-bust cycle. As noted in the previous chapter, fair-value accounting values financial assets based on prices as they appear in the market. As home prices continued to rise through the period 2003–2008, the mortgage-backed securities rose in value because the underlying assets continued to appreciate. In the bust, home prices fell rapidly, bottoming out below stable market value. This forced banks to revalue their assets at market prices, and increased pressure to sell off assets.[148] The banks subsequently lobbied successfully to suspend fair-market-value accounting and to revert to historical-cost accounting.

With the benefit of hindsight, we can recognize that the opponents of regulation put too much faith in the benefits of financial innovation to deliver greater efficiency and safety through hedging strategies, and discounted the possibility that these strategies would increase risk. Mortgage-backed securities allowed investors to insulate themselves from the risks of individual foreclosures because they pooled many loans and thereby spread the risk. But the risks of default of these individual loans were not truly independent of each other; that is, a sharp drop in housing prices could trigger a system-wide crisis that would result in widespread defaults. Furthermore, the regulators did not fully appreciate the possibility that the hedging strategies themselves, plus the ability to hedge further with insurance-like instruments such as credit default swaps, would fuel greater risk-taking.

In sum, this case underlines a core theme of this volume because it illustrates how US regulators committed fundamental errors of market design. The authorities put too much faith in the ability of market players to solve problems and to self-regulate. They believed that private-sector actors would act prudently to protect their reputations, and to preserve their own business and that of their clients. Greenspan famously recanted in his testimony to Congress:

> GREENSPAN: Those of us who have looked to the self-interest of lending institutions to protect shareholder's equity (myself especially) are in a state of shocked disbelief....
>
> CHAIRMAN [HENRY] WAXMAN: The question I had for you is you had an ideology. You had a belief that free, competitive—and this is shown—your statement, "I do have an ideology. My judgment is that free, competitive markets are by far the unrivaled way to organize economies. We have tried regulation, none meaningfully worked." That was your quote. You have the authority to prevent irresponsible lending practices

that led to the subprime mortgage crisis. You were advised to do so by many others. Now, our whole economy is paying its price. You feel that your ideology pushed you to make decisions that you wish you had not made? . . .

GREENSPAN: What I am saying to you is, yes, I found a flaw. . . .[149]

The regulators delegated too much to private agents, such as credit-rating agencies and accounting firms. They relied too heavily on a regulatory distinction between high-worth individuals and institutions with professional support, on the one hand, versus broader financial consumers, on the other. They assumed that they could ease regulations on the former while preserving protection for the latter. But in doing so, they neglected the holistic nature of market design and the interrelationship between different market segments.

Better Markets, a public interest group focused on financial reform, estimates the cost of the financial crisis for the United States alone at $12.8 trillion in actual GDP loss 2008–2018, plus GDP loss avoided only due to emergency fiscal and monetary policy. Yet the macroeconomic figures understate the damage, because the crisis inflicted a very human toll. Unemployment surged from 5% in January 2008 to 10.2% in October 2009. Household wealth declined from $74 trillion in July 2007 to $55 trillion in January 2009. Median family income fell 7.7% from 2007 to 2010, from $49,600 to $45,800. At least 3.7 million homes were foreclosed between 2008 and 2012. And the number of families falling below the poverty line rose from 12.5% in 2007 to 15.1% in 2010.[150]

The US Congress engaged in an extended debate over reforms in the wake of the financial crisis, eventually producing the Dodd-Frank Wall Street Reform and Consumer Protection Act in 2010. The bill addressed many of the problems that contributed to the crisis, including inadequate regulatory authority, too much leeway for banks to engage in risky activity, and banks that were "too big too fail." Yet reform advocates contend that the bill was compromised by concessions made during the legislative process, subsequent rule-making and implementation, and amendments. The bill created a new Consumer Financial Protection Bureau (CFPB) and disbanded the old Office of Thrift Supervision. It established a Financial Stability Oversight Council to coordinate supervision among regulatory agencies with a focus, as the name implies, on overall system stability. It strengthened regulation of derivatives trading, requiring financial institutions to shift most trading to public exchanges. It created additional regulatory requirements for "systemically important financial institutions." And the "Volcker Rule," named for former Fed Chairman Paul Volcker, restricted commercial banks' proprietary trading and investment in hedge funds and private equity, with complex guidelines regarding what types of trades are allowable. Separately from Dodd-Frank, the Basel III international accord also raised bank capital adequacy standards. One report concludes that the Dodd-Frank did not go far enough to consolidate regulatory authority or to strengthen provisions for systemic stability, but that the CFPB and higher capital requirements represent meaningful improvements.[151] From the standpoint of market design, the Financial Stability Oversight Council represents an important step, because the Council has the mandate to monitor the financial system as a whole and to focus on stability as its primary goal. But the Dodd-Frank reform would be more effective with even higher capital requirements, plus a structural solution that channels the spirit of the Glass-Steagall Act by prohibiting deposit-taking institutions from engaging in high-risk speculation. In 2017, however, President Trump issued an executive order designed to restructure major provisions of the Dodd-Frank Act.[152] And the House passed a bill to roll back Dodd-Frank rules, entitled the Finance Choice Act, but the Senate did not follow suit.

At its best, as in the case of the information revolution, the US market system fosters competition and innovation that generates huge leaps in productivity and human welfare. At its worst, as in the case of the financial crisis, it fosters volatility and risk-taking that destroys value and impoverishes ordinary citizens. The United States boasts the closest thing to a "free market" model, and yet this chapter has demonstrated that this model is the product of elaborate market governance, not the lack thereof. In fact, the evidence introduced in this chapter lends support for the stronger version of Proposition 8 from Chapter 1: that an LME like the United States is *more* governed than a CME like Japan. The US economy certainly has more laws and regulations, more elaborate laws and regulations, more lawyers and regulators, and more complex enforcement mechanisms. And there is a logical connection between competitive markets and heavy regulation, as noted in Chapter 1. American-style market reform has replaced monopoly with elaborate pro-competitive regulation and the fabrication of ever-more sophisticated markets, such as the capacity markets for electricity. Antitrust authorities have devised more elaborate models for evaluating, enforcing, and promoting competition. The US government has continuously retooled its marketcraft, with both spectacular successes and devastating failures.

4

Marketcraft Japanese Style

Why It's So Hard to Craft a Liberal Market Economy

In the postwar era, the Japanese government violated many of the precepts of mainstream economic theory—yet it produced the greatest economic success story in the world.[1] It restricted market entry and impeded market exit, regulating the terms of competition through elaborate license and permit regimes. It preferentially allocated credit to certain sectors, deliberately transforming the country's industrial structure. It organized research consortia to develop technology in growth industries, and it sanctioned "recession cartels" to reduce capacity in declining sectors. Meanwhile, Japanese firms collaborated via industry associations, horizontal industry groups, vertical supply chains, and other inter-firm networks. As the economy shifted from boom to bust after 1990, opinion leaders grew critical of these distinctive features of the Japanese model, calling for a dramatic shift toward the liberal market model of the United States.[2]

But what would it really take for Japan to "liberalize" its economy? Here Japan provides a test case for the core argument of this book. According to the market liberal paradigm, the diagnosis and prescription would be simple: the government should just stop interfering and let the free market flourish. In contrast, I contend that the Japanese government would have to do *more*, not less. It would have to build up the legal and regulatory infrastructure to support more competitive capital, labor, and product markets.

Likewise, the market liberal view would suggest that Japanese private-sector actors have collaborated too much, allowing traditional practices and social norms to impede market behavior, so they should abandon these legacies and embrace the free market. The previous chapter has already exposed the flaw in this logic: the liberal market model is itself the product of laws, practices, and norms. So for Japan to "liberalize," firms, banks, and workers would not simply have to reject customary business practices, but to cultivate new ones. Firms would have to develop more competitive patterns of behavior, and the Japanese people would have to adopt more market-oriented norms.

As noted in Chapter 1, an emerging consensus across multiple disciplines applies this logic to the development of market institutions in developing countries and transition economies. Scholars and practitioners have concluded that the challenge for these countries is more a positive one of strengthening government capacity and building market institutions than a negative one of withdrawing the state. Japan is the crucial case, however, for it is an advanced industrial country with the rule of law firmly in place.[3] Yet even for Japan, liberalization does not mean liberation, but rather the construction of market infrastructure.

This chapter illustrates the complex mix of laws, practices, and norms that sustain a modern market economy, and the range of measures required to enhance competition. The next section reviews the core features of Japan's postwar model (1945–1980), following the structure of Chapter 3, but this chapter adds an assessment of what it would take for Japan to transform into a liberal market economy. The subsequent sections examine reforms aimed at transforming Japanese market governance since 1980 in labor relations, finance, corporate governance, antitrust, sector-specific regulation, and intellectual property rights. And the final two sections present case studies of attempts at broader institutional change: Japan's efforts to promote innovation along the lines of the Silicon Valley model and to spur the information technology revolution. These various examples demonstrate that the Japanese government and industry have enacted ambitious market reform programs ostensibly aimed at shifting Japan toward the liberal market model of the United States. Consistent with the core argument of this volume, these reforms were not simply efforts to remove barriers to competition, but rather adventures in market redesign: the construction of new laws and regulations to govern markets, the adoption of new business practices, and the reorientation of social norms. Yet these reforms were less than transformative in four ways: they were designed to adapt the Japanese model to new circumstances more than to overturn it; they addressed some of the measures that might shift Japan toward the liberal market model but not all; formal changes in laws and regulations did not necessarily produce concomitant adjustments in private-sector practices and social norms; and ultimately they did not achieve many of their substantive goals, including promoting competition, growth, innovation, and productivity. Hence the Japanese model evolved, but it did not converge on the liberal market model.

The Postwar Model

In the postwar era, the ruling Liberal Democratic Party (LDP) provided political stability and a strong commitment to economic growth, while the key ministries, particularly the Ministry of Finance (MOF) and the Ministry of International

Trade and Industry (MITI), formulated and implemented specific economic policies. The elite officials within these ministries enjoyed high prestige and legitimacy plus relative autonomy from political pressures, and worked closely with the firms under their jurisdiction.[4] They believed that the government should actively promote and restructure industry, as well as regulate market behavior. They deployed a wide range of policy tools to increase savings and investment, allocate credit to more capital- and skill-intensive sectors, manage competition, and facilitate cooperation among firms. They channeled the personal savings of Japanese citizens deposited in postal savings accounts into government financial institutions to support investment in public infrastructure. And they deployed "administrative guidance" (informal directives) to persuade private banks to channel loans to favored sectors. They diffused technical knowledge to industry and promoted research collaboration across firms. They discouraged "excess competition" because they believed that firms might compete for market share to the point of eliminating profits and threatening the survival of some firms. They engaged in "supply and demand adjustment" (*jukyuu chousei*) through an elaborate system of licenses, permits, and other regulations.[5] Industry associations intermediated between government and industry, and among firms. They not only lobbied the government, but also enforced industry compliance with government directives and organized collaboration, and sometimes collusion, among their members.[6]

Japan was a coordinated market economy in the sense that firms collaborated with each other more extensively than in a liberal market economy like the United States, as illustrated in Figure 4.1. Firms cultivated long-term relationships

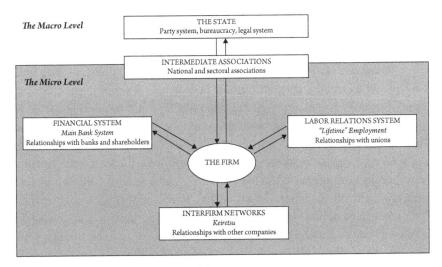

Figure 4.1 Japan's postwar market model.

with their key partners—workers, bankers, and suppliers—so there was less price-based competition in labor, finance, and business-to-business markets.[7] In Albert Hirschman's terms, Japanese firms were less likely to resort to "exit" (sever ties) with these partners and more likely to exercise "voice" (negotiate).[8] And precisely because they were less likely to exit (to lay off workers, cut off a main bank, or abandon a loyal supplier), they cultivated stronger channels for voice. The following paragraphs describe some of the core features of this postwar model: specifically the financial, labor, competition, and innovation regimes, with illustrative examples presented in Table 4.1.

Japan's postwar financial system was credit-based, meaning that firms financed investments primarily by borrowing from banks, rather than by issuing bonds or stocks.[9] Most large firms relied on a "main bank": they gave the main bank a large share of their banking business, including loans and transactions. For firms that were members of a major industrial group, a horizontal *keiretsu* such as the Mitsubishi Group, the group bank served as the main bank.[10] The bank and other group companies held equity stakes in the firm, protecting them from shareholder pressures, and allowing them greater discretion to serve the broader community of stakeholders, particularly creditors and employees. The main banks served as monitors of firm performance, and they would intervene if performance dropped severely and would organize bailouts if necessary. The banks did so not only out of a moral obligation, but also because they had an interest in the firm's survival due to their equity stake in and their business relationship with the firm. And the firm's failure could affect the bank's other client firms, given the network of interlocking business relationships. Japanese banks enjoyed stable revenues because they had access to abundant funds at low cost, thanks to high savings rates and low fixed deposit interest rates.

Under Japan's long-term employment system, large firms were unlikely to poach core ("regular") workers from other firms, and these workers were unlikely to move to rival firms. Japanese labor markets were described as "internal" because regular workers would rotate among plants, divisions, and locations within a firm or a corporate group, but not across firms. Firms cultivated loyalty by tying wage increases primarily to seniority and by offering company-specific benefits such as non-portable pension plans and corporate housing. They were more willing to invest in on-the-job training because they could count on most regular workers to stay with the firm for the long term. Japanese labor unions were organized at the firm level, giving them a common interest with management in improving productivity relative to rival firms. Japanese firms retained flexibility via a starkly tiered employment system, with the regular workers (*shain*) enjoying full membership in the corporate community, while non-regular workers (*hiseiki roudousha*), many of whom worked full-time in skilled positions, received lower wages, fewer benefits, and less job security. The

Table 4.1 **Japanese Market Governance, 1945–1980 (Selected Examples)**

	Laws and Regulations	Practices and Standards	Norms and Beliefs
Accounting	Regulators grant discretion to companies.	Statutory auditor system	Managers should adapt accounting to fit their business strategies.
Banking	MOF regulation of branch expansion, administrative guidance, fixed deposit interest rates	Main bank system	Main banks and their clients should be loyal to each other.
Capital Markets	Tight restrictions on instruments and trading, administrative guidance	Cross-shareholding, stock manipulation	The stock market is unreliable; the real economy should be insulated from it.
Corporate Governance	Ministry of Justice conservative on corporate law; authorities defer to management autonomy	Insider boards	Firms should adhere to the stakeholder model, with insider governance, main bank loyalty, group loyalty.
Antitrust	Weak enforcement, tolerance and support for industry coordination	Substantial industry collaboration, strong business groups	Industry collaboration is good, not bad; government and industry should prioritize growth over competition.
Labor	Strict rules on labor standards and working hours; case law restricts dismissals	Long-term employment, dual labor market (regular and non-regular)	Employers and employees should be loyal to each other; male breadwinner model.
Electricity	Private regional monopolies, price regulation	Regional companies exercise market power.	Electricity companies should stress universal access, safety over low cost.

(continued)

Table 4.1 **Continued**

	Laws and Regulations	Practices and Standards	Norms and Beliefs
Airlines	Price and entry regulation	Market segmentation into three niches	JAL serves as national champion; carriers prioritize quality and safety over price.
Tele-communications	NTT regulates itself; MPT oversight limited	NTT dominance, high investment and R&D	NTT should build the infrastructure and conduct R&D, provide universal access.
Patents	Limited scope of protection and restrictive interpretation by courts	Companies import and diffuse technology, collaborate on R&D.	The government should favor the import and diffusion of technology over patent protection.
Copyrights	Limited protection before 1970; then substantial harmonization with international standards	Companies not strongly constrained by copyright concerns in practice.	The government should favor the diffusion of knowledge over copyright protection.

dual labor system reinforced the gender division of labor, as regular workers were predominantly men, while temporary workers were mostly women.

The Japanese government inherited tough antitrust laws from the United States during the Occupation, but systematically dismantled them afterward. The Occupation forces dissolved the wartime control associations, broke up the prewar industrial groups (*zaibatsu*), and pressed the Diet to pass an anti-monopoly law in 1947. The Japanese authorities then revised the law in 1953, eliminating the Japan Fair Trade Commission's (JFTC) power to break up dominant firms, easing restrictions on anti-competitive practices, and permitting recession cartels, whereby companies in declining industries would agree to reduce capacity in a coordinated manner. In practice, the new law allowed many industries to justify cartels on the basis of some public interest, such as export promotion. MITI was concerned that some of these arrangements still might be vulnerable to challenge by the JFTC, however, so it sponsored laws to sanction cartels in specific industries, and other ministries followed.[11] The JFTC struggled with high evidence requirements to bring cases, limited enforcement powers, a modest budget, and a small staff compared to its US counterparts.[12] Private antitrust suits were not an attractive option due to high costs, small settlements, and a low probability of success.[13] The dismantling of US-imposed antitrust law was critical to the evolution of Japan's postwar model because many forms of coordination—including research consortia, recession cartels, exclusive dealing arrangements, and general trading companies—would violate a stricter regime.

Japanese industry was organized into elaborate interfirm networks. The horizontal industrial groups adhered to the "one set" principle, meaning that they had one firm in most major lines of business, but not direct competitors. They engaged in preferential business relationships, with group firms disproportionately relying on each other for supplies and services.[14] Meanwhile, manufacturers developed vertical *keiretsu* (supply networks) with their subcontractors. They remained loyal to their core suppliers in exchange for efforts to control costs, maintain quality, develop products, deliver supplies in a timely fashion, and provide after-delivery service.

Japan's postwar innovation regime was characterized by government efforts to encourage the transfer and dissemination of foreign technology and to coordinate private-sector development of technological capabilities. MITI leveraged its authority to regulate foreign exchange to restrict foreign direct investment and to promote the purchase of foreign technology and the dissemination of technology among Japanese producers. The government subsidized and coordinated private-sector R&D efforts, with the overwhelming focus on civilian technology, and private-sector organization facilitated the diffusion of technology among industrial group members, between assembly firms and subcontractors, and between manufacturers and their business clients.[15] The government interpreted patent coverage more narrowly than in other countries, giving imitators opportunities to invent around existing patents. And the patent-approval process was slow and costly. Meanwhile, Western governments and multinational firms were relatively lax in enforcing intellectual property rights abroad until the 1980s, and this facilitated Japanese firms' use of foreign technology.[16]

While scholars have debated whether these institutions were rational or cultural, in practice they had both instrumental and normative foundations.[17] Masahiko Aoki, for example, deploys the logic of institutional economics to demonstrate how Japanese firms cultivated long-term relationships with their workers, banks, and suppliers to upgrade workers' skills, reduce the cost of capital, and enhance quality control.[18] Ronald Dore describes similar patterns of behavior, but interprets them in more cultural or sociological terms. He acknowledges the advantages of risk-sharing and long-term ties noted by Aoki and others, but he stresses that these practices cannot be understood without reference to Japanese firms' distinctive loyalty to business partners and preference for high-trust relationships.[19] Mark Granovetter offers a twist on this debate in his famous critique of Oliver Williamson's institutional economic analysis of a firm's choice between vertical integration (making key parts itself) and subcontracting (buying those parts on the market). Williamson argues that this choice hinges on the "asset specificity" of the part: the degree to which it is specific to a particular use and a particular business partner such that it has much less value for another use or for another partner. Manufacturers will favor vertical integration for parts with higher asset specificity.[20] Granovetter contends that Williamson misses the essence of the Japanese supply chain system: that the business partnership between the assembly firm and its suppliers is embedded in dense networks of personal relationships that enhance trust and limit opportunism.[21]

The postwar model represented a stable equilibrium in that there was institutional complementarity among the different elements of the system. Aoki argues, for example, that the financial system characterized by patient bank capital supported the long-term employment system because firms did not have to cater to shareholders who might press for layoffs to bolster financial returns.[22] The logic of complementarity could have two very different implications for institutional change. Some scholars argue that the demise of one element of a system could bring on the collapse of the system as a whole. For example, Wolfgang Streeck suggests that the erosion of the German system of co-determination (whereby capital and labor jointly steward a company) implies the end of the model more broadly.[23] In contrast, I contend here that the Japanese system has not undergone a large-scale transformation because adaptations in one realm do not have their full effect without concomitant changes in many other areas.

Japan's distinctive market institutions fueled its remarkable economic and social performance in the postwar era. Japan not only achieved unprecedented economic growth, but also excelled across various social indicators, including education, public safety, health, and income equality.[24] Scholars have debated the balance of factors that produced high growth, including sound macroeconomic policies, industrial policy, corporate management, labor relations, and interfirm networks. While it is impossible to specify the respective contributions of these various factors, we can identify some of the mechanisms linking these institutions to performance. Political stability plus bureaucratic autonomy and administrative capacity supported pro-growth economic policies. A consensual policy process facilitated the management of policy trade-offs, fostered mutually beneficial bargains among societal actors, and streamlined policy implementation.[25] The government fueled industrial development by promoting high savings, maintaining low interest rates, and channeling investment toward developmental purposes, such as infrastructure investment and R&D.[26] Long-term employment and strong labor-management relations minimized labor conflict, enhanced collaboration, and enabled firms to invest in training their workers in company-specific skills. Supply networks linking assembly firms with subcontractors sustained the lean production model that revolutionized manufacturing, particularly in the auto sector.[27]

By 1980, as growth slowed and the budget deficit soared, some Japanese leaders began calling for economic reforms.[28] The administrative reform program (1981–1983) included a broad range of reforms, including fiscal reform, the privatization of public corporations, and regulatory reform. And in 1986, a blue-ribbon commission chaired by former Bank of Japan governor Haruo Maekawa advocated a shift from an export-led strategy toward a consumption-driven model of growth, including regulatory and tax reforms—but the government never fully embraced the commission's proposals.

The financial crisis of the 1990s fundamentally transformed the debate. As in the US case presented in the previous chapter, the combination of financial liberalization (discussed further later in the chapter) without stronger prudential regulation contributed to the crisis. But macroeconomic policy errors played an even more central role in Japan: the authorities allowed the asset bubble to inflate to extraordinary heights in the late 1980s, and responded too slowly and tentatively with fiscal and monetary stimulus after it burst in the early 1990s. Investors continued to pour funds into real estate and stock markets in the bubble years, in part because they had confidence in the government authorities to manage the economy. As the Japanese economy descended into stagnation, government and private-sector reports analyzed Japan's failures and US successes, and recommended bold market reforms.

This chapter reviews reforms since 1980 in subsequent sections, but let us first return to the original question: What would it take for Japan to develop more competitive capital, labor, and product markets? (See Table 4.2 for selected examples.[29]) Let me be clear: I am making an empirical claim here about what Japan would need to do to converge upon the liberal market model because this is critical to the broader argument of this volume, that market reform requires marketcraft. But I am not making a normative claim that Japan should do so. In fact, I would argue that Japanese government and industry were wise to favor incremental adjustments over drastic liberal reforms. I return to an assessment of Japan's adopted strategies in the conclusion to this chapter.

With respect to capital markets, the government would need to promote competition in financial services; strengthen accounting rules so that investors would have more tools to value companies; transform corporate law so that companies would focus more on shareholder returns; and revise regulations to discourage cross-shareholding and other practices that impede takeovers and to foster financial mechanisms that facilitate them. Corporate boards would have to cater more to shareholders, seeking to maximize returns rather than market share or firm survival. And shareholders would have to press for higher returns.

Table 4.2 What Would It Take to Turn Japan into a Liberal Market Economy? (Selected Examples)

	Laws and Regulations	Practices and Standards	Norms and Beliefs
LABOR	• Reform labor law • Reform corporate law • Promote pension portability • Permit employers more freedom with dismissals • Strengthen social safety net	• Lay off workers when necessary • Stop favoring new graduates over mid-career hires • Shift from seniority to merit-based pay • Introduce stock options	• The government should not use regulation to preserve employment. • Companies should not preserve employment at the expense of profits. • Employees should pursue opportunities in the labor market.
FINANCE	• Reform financial system • Reform corporate law • Reform pension system • Lift holding company ban • Give financial institutions freedom to develop new financial instruments • Do not favor domestic financial institutions	• Make lending decisions and price loans on the basis of risk • Stop lending to insolvent firms • Sell off cross-held shares • Companies restructure to improve financial returns	• The government should not protect banks. • The government should not manipulate financial markets. • Companies should maximize shareholder value. • Institutional investors should actively steward their investments.
COMPETITION	• Enhance antitrust law and enforcement • Strengthen pro-competitive regulation • Reform bankruptcy law • Fortify social safety net • Upgrade economic analysis of collusion and anti-competitive practices	• Choose business partners on the basis of price, not relationships • Do not cooperate or collude with competitors • Refuse to bail out failing firms	• Firms should compete, not collude. • Companies should not favor long-term business partners.

The financial sector would have to develop the human capital to support a market for corporate control, including sophisticated institutional investors, consultants, lawyers, and analysts. And managers and shareholders would have to embrace the view that firms should maximize shareholder value.

With regard to labor markets, the government would have to revise labor laws to facilitate dismissals, and/or the courts would have to become more permissive with regard to conditions for dismissal. The government would have to revise regulations to enhance job mobility, such as encouraging portable pensions like US 401(k) plans. The government and/or the private sector would have to develop better mechanisms for disseminating employment information and cultivate job-matching organizations such as employment agencies and head-hunting firms. Employers would have to hire more mid-career workers and not only entry-level recruits, and they would have to offer competitive wages. And companies would have to moderate internal labor market practices to generate more active external labor markets. Firms would have to be less loyal to their workers, and workers less loyal to their firms.

With respect to product and service markets, the government would have to strengthen antitrust policy and its enforcement. It would need to actively promote competition in regulated sectors such as transport and utilities. And it would have to revise bankruptcy law to facilitate market exit. Companies would have to reduce cross-shareholdings, unravel preferential business agreements, and provide more information to each other about costs and prices. Firms and their business partners would have to become less loyal to each other. Overall, Japanese companies would need to cooperate with each other less, and compete more aggressively.

The government and industry have deliberately addressed many of the issues outlined in Table 4.2 since the 1990s, yet they have crafted reforms to facilitate adjustment without undermining valued institutions. I explain the political factors underpinning this distinctive approach to market reforms during this period at greater length in a previous book, but for present purposes I can summarize the argument as follows.[30] Japanese firms sought modest reforms to facilitate restructuring without jeopardizing valued institutions. Hence they lobbied the government for reforms that would expand their options for restructuring but would not undermine long-term cooperative relationships with workers, banks, and other business partners. Moreover, reform advocates could not forge a strong political coalition because the major political parties and industry associations incorporated both the potential winners and potential losers from reform. As a result, Japan wound up with a distinctive pattern of reform: government officials proceeded incrementally, packaging delicate compromises; they designed reforms to preserve the core institutions of the model as much as possible; and they sought novel ways to build on the strengths of Japan's distinctive market institutions. The following sections of this chapter review these reforms since 1980 in more detail, as illustrated in Table 4.3.

Table 4.3 **Reforms of Japanese Market Governance, 1980–Present (Selected Examples)**

	Laws and Regulations	Practices and Standards	Norms and Beliefs
Accounting	Consolidated accounting; mark-to-market accounting 2000	Financial Accounting Standards Foundation 2001, partial adoption of fair-value accounting	Companies maintain some discretion in reporting, ability to smooth over returns.
Banking	Deposit interest rates liberalized 1985–1994; Financial System Reform 1992; Big Bang 1996	Financial holding companies, megabanks	MOF authority declines; main banks maintain loyalty to major clients.
Capital Markets	Financial System Reform 1992; brokerage commissions liberalized 1994; Big Bang 1996; Financial Instruments and Exchange Law 2006	Financial holding companies, megabanks	MOF authority declines; shift toward shareholder value more in form than practice
Corporate Governance	Commercial Code revisions, especially 1993–2005; takeover guidelines 2005; stewardship code 2014; corporate governance code 2015	Corporate restructuring, M&A, buybacks, stock options, outside directors	Shift toward shareholder value more in form than practice
Antitrust	Holding company ban removed 1997; Antimonopoly Law revised 1990, 2000, 2005 and 2009	M&A increases after 1990; corporate groups restructure	Greater appreciation for the benefits of competition
Labor	Labor Standards Law 1998 and 2003; Temporary Work Agency Law 1999; Labor Contract Law 2007	Labor adjustment without layoffs, rise of temp agencies, private employment agencies	Some weakening of "lifetime" employment and male breadwinner norms

Table 4.3 **Continued**

	Laws and Regulations	Practices and Standards	Norms and Beliefs
Electricity	Reforms 1994 and 2012–2014	Slow growth of independent generators; core utilities flex power	MITI-Tepco nexus discredited post–2011; shift to smart grid model
Airlines	Reforms 1986 and 1994	Modest increase in competition	Some erosion in preference for quality and safety over price
Tele-communications	NTT privatization and liberalization 1985; pro-competitive regulation, especially 2001	Dominant carrier obstruction; Softbank engages in aggressive price competition after 2000	Growing appreciation for price competition
Patents	"Japanese Bayh-Dole" 1999	Increased R&D and patent applications first decade of 2000s	Increased commitment to patent protection
Copyrights	Multiple revisions since the 1990s: strengthening enforcement and adapting to the digital age	More entities claim copyrights, including individuals.	Public attitudes shift gradually toward open-access norms since the late 1990s.

Financial Reform

More than three decades of financial reform have eroded the Japanese authorities' ability to control the allocation of credit and have produced more price-based competition in the financial sector, cross-entry across the various segments of the industry, a reorganized and consolidated set of megabanks, and a greater foreign presence. Moreover, financial reforms combined with corporate governance reforms (discussed in the following section) to address many of the steps outlined earlier that could provide the foundation for a market for corporate control in which hostile bidders could take over a firm and oust the management team. In fact, Ulrike Schaede argues that these measures combined with changes in corporate strategy to produce a "strategic inflection point" in the period from 1998 to 2006 that fundamentally transformed the logic of Japanese capitalism toward one in which firms actively restructure to maximize returns for share-holders.[31] In contrast, I find that Japanese firms resisted wholesale reform, both in the political arena and in their own business strategies, leaving a subtle blend of continuity with change.

The MOF embarked on financial reform in the 1980s under pressure from the United States. American manufacturers claimed that the dollar was overvalued relative to the yen, and that Japanese financial liberalization could help to correct this imbalance. Under the Yen-Dollar Agreement of 1984, Japan pledged to allow foreign financial institutions to set up trust subsidiaries in Japan, to create a Euroyen bond market (an offshore bond market denominated in yen), to liberalize money markets, and to remove deposit interest rate ceilings. They moved quickly on the first three of these items, but phased in deposit interest-rate liberalization gradually from 1985 to 1994 to give banks time to adjust. The MOF took on the segmentation of the financial system in the late 1980s, eventually deciding in 1992 to allow commercial banks and securities houses to enter each others' lines of business via separate subsidiaries.[32] The ministry also phased out fixed brokerage commissions—forcing brokerage firms to compete on price—gradually reducing rates from 1985 through 1990 and then beginning liberalization in 1994 with trades over 1 billion yen. Financial reforms contributed to the financial crisis of the 1990s by increasing competition in the financial sector and giving financial institutions greater freedom to make risky investments without increasing prudential supervision.

In the wake of the financial crisis, Japan's financial "Big Bang" of 1996 (named after the British reforms of 1986) and related reforms opened mutual fund, pension, and trust markets; approved new financial instruments; allowed securities houses and commercial banks to enter each other's core business lines via holding companies; and eased foreign exchange restrictions.[33] Reform proponents viewed the various measures as interrelated steps that would generate synergies among them. For example, removing foreign exchange controls would promote cross-border financial transactions that would open up the financial system, producing economic and political pressure for further reform. The MOF and the banks were not in a strong position to resist reforms given their complicity in the financial crisis.[34] The government also created a new financial regulator, the Financial Services Agency (FSA), outside the ministry. Former ministry officials comprised a substantial share of the staff of the new agency, but they ceased being ministry officials once they were transferred, and they were not allowed to return. As a whole, the Big Bang reforms increased competition in the financial-services sector, facilitated the reorganization of the sector, enhanced foreign financial institutions' access to the market and Japanese investors' ability to invest in foreign equity markets, and made it easier for firms to raise funds in capital markets.

The Big Bang package reached the realm of accounting in 2000, when the government shifted to consolidated reporting. This meant that the firm at the center of a business group would have to report not only its own financial results, but also those of its subsidiaries above a certain threshold of ownership. This made it harder for companies to hide losses in subsidiaries, and pushed them to assess value by the corporate group as a whole. It diluted the incentive to vertically integrate and gave would-be acquirers a more accurate view of corporate value.[35] In 2001, the FSA transferred the authority to set accounting standards to a private-sector body, the Financial Accounting Standards Foundation.[36] It introduced mark-to-market accounting, which is based on market value rather than purchase price, for real estate and securities in 2000. This encouraged corporations to sell off assets that were not contributing to profits, and added pressure on companies to increase financial returns. Some observers suggested that this would open up a market for corporate control, as more shares would become available for sale and shareholders would demand higher returns for their investments.[37]

Prime Minister Junichiro Koizumi's (2001–2006) extraordinary battle over the privatization of the postal system also affected the financial system because the postal savings system took in a huge share of savings deposits and financed a substantial amount of government activity via the Fiscal Investment and Loan Program (FILP). The postal savings system was a core pillar in Japan's postwar political and economic system that enabled bureaucrats to channel domestic savings toward developmental goals, especially infrastructure investment, and allowed politicians to allocate resources to their constituents.[38] Reform proponents contended that Japanese financial markets could not be modernized effectively unless more savings were channeled through private financial institutions and invested on a market basis. Koizumi made postal reform the centerpiece of his "structural reform" program, arguing that the postal savings system impeded the efficient allocation of credit, crowded out private financial activity, and fueled the public works political machine. The Cabinet approved a bill in 2005 that broke Japan Post into four units under a holding company: postal savings, postal life insurance, mail delivery, and post office network management. The government sold off shares in Japan Post Holdings in November 2015 and September 2017, still leaving it with a majority ownership stake.

The financial authorities sought to invigorate Japanese stock markets with the Financial Instruments and Exchange Law (*kinyuu shouhin torihiki-hou*) of 2006. They aimed to give experienced investors greater access to sophisticated financial instruments while strengthening protection for retail investors. The bill shifted from an industry-based approach to financial regulation (organized by the sub-sectors of the financial industry) to an instrument-based approach (organized by the financial instruments being regulated), and overhauled securities regulation, including disclosure requirements, investor protections, and stock exchange governance. It also included provisions on internal controls and independent audits, referred to as "J-SOX" for the Japanese version of the US Sarbanes-Oxley Bill. The bill contributed to the evolution of corporate governance practices, discussed in the following section, by making managers more sensitive to short-term financial results and by clarifying procedures for takeovers.[39]

The Japanese financial system has transformed since the 1990s, yet not nec-essarily in the direction of a liberal market economy. Japan's largest corporations began to wean themselves from their main banks (*ginkou banare*) in the 1980s, yet many returned to their main banks (*ginkou gaeri*) in the 1990s as their bond ratings plummeted so low that they could not issue corporate bonds. And while banks certainly sold off shares in client firms and some even refused to partic-ipate in costly bailouts, many continued to extend credit to these firms, effec-tively providing life support for the famed "zombie" firms. Hardie et al. argue that the classic dichotomy between "equity-based" financial systems (such as the United States and Britain) and "bank-based" financial systems (such as Germany and Japan) no longer holds because most major industrial countries have con-verged on market-based banking models—yet they concede that Japan defies this trend. Japanese banks rely less than other countries on financial markets as a source for their funds and as a target for their investments.[40] Japan's largest and most profitable companies have shifted toward more arms-length relationships with their banks, but smaller and more vulnerable companies have preserved the mutual loyalty of main-bank relationships with their banks.[41] Meanwhile, the financial crisis produced a major restructuring of the financial sector across tra-ditional *keiretsu* lines, leaving the sector dominated by three megabank groups.

Corporate Governance Reform

The Japanese government enacted a daunting array of legal reforms from the mid-1990s through the mid-2000s, giving corporations more options for restructuring and strengthening accountability to shareholders.[42] Corporations emulated American business practices—such as stock options, buybacks, outside directors, mergers and acquisitions, and downsizing—that had not proven to improve performance in the United States, as noted in the previous chapter.[43] Government officials saw corporate law reform as part of a larger effort—including industrial revitalization and accounting reforms—to facili-tate corporate adjustment by modernizing Japan's market infrastructure. The government and industry embraced shareholder value in principle, yet they favored cautious reforms and incremental adjustments in practice. The government designed reforms to offer corporations new options without binding requirements, and followed up by issuing non-binding governance codes and forging networks to promote communication between managers and investors.

In 1993, the government enhanced the statutory auditor system, expanded shareholder rights, and reduced the fees required to file shareholder suits. In 1995, it allowed companies to buy back their own shares, giving managers a tool to prop up share prices and fend off hostile takeovers.[44] In 1997, it simplified procedures for mergers and introduced stock options. In 2000, it followed with the Corporate Spinoff Law (*kaisha bunkatsuhou*) to make it easier for corporations to spin off divisions into new subsidiaries or to sell them off.[45] In 2001, it strengthened the statutory auditing system but also limited directors' liability in shareholder suits. The Japanese Business Federation (*keizai dantai rengoukai*, or Keidanren for short) had been concerned about the rise in shareholder suits, and lobbied hard for limits on liability. In the same year, the government limited banks' stock ownership such that Tier 2 capital (ownership in other firms) could not exceed Tier 1 capital (the bank's own equity). This was meant to improve the stability of the banking system, but it also had the effect of reducing banks' holdings of other firms, thus accelerating the unwinding of stable shareholdings.[46]

In 2002, the government permitted large firms to adopt a US-style committee system board. Firms that chose this form would abolish the statutory audit board, and would establish new audit, nomination, and compensation committees. Each committee would have at least three members, a majority of whom would be outside directors. The commercial code's definition of outside director, however, included employees of a parent company, a subsidiary of the parent company, or a major shareholder. Keidanren lobbied successfully against requiring firms to adopt the committee system, and also fought off a proposal to require all companies to appoint at least one outside director.

Hedge funds, both Japanese and foreign, became more aggressive in pressing companies for higher dividends, share buybacks, and business strategies designed to maximize returns for shareholders after 2000, and some even launched hostile takeover bids. Industry leaders grew concerned that they were vulnerable to takeover in this environment, so the Ministry of Economy, Trade, and Industry (METI) organized a panel to issue guidelines for takeover defenses in 2005 to help companies determine which strategies would be legal and appropriate. "We had some severe battles between those who wanted the guidelines to facilitate takeovers and those who wanted them to impede takeovers," recalls Noriyuki Yanagawa, a University of Tokyo economics professor and a member of the panel. "But ultimately these were just guidelines, not binding rules."[47] Buchanan, Chai, and Deakin conclude that the hedge funds achieved modest returns from activist strategies in the early 2000s, but that their efforts subsequently stalled. Moreover, the hedge funds failed in their broader effort to reorient the business strategies of the target firms.[48]

The Diet passed a major revision of the commercial code in 2005 that eliminated the minimal capital requirements for a stock company to encourage start-ups. The bill broadened the discretionary power of boards of directors, and facilitated mergers and acquisitions, while also expanding companies options' for takeover defenses. It also clarified the designation of the major corporate forms: the stock corporation, the limited liability company, the unlimited partnership, and the limited partnership.[49]

Foreign shareholder groups became more influential in the corporate governance debate as their stock ownership increased and domestic stable shareholdings declined.[50] The American Chamber of Commerce in Japan (ACCJ) produced an influential report asking the government to issue listing rules that require at least one-third of directors on corporate boards to be outside directors and to ensure that these directors are truly independent.[51] The Ministry of Justice's Legislative Subcommittee recommended a requirement of at least one outside director in an interim report in 2011. Keidanren strenuously opposed this requirement, so the subcommittee subsequently proposed that companies be allowed to forego outside directors on the condition that they publicly justify this choice. In 2009, the Democratic Party of Japan (DPJ) had ousted the LDP, which had dominated Japanese politics for more than 50 years. The DPJ administration drafted legislation reflecting the subcommittee report in 2012, but it lost power before it was able to pass the bill.[52]

The LDP returned under Prime Minister Shinzo Abe in December 2012, and incorporated corporate governance reform into its growth strategy, the famed "Third Arrow" of Abenomics. The government recognized that the business community opposed an outright requirement for outside directors, so it opted for a softer approach: altering corporate governance practice by developing best-practice codes. An FSA council of experts established a stewardship code in 2014 that set out standards for how institutional investors should engage with investee companies to maximize returns for their clients.[53] "The stewardship code is like herbal medicine (*kanpouyaku*)," declares the FSA's Ryozo Himino, "it induces change slowly but steadily."[54]

The Diet passed a bill in June 2014 that adopted the British "comply or explain" approach to corporate governance standards: listed companies would need to either have two outside directors, or publicly explain why they do not at a shareholder meeting. "We want to make Japanese companies stronger, but we cannot just tell them how to behave and expect them to do it," explains Yasuhisa Shiozaki, acting chair of the LDP's Policy Research Council. "So we are using the corporate governance code as a sort of sales pitch."[55] Companies would be permitted to select a third corporate governance structure in addition to the traditional statutory auditor system (*kansayakukai secchigaisha*) board and the US-style committee board (*shimeiiinkaitou secchigaisha*): one with an audit committee with supervisory functions (*kansatouiinkai secchigaisha*). Under this new structure, the audit committee would be given supervisory functions regarding the nomination and compensation of directors. An FSA-Tokyo Stock Exchange (TSE) joint council then fleshed out the corporate governance code, and the TSE followed with new listing requirements. Listed firms would not only have to comply or explain with respect to outside directors, but they would have to publish their principles for holding other firms' shares, criteria for voting as shareholders, basic management philosophy, and policies on executive appointments, remuneration, and shareholder relations.[56] Meanwhile, a METI council recommended that firms and investors engage in a dialogue about how to raise share value over the medium and long term, and METI organized working groups for this purpose.[57]

In essence, the government sought to facilitate corporate restructuring and to make Japanese firms more attractive to foreign investors without jeopardizing managers' autonomy or undermining valued management practices. The Big Bang reforms integrated Japanese financial markets further into global markets; accounting reforms increased pressure on managers to improve returns for shareholders; and corporate law reforms facilitated restructuring and offered new models for corporate boards. Keidanren and other interest groups fought to ensure that committee-style boards were not required; that companies retained viable mechanisms to defend against hostile takeovers; and that companies continued to serve a broader array of stakeholders, not only shareholders. Lawyers contend that the legal structure for a market for corporate control is still not in place. For example, companies do not have a legal duty to the bidder that offers the best price.[58]

Japanese corporate governance practices have evolved gradually in response to these legal changes and codes. Most Japanese firms have reduced the size of their boards and have adopted an executive officer (*shikkou yakuin*) system that permits those excluded from the board to preserve their social status while allowing the companies to streamline decision-making. Yet only 70 of 3507 TSE listed companies had committee boards as of 2016, less than 2% of the total.[59] Managers remain reluctant to empower shareholders further, and many institutional investors do not exercise their rights anyway. Almost all listed firms have added outside directors, but some managers feel that outside directors are more likely to undermine good management than to enhance it, so they do not provide directors with the information they would need to be more effective.[60] Japan also faces a shortage of qualified board candidates who could be effective and independent. Companies have taken advantage of the new options for restructuring, and mergers and acquisitions (M&A) activity has increased. The courts supported takeover defenses in several key cases, such as US hedge fund Steel Partners' attempt to acquire Japan's Bull-Dog Sauce Company in 2007, so this has deterred hostile takeover attempts in subsequent years. Hostile takeover bids remain rare, and very few to none have been successful—depending on one's definition of "hostile."[61]

Labor Market Reform

The Japanese government has substantially reformed labor regulation since the late 1990s: enhancing firms' flexibility to employ non-regular workers and giving them more options for labor adjustment short of layoffs, yet preserving long-term employment for the shrinking core of regular workers. Specifically, it eased restrictions on private employment agencies; opened up a new category of non-regular workers—agency temps; permitted portable pension plans; and loosened restrictions on working hours and other working conditions. But it did not make it any easier for firms to dismiss regular workers.

Members of the Deregulation Committee of the Administrative Reform Council turned to labor issues in 1995, and their recommendations prompted a series of reforms. They felt that regulatory reform in other sectors was likely to cause labor dislocation, so they wanted to reform labor markets to facilitate the reallocation of workers. In 1997, the government amended the Equal Employment Opportunity Act to remove some special protections for female workers, such as those governing overtime and nighttime work. In 1998, it revised the Labor Standards Law to give employers more flexibility with work-hour rules. The Japan Trade Union Confederation (*nihon roudoukumiai sourengoukai*, or Rengo for short) succeeded in imposing conditions, however, such as requiring worker consent, that made it difficult for employers to exercise this flexibility.[62]

In 1999, the government revised the Temporary Work Agency Law and the Employment Security Law to allow employers greater freedom in hiring agency temps, to permit private companies to provide employment placement services, and to increase legal protection for job seekers. Agency temps gave employers a category of workers beyond the existing tier of non-regular employees whom they could deploy for shorter periods of time with lower levels of benefits and job security. In 2003, the government allowed the use of agency temps in manufacturing, extending the maximum contract period for which employers could employ them without hiring them for good from one to three years, and allowing local governments to provide job placement services for free. The government also decreed that temporary workers performing comparable work to permanent workers should be given comparable treatment.[63]

Meanwhile, the government revised the Labor Standards Law to codify guidelines for dismissing workers. Court decisions had generally supported the long-term employment system by ruling that employers could not dismiss workers without cause unless they met fairly stringent criteria for economic hardship. Moreover, the courts tended to presume that large companies should reallocate workers within the corporate group if possible, following Japanese custom, rather than laying them off. The new legislation required employers to publish guidelines for dismissal in their employee handbooks and to specify reasons for dismissal in writing upon request by the employee. The DPJ successfully amended the language of the bill so that it would not imply that firms had a basic right to lay off workers.[64]

Japanese dismissal rules nicely illustrate the broader argument of this book, for if the Japanese government really wanted to give employers more freedom to lay off workers, it would have to do *more*, not less—that is, the restrictions on dismissals reflect corporate practices and social norms, which are in turn reflected in case law. So the government would have to actively intervene to change them.[65] Noriyuki Yanagawa argues that it might take drastic reform to foster a labor market for mid-career executives, so he proposes setting the retirement age at 40, thereby forcing companies and workers to renegotiate their contracts at that point. While Yanagawa concedes that the government is not likely to do this, the proposal reinforces the point that it would require decisive action—not deregulation—to invigorate these labor markets.[66]

The government made some modest adjustments in welfare provisions for unemployed workers, but it did not substantially bolster the social safety net.[67] It continued to rely more on government policies and private-sector practices that maintain employment (job protection) than on policies to support those who lose their jobs (worker protection). And in 2001, it restructured conventional defined-benefit plans and introduced defined-contribution systems similar to US 401(k) plans. The defined-contribution plans were expected to enhance labor mobility because benefits would be portable from one employer to another.

By 2005, the media were sounding the alarm over increasing economic inequality in Japan, and some critics were blaming Prime Minister Koizumi's economic reforms, especially labor market reforms such as the liberalization of agency temps.[68] Under Koizumi's successor, Shinzo Abe (2006–2007), the government revised the Part-Time Labor Law to establish the principle of balanced treatment for regular and non-regular workers, but it left some room for "legitimate" discrimination in a distinctively Japanese way. In the Japanese context, the two categories of workers are distinguished not only by job duties, but also by their levels of "constraint" (*kousokusei*). That is, the (mostly male) regular workers are expected to comply with employer demands for overtime work or transfers, whereas (mostly female) non-regular workers are not. The bill viewed non-regular workers as equivalent to regular workers if they have the same responsibilities, indefinite work contracts, *and* the same terms for changes in assignments. In practice, this meant that very few non-regular workers were judged to be equivalent to regular workers—even if they were performing similar duties—and thus they would not be entitled to receive equal pay and benefits.[69]

The second Abe administration (2012–) incorporated labor market reforms into its growth strategy, revisiting two proposals abandoned during the first Abe administration: a white-collar exemption for working-hour restrictions and a proposal to allow monetary compensation to settle disputes regarding unfair dismissals.[70] The administration submitted the white-collar exemption to over-time rules under the Labor Standards Law to the Diet in April 2015, but then abandoned the effort due to strong opposition. Some commentators charged that the compensation scheme revealed the employers' intent to engage in massive layoffs, but in fact employers were only seeking an added tool for the relatively rare cases of a dispute. The government also announced that it would create more flexible labor rules in six special economic zones in large cities, but Ministry of Health, Labor, and Welfare (MHLW) officials successfully fought off the proposal, arguing that the country could not have two sets of labor laws for different parts of the country. Instead, they proposed to set up special employment assistance offices for foreign companies in these zones and to enact more modest amendments to the Temp Agency Law that would apply nationwide.

Employers actually asked the government to *strengthen* regulation of the temp agency business, because the public image of the business was so poor. The Diet passed a bill in 2015 to increase the level of regulation from "registration" (*todokede*) to "permit" (*kyoka*); to eliminate the job category restrictions on agency temps; and to shift from a system that regulates agency contracts to one that focuses more on individual workers.[71] Meanwhile, the Abe team publicly pledged to promote "Womenomics," including policies to make it easier for mothers to work outside the home and to encourage companies to appoint more female executives and board directors. The Diet passed the Promotion of Women's Participation and Advancement in the Workplace Law in 2015, requiring large companies to publish data on the number and status of female employees and to develop action plans for promoting women in the workforce.

By 2016, the Abe administration shifted course from enhancing labor market flexibility to strengthening labor protection. The earlier labor market reforms had led companies to increase the non-regular share of their workforce, to incorporate agency temps into their mix of non-regular workers, and to impose wage restraint overall. "Given the polarization of Japanese employment into two groups, regular and non-regular workers," explains one MHLW official, "labor deregulation only exacerbated that gap, dampened demand, and undermined competitiveness. So we need to moderate this polarization before proceeding further with market reform."[72] So the government sought to support the macro economy by making workers feel more secure and raising wages to give them more disposable income. And it hoped to encourage more women and elderly to participate in the labor force to sustain the labor supply and support economic growth in an era of population decline. It announced a "work style reform" (*hata-rakikata kaikaku*) that included measures to narrow the status gap between regular and non-regular employees and the wage gap between males and females, to improve childcare and elder-care leave policies, and to limit excessive overtime work. The government moved beyond setting guidelines to actively monitoring corporate compliance through its regional branches, publicizing model behavior, and sanctioning violations. Yasuhisa Shiozaki, who was Minister of Health, Labor and Welfare from 2014 to 2017, reports that the equal pay for equal work measures encountered resistance from both industry (Keidanren) and labor (Rengo) organizations that represent the vested interests of the core (regular) workers. "The Prime Minister's Office made it clear that they did not want to touch the core employees," he recalls, "so I had to work hard to persuade them to go along with some of the language we put in the guidelines."[73]

Japanese employers generally have not pressed for greater freedom to hire and fire regular workers. Keidanren Vice Chairman Yoshio Nakamura puts it this way: "We support voluntary reductions but not forced layoffs. Companies would not resort to mass layoffs even if they had the freedom to do so, because Japanese managers have a strong commitment to employment stability."[74] Many Japanese firms value the long-term employment system because they benefit from employee loyalty, collaborative labor-management relations, and the ability to invest in training workers in firm-specific skills. They have preferred to maintain the combination of a long-term employment system with the flexibility of a dual labor market, and they have pressed for reforms that would give them greater flexibility within this structure.

Japanese firms have taken advantage of those reforms that have passed, employing a rising number of agency temps, for example. Some allocated stock options to top executives, but the coverage and the scale of these allocations remained modest in comparison to the United States.[75] Some firms gradually increased mid-career hires, but there is still not an active market for executives in large companies.[76] Many firms introduced more performance-based pay, but some deployed these systems as camouflage for wage restraint. Overall, Japanese firms have charted a distinctive pattern of employment adjustment, designed to cut costs without laying off workers.[77] They have favored moderate measures such as restraining wages, cutting bonuses, and reducing overtime. They have seconded workers to affiliated firms, using corporate groups as employment networks. Corporations have also diverged more from each other in strategy since the 1990s: those firms that benefited the most from long-term employment, such as manufacturers, adhered to it; while those who benefited the least, such as retailers, abandoned it.[78] As Japan has shifted from labor surplus to labor shortage, however, some Japanese firms have embraced the spirit of the work style reforms, focusing less on how to shed excess workers and more on how to recruit and retain quality workers.

Government and industry have avoided major labor dislocation by favoring modest policy reforms and gradual labor adjustment strategies, yet these measures have taken a toll over time. For example, many firms have reduced employment via attrition rather than layoffs, but this has created a generation gap between older workers, who still have permanent positions, and younger ones, who increasingly do not. Likewise, firms have increased the share of temporary workers rather than abandoning core workers, but this has still undermined employment security overall. Over the long term, this cost-cutting has reduced employee welfare, undermined labor-management relations, and weakened macroeconomic performance.

Antitrust Reform

The Japanese government has gradually strengthened antitrust enforcement since the 1990s, but this has not substantially impaired firms' ability to coordinate through industry associations, standards-setting bodies, or research consortia. Nevertheless, Japan's distinctive pattern of long-term relationships among firms has evolved in the wake of the financial crisis of the 1990s, as firms reduced levels of cross-shareholdings and manufacturers rationalized their supply networks.

In the late 1980s, the US government pressured Japan for stronger antitrust enforcement under the bilateral Structural Impediments Initiative (SII) talks. American negotiators charged that Japanese private-sector practices, such as dealership networks and vertical supply chains, constituted discriminatory practices that shut out US competitors. Keidanren was ambivalent about antitrust and regulatory reform, reflecting the divisions within its own ranks. Many competitive manufacturers favored reform because it could lower prices (for utilities or distribution, for example) and reduce trade friction with the United States, but less competitive manufacturers and service-sector firms resisted. MITI gradually grew more favorable toward reform, as some officials became less wedded to traditional industrial policy goals and more amenable to competition as a means to enhance international competitiveness.[79]

The biggest single change in antitrust policy, the removal of the ban on holding companies in 1997, did not promote competition but rather permitted further consolidation. The US Occupation forces had enacted the ban when they broke up the prewar industrial groups (*zaibatsu*). By the 1990s, company executives began to feel that holding companies could help them with financial management by allowing them to hedge the risk of any single business line. They could reduce labor costs by differentiating wages and benefits across companies; reorganize internally by turning divisions into separate companies; or merge with other companies more easily by using a holding company structure. Few firms formed holding companies immediately after the reform passed in 1997, in part because they could not fully take advantage of this structure until the government introduced a consolidated tax system in 2003.[80] Yet the government used holding companies to resolve tricky policy problems in key sectors. In telecommunications, for example, it reorganized Nippon Telegraph & Telephone (NTT), preserving some integration with a holding company while breaking up NTT into two regional local telephone companies, a long-distance and international carrier, wireless communications, and data services. MOF officials had explored the holding company option for financial-sector desegmentation in the late 1980s, but they ruled it out because they judged that it was not feasible politically. But once the ban was lifted, they allowed commercial banks, securities houses, and insurance companies to enter each other's lines of business via a holding company structure.

In the early 2000s, the government prepared legislation to strengthen antitrust policy by expanding the JFTC's investigative powers, doubling penalties for price-fixing to 12% of sales obtained from anti-competitive practices, and offering leniency to firms that blow the whistle on their partners in collusion.[81] Keidanren strongly opposed these measures, however, arguing that the government was acting too quickly; that the penalty increase was unreasonable; that the penalties were unconstitutional because they could subject executives to double punishment (civil and criminal); that the JFTC would be acting as both prosecutor and judge if firms filed appeals to the JFTC; and that the proposals failed to address the government's own role in fomenting collusion, especially via public procurement practices.[82] The Diet forged a compromise in 2005, passing a bill to increase fines to 10% for large companies and 4% for smaller companies, to encourage whistle-blowing by waiving fines for the first company to admit illegal activity and reducing fines for the second and third; and strengthening the JFTC's powers to conduct criminal investigations.[83] The Diet further amended the Antimonopoly Act in 2009, increasing penalties for violations, broadening the range of violations subject to surcharges, and increasing the maximum criminal penalty from three to five years in prison. The JFTC shifted toward a more sophisticated economic analysis of mergers, and broadened and strengthened its staff expertise.[84] The JFTC gradually increased its staff from 150 in 1990 to 672 in 2004 and 842 in 2017, and its budget from ¥5.24 billion in 1995 to

¥7.81 billion in 2004 and ¥11.2 billion in 2017.[85] American authorities claim that Japanese enforcement remains lax by international standards, and that the JFTC's capacity for economic analysis of anticompetitive behavior lags that of the United States and the European Union.[86]

While antitrust reform has proceeded incrementally and not uniformly in the direction of promoting competition, Japanese companies have none-theless reorganized their business relationships since the 1990s, largely in response to market pressures. The horizontal groups have reconfigured due to mergers across group lines, and member companies have reduced their cross-holdings.[87] Manufacturers have restructured their relationships with suppliers, reinforcing ties with core suppliers while reducing the number of suppliers in their groups.[88] Japanese firms now give greater weight to price factors in business-to-business transactions. Many firms have abandoned the traditional after-pricing system whereby the two parties to a transaction negotiate the price after the fact so as to give each other more flexibility with market fluc-tuations.[89] Even with these adjustments, Japanese companies retain a propen-sity to rely on long-term business partnerships and to coordinate strategies via industry associations.

Regulatory Reform

The Japanese government has been working on "deregulation" since the adminis-trative reform (*gyousei kaikaku*) movement of the early 1980s, when it privatized NTT, the Japan National Railways, and Japan Tobacco & Salt. Yet Japanese-style regulatory reform followed a common pattern across sectors, with the central ministries maintaining regulatory authority and carefully managing the process of introducing competition.[90]

In telecommunications, the government liberalized the market for value-added network (VAN) services in 1982, and then privatized NTT and liberalized tele-communications services in 1985. Ministry of Posts and Telecommunications (MPT) officials had advocated competition in telecommunications since the 1970s because they recognized that they could augment their own power and status by allowing competition with NTT.[91] Under the new regime, they took over some policy functions from NTT, including R&D and infrastructure invest-ment. They also orchestrated the entry of new competitors into each market seg-ment: long-distance, international, and mobile. And they micro-managed the competition by evaluating price and service changes for their potential impact on the competitive balance. The ministry then strengthened pro-competitive regulation after 2000, as described in the information technology section at the end of this chapter.

In the airline sector, Ministry of Transportation (MoT) officials took the art of government-managed "deregulation" to its highest form.[92] The MoT had developed the market with clear niches for three major players: Japan Air Lines (JAL) monopolized international routes; All Nippon Airways (ANA) dominated the main domestic routes; and Japan Air System (JAS) specialized in local routes. In 1986, ministry officials slowly began to allow second or third carriers to operate on those routes where demand was greatest, with each carrier receiving approximately one new route for every one of its own routes on which it would have to tolerate a competitor. In 1989, they allowed airlines to adjust fares within plus or minus 10% of a specified pricing curve based on distance. Then in 1994, they reduced the level of regulation over price changes from permit to notification, allowing carriers to lower prices substantially. Even so, ministry officials retained substantial regulatory control, contending that Japan had a shortage of facilities and airspace so that further price and entry liberalization would lead to higher prices, not lower ones.

In electricity, MITI created a wholesale market and marginally liberalized prices in 1995. It allowed non-electric companies with their own generators to sell excess supply to electric companies and required electric companies to transport this electricity over their own power lines. And it opened the electricity market for commercial users in 2005. The regulatory regime came under intense pressure for reform after the 2011 earthquake, tsunami, and Fukushima nuclear plant crisis. The government responded with a three-stage reform: creating a new regulatory body, liberalizing retail sales, and unbundling production and distribution. It created the new nuclear safety regulator in 2012 and established an agency to regulate electricity competition in 2015; it permitted competition in the retail market by the regional monopolies across jurisdictions and from new entrants in 2016; and it passed legislation in 2015 to hive off transmission and distribution divisions from the regional power monopolies and to establish them as separate companies by 2020. METI officials wanted to seize the window of opportunity to publicly commit to the full package of reforms right away, but also to phase in the implementation to give themselves and the electric companies time to prepare, especially for the unbundling in the third phase. They would need time to evaluate progress at each stage and to recalibrate before proceeding with the next steps. And the electric companies would have to prepare their IT and management systems for reorganization.[93]

The Japanese government keeps a tally of total regulations, providing a crude test of the "free markets and more rules" thesis. The total number of regulations has in fact increased despite numerous "deregulation" programs, rising from 10,621 in 2002 to 14,908 in 2015. But the government contends that the stringency of these regulations has declined.[94] As stressed throughout this volume, however, formal regulatory change is only part of the story. Ulrike Schaede argues that Japan's regulatory reform tended to foster self-regulation via indus-try associations in a variety of sectors, including trucking, investment banking, commercial banking, and insurance.[95] Strikingly, Hoshi and Kashyap find that "deregulation" in the 1995–2005 period did not correlate with improvement in total factor productivity.[96] The analysis here suggests three hypotheses that might account for this result. First, government regulation may be supplanted by private coordination or collusion so that reducing it has no net effect on pro-ductivity. Second, regulation may interact with so many other facets of market governance that it has no clear independent effect on productivity. Third, some regulations may enhance productivity while others undermine it, leaving no measurable net effect.

Intellectual Property Rights

As Japan advanced from technology catch-up in the early postwar era to the frontier after 1980, the authorities placed greater emphasis on IPR protection as an incentive for innovation. By the late 1990s, the government began to reform the IPR system to adapt to the digital age, yet reform efforts remained incremen-tal, impeding the development of Internet services.

The government responded to both international and domestic pressures for stronger IPR protection. Japan participated in international harmonization efforts such as the Paris Convention (since 1883), the Patent Cooperation Treaty (1970), Trilateral Co-operation (a US-Europe-Japan forum since 1983), and the Agreement on Trade-Related Aspects of Intellectual Property Rights (TRIPS, since 1994). It forged bilateral agreements with the United States, which com-plained that the Japanese patent system insufficiently protected foreign inven-tions and discouraged high-tech imports. And domestic lobby groups in specific sectors pushed the government toward stronger IPR protection.[97]

Beginning in the 1980s, METI and the Japan Patent Office increased damage awards, accelerated the dispute resolution process, and expanded patent protec-tion to new spheres in the IT and biotech fields. The government first granted patent protection to software in 2000, and extended protection to business mod-els, such as e-commerce auctions and settlement systems. It increased damage claim amounts for patent infringements in 1999 and 2000, and revised the pat-ent dispute system and legal judgment procedures. It enacted the Technology Transfer Promotion Law in 1998 and the "Japanese Bayh-Dole Act" in 1999 to promote the transfer of technology from universities to the commercial sector, and many private universities subsequently set up technology transfer offices. Public universities could not participate until 2004, when they were par-tially privatized so that faculty members would have greater liberty to pursue commercial activities.[98] The Japan Patent Office favored university technology transfer offices by discounting or waiving fees and expediting the approval process.[99]

The government moved on to more comprehensive reform to strengthen Japan's industrial competitiveness with the Basic Law on Intellectual Property of 2002. It created a new IP Strategy Headquarters, a commission with a staff housed in the Cabinet Secretariat, and began issuing annual action plans to promote the creation, dissemination, and exploitation of intellectual property. The Headquarters does not execute the plans, but it specifies which ministries are responsible and deploys its own task force to promote implementation. The first Strategic Framework Plan promoted patenting by universities and public research institutions, revised the regulation of staff inventions within businesses, and reformed the Unfair Competition Prevention Law to prevent technology drain overseas. In 2005, the government established the Intellectual Property High Court, with specially trained judges. The government gradually enhanced the IP regime, including the patent application process, the dispute resolution system, anti-counterfeiting and piracy measures, training for IP experts and lawyers, and the university technology transfer system.

While these reforms strengthened patent rights, they have only contributed to modest increases in R&D effort and innovative output.[100] Surveys of electrical machinery, pharmaceutical, and software firms show that reforms have resulted in higher R&D expenditures and more patent applications.[101] And the number of patents from university-industry collaborations increased, without a decrease in patent quality.[102] Yet small and medium-sized enterprises (SMEs) have not responded to the changes in policy.[103] And Japan has not developed a market for patents like that in the United States, as Japanese firms remain reluctant to sell their proprietary technology. "We have made substantial progress in strengthening the protection regime," reports one IP Headquarters official, "but Japanese companies still do not make full use of their intellectual property."[104]

The Japanese government has also reformed copyright regulation to adapt to the information age. Critics argued that the Copyright Act of Japan of 1970 was incompatible with the digital environment: it hindered new business entrants, and its lack of fair-use provisions left a large gray area between infringing and non-infringing activity, creating legal uncertainty that hampered investment.[105] In preparation for accession to the World Intellectual Property Organization (WIPO) Copyright Treaty, in 1999 Japan added criminal penalties for producing and distributing devices designed to circumvent copyrights and for illegally revising copyright management information to make a profit. The government raised the cap on fines for criminal copyright infringement from 1 to 3 million yen in 1996 and then to 10 million yen by 2006. A government project to create a new national search engine in 2006 encountered an unexpected roadblock from copyright law, which prohibited the copying of copyrighted material into a browser cache (a repository for stored data that allows speedier retrieval). The government did not amend copyright law to allow this until 2009.[106] The Diet amended Japan's fair use rules in 2009 and 2012, but fair use rights remained more restricted than in the United States. Having achieved its goals of strengthening intellectual property protection and streamlining procedures in its first 10 years, the IP Headquarters began to shift in a direction more favorable toward users with a more open innovation model by 2015. It would expand rights to fair use of copyrighted material, facilitate industry-academia-government collaboration, and promote the international harmonization of technical standards.[107]

Marketcraft for Innovation

Let us now turn to two case studies in which the Japanese government and industry have attempted to reshape market institutions for a changing competitive environment: the efforts to foster entrepreneurship and to promote the information revolution. Superficially one might characterize these as attempts to liberalize the market, yet they are more accurately viewed as adventures in marketcraft. The Japanese government sought to emulate the liberal market model of the United States, yet to do so, it increased regulation, launched new initiatives, prodded businesses to change their practices, and campaigned to alter social norms. In both cases, government officials devised comprehensive reform visions to transform market governance; they successfully implemented many of these reforms; they made progress toward specific goals—and yet they failed in their larger projects of emulating the US model and closing the performance gap with the United States.

The Japanese government has adopted a multitude of strategies to stimulate innovation in response to economic stagnation since the 1990s, including government-sponsored R&D, government-industry and university-industry partnerships, regional industrial clusters, legal reforms to facilitate venture formation and venture capital, and public campaigns to foster entrepreneurial spirit. Japan has faced increasing pressure to boost productivity as economic growth slowed, population growth declined and ultimately reversed, labor costs increased, the yen appreciated, and the dominant technological paradigm shifted away from areas of Japan's competitive strength. Yet despite these heroic efforts, Japan has failed to replicate the Silicon Valley ecosystem, including its unique venture-capital sector, dynamic labor markets, and radical innovation. Hall and Soskice contend that liberal market economies like the United States excel in radical innovation that is critical in dynamic technology sectors such as biotechnology, semiconductors, and software; system-based products, such as telecommunications or defense systems; and service sectors, such as advertising, corporate finance, or entertainment. Coordinated market economies like Japan favor incremental innovation that is essential for capital goods manufacturing, such as machine tools, consumer durables, engines, and specialized transport equipment.[108] In addition, Japan's dominant norms of social order, egalitarianism, and techno-nationalism have encouraged risk-sharing behavior while discouraging risk-taking.[109]

MITI began supporting small businesses in the 1960s via subsidized loans from government financial institutions. Given the Japanese political context, however, the government offered its strongest support to the large numbers of retailers, rather than to the small numbers of entrepreneurial technology firms. The authorities viewed the weakness of SMEs as an impediment to strengthening the competitiveness of industry as a whole.[110] The government sponsored three small business investment companies (SBIC) beginning in 1963, and these have continued to provide a major source of venture finance. It not only provided financial incentives, but also sponsored training programs to train entrepreneurs and public education campaigns to spur entrepreneurship.[111]

By the 1970s, MITI had begun trying to cultivate a venture capital industry on the Silicon Valley model. Japan first introduced venture capital financing in 1971, but the JFTC imposed severe conditions that remained in place until 1998. Venture capital companies could not hold more than 49% of shares, transfer directors to the company, or invest in existing stock. Each of these provisions prevented venture capital financing as practiced in the United States, and impeded the development of the sector.[112] In 1999, the government facilitated the pooling of investments into venture funds under the Limited Partnership Act for Venture Capital Investment.[113] The government also used capital injections from government financial institutions to spur private venture capital investments, and developed tax-incentive programs to encourage individual "angel" investors to fund new ventures. Early venture capital firms did more lending than investment, but they shifted to investment in the 1990s.[114] Even so, Japanese venture capital firms still differed from their US counterparts in that they were more likely to be affiliates of large financial institutions; they invested a larger proportion of their own funds (as opposed to third-party investments); they financed at a later stage; they spread their investments across a larger portfolio of investments; and they took a less active role in monitoring and mentoring venture managers.

By the late 1990s, METI sought to shift the innovation system from one dominated by in-house R&D conducted at major corporations toward one based on networks among innovators by strengthening ties between university research laboratories and venture firms. Policy reforms produced a significant increase in joint research projects between universities and firms, university-industry cooperative research centers, and university-based startups. The government promoted the formation of business incubators under the 1999 New Business Creation Promotion Law. Incubation facilities increased from 30 in 1999 to 498 in 2013.[115] Early incubators lacked managerial expertise and other support services, in contrast to the United States, where incubator managers often function as a bridge between firms and venture capital, sales and marketing, and other resources.[116] Although the government addressed these problems through training programs to improve managers' skills, incubators still had trouble recruiting managers with private-sector experience. Some successful incubators emerged, but many failed.[117] In 2001, the government announced a target to create 1,000 academic spin-offs in three years.[118] It met this goal, but the momentum faltered in the latter half of the first decade of the 2000s, with the number of university spin-offs that closed or went bankrupt surpassing the number of newly founded ones.[119]

In 2001, METI announced a "Regional Cluster Plan" to foster centers of innovation bridging government, industry, and universities. It sought to link 5,000 SMEs and 200 universities with regional METI bureaus and other organizations in 19 clusters across nine geographical regions.[120] In contrast to previous regional innovation policies, the cluster plan supported the autonomous development of regional industries without direct government management of the clustering process. By 2005, METI had created regional networks among 6,100 firms and 250 universities in 17 clusters.[121] One assessment of the industrial clusters found that participation in the cluster project alone did not increase R&D productivity and that research collaboration with a partner in the same cluster region actually decreased R&D productivity, both in terms of the quantity and quality of patents.[122] Kathryn Ibata-Arens argues that the cluster plan focused on creating the formal institutions undergirding clusters, but METI lacked the social capital to foster a shared national-local vision among community stakeholders or to facilitate civic entrepreneurship.[123]

In December 1999, the Diet passed the Civil Rehabilitation Law (*minji saiseihou*) to streamline bankruptcy procedures to make it easier for companies to declare bankruptcy and pay off creditors without being forced to liquidate the enterprise. The authorities hoped that better bankruptcy procedures would moderate risk for entrepreneurs and thereby generate more startups. The new law lowered the requirement for creditor consent for a reorganization plan from near unanimity to a simple majority. It allowed creditors to enforce a settlement under continuing court supervision, rather than having to initiate new proceedings. And most critically, it allowed managers to remain in place in most cases, encouraging them to endure rehabilitation since it would not cost them their jobs. In 2001, the government issued new guidelines for out-of-court workouts, specifying how to structure debt relief in cases with multiple lenders and uncertain claims. In 2003, it revised the Corporate Reorganization Law (*kaisha kouseihou*) to allow turnarounds adjudicated in court. And in 2004, it revised the Liquidation Law (*hasanhou*) to simplify procedures for selling off assets. Thus the government streamlined the three main avenues for dealing with failing companies: shutdown, reorganization, and informal workout.[124] Eberhart, Eesley, and Eisenhardt find that streamlining bankruptcy procedures increased the number and quality of new market entrants.[125]

Japan established several stock exchanges to foster smaller initial public offerings beginning in 1999, including MOTHERS, NASDAQ-Japan, Hercules, and JASDAQ. Black and Gilson had identified the lack of a liquid initial public offering (IPO) market in Japan as a critical factor impeding venture capital in Japan.[126] The creation of new exchanges at least partially addressed that problem, but did not substantially boost Japan's venture capital sector.

In April 2003, METI set up a study group to look at start-ups spun off from large corporations. The study group concluded that venture spin-offs would be more likely to succeed in Japan than independent start-ups. Subsequent studies have found that spin-off subsidiaries tend to exhibit stronger short-to-medium growth than their parents. Profitability growth performance after 10 years correlates with diversification, with subsidiaries operating in the parent's industry underperforming the parent and subsidiaries in different industries outperforming their parents.[127] Many experts remain skeptical, however, because Japanese parent companies tend to exercise so much control that spin-offs lack a truly entrepreneurial spirit.[128]

Prime Minister Abe sought to promote innovation under his Innovation 25 scheme in 2007, but he was not in office long enough to follow through. When he returned as prime minister in 2012, however, he incorporated this theme into the Third Arrow of Abenomics. The strategy included tax incentives for large firms to invest in venture capital funds, legal reforms to allow four national universities to create venture capital companies, and mentorship programs for young entrepreneurs. METI put particular emphasis on using public research institutes, such as the National Institute of Advanced Industrial Science and Technology (AIST), to forge bridges between universities and industry, especially smaller businesses.[129]

The Japanese government has addressed some of the major legal prerequisites for a vibrant venture-capital sector through the corporate law reforms addressed earlier in this chapter, including the introduction of stock options, limits on director liability, and reducing listing requirements. Stock options facilitate US-style venture capital as a vehicle for equity incentives: founders and managers may be willing to forgo salary in the short term in exchange for the possibility of substantial equity gains. Meanwhile, limits on liability were expected to make Japanese venture capitalists less reluctant to take an active role in monitoring ventures, the common practice in the United States. The corporate law reforms that facilitated the formation of companies were effective in increasing the number of start-ups, but they also brought in more low-quality start-ups due to the lower threshold.[130] The Japanese corporate law revisions of 2000 and 2001 also loosened restrictions on preferred stock. American venture capitalists use preferred stock (as opposed to common stock) to finance ventures because it helps them to prevent dilution of their stock in subsequent financing rounds and to protect themselves by giving the owners of preferred stock "deemed liquidation," meaning preferential compensation in the case of liquidation. But Japanese firms for the most part have not used preferred shares because the law does not allow deemed liquidation, and the tax authorities have not worked out how to account for the difference between preferred and common shares.[131] The venture capital market is also constrained because Japan does not have a standard approach to the valuation of intangible firm assets, such as intellectual property.

Thus the Japanese government has effectively put in place several of the institutional prerequisites for Silicon Valley–style venture capital, yet those piecemeal efforts have not produced the desired result of a flourishing venture capital industry and growth in startups.[132] Zen Shishido argues that Japan has moved toward the US model in three key respects: (1) the growth of IPO markets (the new stock exchanges); (2) the reform of corporate law, especially the introduction of stock options and preferred stock, plus limits on director liability, and (3) the development of start-up communities. Nonetheless, the fundamental logic of the venture capital business still differs from that of the United States because Japanese entrepreneurs cede less management control to venture capitalists and reap fewer rewards from success via equity stakes. Shishido attributes this to remaining differences in law as well as market culture (greater risk aversion), business practices (a bank-centered capital market), and market development (an immature reputational market for venture capital). Specifically, Japanese corporate law makes a majority stock share more important than it is in the United States, so entrepreneurs are less willing to cede a majority to venture capitalists. And director liability remains greater, so venture capitalists are less willing to take board positions in start-ups.[133] This nicely illustrates the broader argument of this chapter: piecemeal reforms are not likely to produce convergence on a foreign model because market governance systems constitute complex combinations of interconnected laws, practices, and norms. "We recognize we cannot create a Silicon Valley in Japan," concedes one METI official. "So now we are trying to build bridges between Japanese entrepreneurs and Silicon Valley itself."[134]

As a result, Japan still has a relatively low level of start-ups, and these start-ups contribute less to innovation.[135] Japan ranks third in the world in venture capital investments at $1.4 billion, but remains far behind the United

States at $66.2 billion.[136] Japan ranks 22nd in venture capital investments as a share of GDP, with Israel, the United States, and Canada in the top three spots.[137] Japan's rates of business entry and exit are both low by international standards: 5.2% and 3.8%, respectively, compared to 10.2% and 8.8% for the United States.[138] Given the impossibility of replicating the Silicon Valley ecosystem, government and industry would be better off focusing on ways to adjust Japan's existing institutional strengths to the changing environment. This could mean leveraging strong government-industry ties and industry links to promote technological development in key sectors. Or it could mean leveraging the financial and human resources of large firms to support corporate spin-off ventures, but structuring these ventures so that they are more independent in terms of finances and human resources and they act more like true ventures.

Marketcraft for a Japanese IT Revolution

In the previous chapter, we reviewed the US institutional roots of the information revolution. But how could Japan best propel this revolution at home? Should it emulate US market architecture, or design something distinctively Japanese? The Japanese government has responded to the IT challenge with a series of reform initiatives designed to emulate the US model and to accelerate the information revolution. Its strategy, consistent with the overall argument of this chapter, was to strengthen regulation and enhance the government role in the sector, not to liberate businesses to innovate on their own. Nevertheless, I contend that the Japanese government ultimately produced the wrong mix of industrial promotion and market reform in its IT strategy. It failed to deliver strong state support where it was most needed, such as in sectors that require massive investment, like liquid crystal displays and solar panels. It moved too cautiously with pro-competitive policies where they were most appropriate, such as in telecommunications. And it was not aggressive enough in promoting IT diffusion in schools, government, and society at large. In contrast, for example, the South Korean and Nordic country governments have devised more effective combinations of government policies for IT sectors.[139]

The IT revolution poses a particular conundrum for Japan because it undermines many of Japan's institutional strengths and exacerbates its weaknesses.[140] Japan has lost its edge in some areas of its greatest competitive strength, such as IT hardware, and it has failed to challenge the global leaders in areas of weakness, such as IT software and services. Japan's world market share has plummeted in key products such as DRAM chips, liquid crystal displays, and solar panels, and its share of global information and communications technology (ICT) exports dropped from 10.9% in 2000 to 2.7% in 2015.[141] Meanwhile, US firms dominate in software and services, including operating systems, business software, and search engines, as noted in the previous chapter.

We should not be too surprised that the information revolution has not played to Japanese strengths. Japanese market institutions fostered the lean production revolution, and Japanese companies led the shift to that paradigm and profited from it. Likewise, US market institutions nurtured the Internet revolution, and US companies have played the leading role and have enjoyed the enormous first-mover advantages characteristic of the information economy. The IT revolution has tested Japanese manufacturers because it relies on capabilities in areas of weakness—such as services, software, and system integration. The decomposition of production (modularization) has undermined the competitive advantage of Japanese business models that rely on integral production plus long-term relationships with suppliers, banks, and workers to foster incremental advances in production processes. Japan's integrated electronic companies favored proprietary technology, and they had considerable success with this model in Japan's high-growth years. Yet the information economy operates on a different logic, with more open interfaces and user-driven innovation.

Japanese electronics producers have been slow to embrace these changes. Japan's IT-hardware sector has been dominated by NTT "family" firms, such as NEC Corporation and Fujitsu, that worked closely with NTT, the dominant telecommunications service provider, in building up Japan's communications infrastructure and developing high-quality equipment. These firms focused first and foremost on serving NTT and the large domestic market, and this impeded them from adjusting rapidly to the discontinuous technology of the Internet. NTT was strongly committed to its own network technology, so it was late in adopting the core communication protocol for the Internet, TCP/IP. Japanese cellular telephone makers gave priority to developing phones for NTT DoCoMo's standards, undermining their ability to compete in the global market.[142]

Japan has also been challenged by what Breznitz and Zysman call the "services transformation": the integration of service functions into manufacturing.[143] This transformation involves the substantial use of advanced software embedded in manufacturing, yet Japan lags in many areas of software development.[144] Arora, Branstetter, and Drev contend that this shift is the single most important factor in Japan's competitive decline in the IT sector relative to the United States. They find that US firms improved their relative performance over the course of the 1990s, but advanced most dramatically in those areas where software competence was critical. Moreover, IT patents granted by the US government—including hardware patents—increasingly cited software technology, yet Japanese firms were less likely to cite software than their competitors, suggesting that their innovations were less reliant on advances in software.[145]

Japanese firms' strong orientation toward the domestic market rather than the global marketplace has hindered their ability to adapt to the decomposition of production and the services transformation. Commentators now commonly refer to this as the "Galapagos" phenomenon—that is, Japanese manufacturers develop high-quality products that are only suited for the Japanese market.[146] In a classic example, Japanese electronics companies produced some of the most sophisticated cellular telephones in the world, yet they did not succeed in world markets because the handsets were not suited to global technical standards, their features were tailored to Japanese tastes, and their prices were too high.

Critically, Japanese firms lag behind their US counterparts in the use of sophisticated IT systems. Kyoji Fukao estimates that Japanese firms' failure to fully leverage IT for productivity gains costs Japan as much as 0.7% a year in GDP growth.[147] One survey found that Japanese companies deployed IT more for defensive purposes, such as cutting costs, whereas US companies leveraged it more for strategic goals, such as raising productivity. And only 18.5% of Japanese companies had begun to use big data as of 2014, compared to 72.7% for US firms.[148]

The government formed an IT Strategy Headquarters within the Cabinet Office in 2000, and unveiled its "e-Japan Strategy" in 2001 to bolster Japan's IT sector, combining pro-competitive regulation, investment in infrastructure, improvements in the legal apparatus supporting electronic commerce, and measures to support electronic government. The ministry pressed NTT to lower interconnection charges and to lease unused capacity, fueling a remarkable price war in digital subscriber lines (DSL). Softbank aggressively cut prices for its DSL service to challenge NTT and to raise demand for its Internet-based services. NTT and other competitors fought back with even faster fiber-to-the-home service.[149] Japan's broadband service rates dropped to the lowest in the world by 2002.[150] And Internet penetration surged from 30% in 2000 to 92% in 2016.[151] MIC published guidelines that would allow mobile virtual network operators (MVNOs) to provide service using the networks of existing mobile operators in 2002, but this policy did not bear fruit until MIC required the operators to negotiate with the MVNOs and stipulated procedures for arbitration if the two sides could not reach agreement in 2007.[152] The IT Strategy Headquarters followed with "e-Japan II" in 2003, but it confronted bureaucratic rivalries and struggled to develop concrete goals. The MIC proposed its own "u-Japan Strategy" to promote IT use in health care, electricity, transport, and education sectors, but the ministries in charge of those sectors preferred to develop their own plans.[153]

By 2010, METI and MIC officials were remarkably candid in their assessment of Japan's declining competitiveness, and they were proposing some creative policy responses.[154] One METI report offered three explanations for Japan's weakness in IT: insufficient investment, a flawed strategy on standards, and too much focus on the domestic market.[155] METI officials proposed that the government should resurrect elements of an industrial policy: increasing financial support for research, actively coordinating Japanese companies, and aggressively marketing Japanese products abroad. Both METI and MIC advocated a dramatic increase in investment in IT.

The Abe administration incorporated IT strategy into its growth strategy, creating a new post of chief information officer in 2013 to oversee IT investment and market reform. The government's ICT National Strategy Headquarters proclaimed the goal of becoming the world's most advanced IT nation by increasing IT usage in government services and the private sector, especially the deployment of "big data." Yet this grand vision was not followed with major changes in policy or budgetary commitment. By 2015, both the ICT Headquarters and METI shifted emphasis toward the promotion of the "Internet of Things" (the interconnection of smart devices with the Internet).[156]

Nonetheless, government efforts to invest in the telecommunications infrastructure and to promote competition have paid off over time. By 2016, Japan led the world with 74.9% of broadband subscribers with fiber to the home, compared to 11.2% for the United States. As of 2014 Japan's monthly cost for broadband service per Mbps was also the lowest in the world, at 2 cents, compared to 59 cents for the United States.[157] The fierce price competition of cellular and broadband of the early 2000s subsided, however, and the NTT Group has continued to dominate some subsectors, including (non-broadband) fixed line service (90%), Internet protocol (IP) telephone service (56%) and fiber to the home service (69%).[158]

In sum, the Japanese government successfully promoted telecommunications competition and the infrastructure buildout, giving Japan a low-cost and high-quality broadband network. But it was unable to prevent a sharp decline in Japan's IT hardware sector, or to challenge US supremacy in business software, IT systems, operating systems, or search engines. And the Japanese government, firms, and schools lag behind the world leaders in the use of sophisticated IT systems.

The financial crisis of the 1990s drove a massive effort at policy reform and corporate restructuring designed to shift the country toward the liberal market model of the United States. This offered an ideal window to explore a central question of this book: What does it take to make competitive labor, finance, and product markets? And this chapter provides a clear answer: It requires the construction of a broad spectrum of laws and regulations that sustain competition in modern markets, combined with a fundamental shift in business practices and social norms.

The Japanese government and corporations have experimented with a wide range of reforms, as outlined in Table 4.3, but they have produced incremental change in some areas rather than a drastic overhaul. And formal changes in laws and regulations have not always resulted in the expected transformations in business practices and social norms. For example, the government has enacted major financial and corporate governance reforms, yet Japan has not developed a full-fledged market for corporate control. It has passed major labor reforms, yet Japan still lacks an active labor market for executives at large firms. And it has strengthened antitrust enforcement and adopted pro-competitive regulation in some sectors, yet Japanese firms retain a strong propensity toward networks of alliances via industry groups and coordination via industry associations.

So let us return to the question raised earlier in the chapter: Should Japan have enacted more drastic liberal market reforms? The logic of this volume suggests not. Given the strong complementarity among the different elements of the system and the impossibility of an instantaneous transition along all possible dimensions, more dramatic reform would probably have been more disruptive than productive. And formal changes would not have had their intended impact without adjustments in informal practices and norms, which cannot be legislated. Moreover, as we discovered in the previous chapter, many of the neoliberal reforms advocated for Japan—such as stock options or mass layoffs—have not proven to improve economic performance, even in the United States. So the Japanese government and industry were probably wise to opt for more incremental reforms, but to give firms more flexibility to adjust to a harsher economic climate. In some cases, however, they may have gone too far with market reforms, undermining employment security and allowing economic inequality to rise. Financial reforms in the 1980s, for example, contributed to the financial crisis in the 1990s. Corporate governance reforms permitted companies greater leeway to engage in business practices that have not improved corporate performance and to shift toward a narrow approach to restructuring focused on selling assets and reducing labor costs. And labor reforms have exacerbated the gap between regular and non-regular workers, have increased economic inequality, and have undermined employment security.

The final two case studies—Japan's efforts to replicate Silicon Valley and to emulate the US information revolution—bear a different normative lesson. These are cases of unsuccessful adaptation because the Japanese government tried to reproduce institutional ecosystems that were not appropriate to the Japanese environment. Instead, Japan would have been better off adapting its own strengths—including a competent bureaucracy, strong government-industry ties, and close collaboration among firms, banks, and workers—rather than trying to emulate a foreign model.

Marketcraft in Theory and Practice

The proposition that markets are institutions governed by laws, practices, and norms may appear patently obvious, almost banal. Yet most policy debates over economic issues disregard this common sense; much scholarly analysis fails to appreciate the implications; and linguistic conventions entrench the confusion. Economic policy debates are framed by the dichotomy between government and market as if more of one implied less of the other. Participants in partisan debates often frame their positions this way, yet their substantive differences are more often about how to govern markets than about restricting either governments or markets. Those favoring market solutions may be particularly wedded to this framing, but those advocating for a government role fall into this trap as well. While many scholars and pundits have sought to debunk the government-versus-market dichotomy, their efforts have yet to dislodge this basic assumption from popular discourse.[1]

Rhetoric

The conventional framing of economic debates relies on a conceptual shorthand embedded in our language that inhibits a deeper understanding of real-world markets. The elegant juxtaposition of the words *free* and *market* evokes many of the presumptions challenged in this book: that markets are natural; that markets arise spontaneously; that markets inherently constitute an arena of freedom; and that government action necessarily constrains this freedom.[2] The presumption of free markets is evident in many other linguistic conventions, such as the common phrases that one should "leave" things to the market, "rely" on market forces, or "trust" the market. In many cases, it would be more accurate to use active language to describe the relationship: governments "create," "empower," and "sustain" markets.

The common use of the term "intervention" to describe the government role in markets implies both an analytical stance and a normative judgment. It suggests that government and market are distinct realms, both empirically and conceptually; that the market would function and flourish without government action; and that government action is unnatural and/or undesirable. In some cases, the term "intervention" may be appropriate. For example, when a central bank intervenes in foreign exchange markets by buying or selling currency, one could reasonably view this as a government intrusion into what is normally a private market activity. But commentators use the term to refer to any government role in the economy, including actions such as those portrayed in this book that support markets. If governments make markets work in the first place, however, it does not make sense to refer to this role as "intervention" in markets.

Oddly enough, even the advocates of government "intervention" in policy debates and scholars of market institutions embrace this language, seemingly unaware that this linguistic choice undermines the power of their case.[3] Monica Prasad, for example, powerfully demonstrates that the US government played a central role in shaping markets, yet she repeatedly deploys the language of "intervention" to describe this role. I concur with the essential point she is making when she asserts that "we should not presume that state intervention always undermines the market."[4] At the risk of splitting hairs over the choice of words, however, I would suggest that this language comes perilously close to the self-contradictory statement that "state interference does not interfere with the market." Yet if we simply replace the word "intervention" with a more neutral term such as "action," the sentence transforms from almost self-contradictory to virtually self-evident. David George finds that the *New York Times*, not exactly a bastion of libertarian ideology, has increasingly used the terms government "intervention" or "interference" relative to the term "action" over the period 1900 through 2009. He also notes, not surprisingly, that it depicts "intervention" and "interference" more negatively than "action."[5]

Likewise, analysts often depict government action as a "distortion" of markets. This language shares some of the presumptions underlying "free market" and "government intervention," but it evokes two particular nuances common in policy debates: that markets are pure, so that government action taints this purity; and that markets are tightly wound, so that government action undermines the efficient allocation of resources. Yet real-world markets are not pristine, but rather are thoroughly contaminated by society and politics. They are distorted, for example, by imbalances of private power, abuses of power, fraud, and waste. So government action does not necessarily add to the distortions, and may even modify them. Moreover, real-world markets are not so tightly wound that government regulation necessarily undermines them. After all, markets derive their greatest power not from the ability to convey perfect information— which they cannot—but from giving the players in the market the incentive to act more efficiently. As Charles Lindblom notes, the market does not provide such clear and powerful signals that it forces firms toward a single equilibrium strategy to satisfy consumer demand. Rather, firms retain a realm of discretion wherein they can choose among different options, all of which may be equally efficient. So within this realm of discretion, the government could adjust regulation in any direction without compromising efficiency prices.[6]

Even those scholars who favor an institutional perspective on markets sometimes unwittingly deploy language that obscures the relationship between governments and markets, or otherwise undermines their case. For example, Azfar and Cadwell stress that governments are essential for market governance, yet they undercut their point by framing the project with the term "market-augmenting government." This language implies that markets exist prior to or separate from government action, and that the government's role is supplemental rather than constitutive.[7] The term "market-enabling," for example, would be more accurate and instructive.[8]

Likewise, many scholars employ the language of "non-market institutions," yet many of the things that they describe as "non-market"—such as laws, practices, and norms—are in fact inherent to those markets.[9] These institutions are *market* institutions—institutions that define markets—not *non-market* institutions. So labeling them as the latter only obfuscates the position the authors are trying to assert. The language of *market institutions* would be simpler, more accurate, and more consistent with the position they are taking.

Scholars in the varieties of capitalism school sometimes deploy the terms "embedded" and "disembedded" to refer to liberal market and coordinated market economies, respectively. They have also juxtaposed "disorganized" versus "organized" and "uncoordinated" versus "coordinated."[10] Crouch and Streeck even describe CMEs as "institutional" economies—as if LMEs were not institutional—and refer to LMEs as "free market" or "unregulated" economies.[11] Here again, the language undermines the argument, for if all markets are embedded in laws, practices, and norms, then why would we refer to one group as "disembedded" or "unregulated"? The scholars tend to describe liberal market economies in negative terms, as systems lacking embeddedness or coordination or organization, as if their markets were less governed than those of other countries. Yet liberal market economies are not *disembedded*, but rather *differently embedded* (as elaborated later in this chapter, under "Markets as Institutions").

Fortunately, we do not have to reinvent the English language to find more accurate and more analytically useful vocabulary to describe and interpret real-world markets (Table 5.1). We just have to carefully choose our words. Consider, for example, the most common terms for market reform: *privatization, liberalization,* and *deregulation.* While all three terms may be applied to all countries, *privatization* is typically deployed as a code-word for market reform

Table 5.1 **The Language of Markets: Free-Market-Speak versus Plain English**

Free-Market-Speak	Plain English
Leave it to markets	Enable markets
Rely on markets	Empower markets
Trust markets	
Intervention (by government in markets)	Regulation or action
Distortion (by government of markets)	Regulation or action
Privatization (in post-communist economies)	Market transition
Liberalization (in developing economies)	Market development
Deregulation (in advanced economies)	Market reform
Redistribution	Distribution

in transitional economies; *liberalization* for developing economies; and *deregulation* for advanced industrial countries—that is, market liberals contend that the former command economies should *privatize*; developing economies should *liberalize*; and industrial economies should *deregulate*. Yet this language reflects the very assumptions critiqued in this volume, and mischaracterizes the challenges these countries face and the nature of the transitions they undergo. As noted in Chapter 1, scholars have achieved a rough consensus that economies transitioning from plan to market do not simply need to sell off state assets (privatization), but to establish the rule of law, develop financial systems, and enhance market governance capabilities (market transition). Likewise, developing countries do not simply need to lower trade barriers, reduce regulation, and cut government spending (liberalization), but to build market institutions (market development). The term *liberalization* is particularly problematic because it evokes an image of liberation from constraint, when in practice market development requires *more* governance: greater administrative capacity, government regulation, private-sector coordination, and socialization to market norms. Likewise, as noted in Chapter 1, the advanced countries do not need to reduce regulation (deregulation) so much as they need to strengthen the market infrastructure and enhance pro-competitive regulation (market reform) to empower markets. Hence my modest recommendation would be to replace the language of privatization, liberalization, and deregulation with the more neutral and more accurate language of *market transition, market development,* and *market reform.* This simple change in language could contribute to more precise scholarly analysis and more appropriate policy prescription.

Moreover, I would propose greater use of the term *governance* in addition to *regulation* because it refers to market governance more holistically, including private-sector governance as well as government regulation. It allows us to speak about market governance without restricting ourselves to governance by government. And this in turn facilitates the exploration of real-world market governance, including shifts from public to private and combinations of the two, without the language presupposing one or the other. The term *governance* also covers both the empowerment and constraint of markets, whereas the term *regulation* implies constraint. Similarly, the French Regulation School deploys the term "régulation" as governance in a very broad sense, while using "réglementation" in the narrower sense of government regulation.[12] The term *market design* also nicely captures the essence of the market governance challenge.[13]

Finally, US commentators often use the term "redistribution" to frame debates over economic policy. Yet the conventional usage of the term implies that the market allocates wealth and then the government redistributes it. This focuses debate on policy choices after (or external to) the initial allocation of wealth, rather than on the policy choices that govern markets and therefore determine the distribution of wealth in the first place. Once again, this language implies that the market constitutes a sort of natural order separate from government; that this is a realm of free exchange among private actors; and that this realm determines the distribution of wealth in the absence of government redistribution. Yet this is a wildly misleading way to view the relationship between governments and markets, and it misses the heart of the action: how the government and private-sector actors govern the markets that distribute the wealth, and the myriad choices that shape that governance.[14] I modestly propose to shift from a language of *redistribution* (by the government of market-determined allocations) to *distribution* (by inherently governed markets). Thus we would assert, for example, that people disagree not only about whether the government should redistribute wealth, but also about how the government should craft the markets that distribute wealth—and perhaps we might add: and whom those markets should benefit.

Economics

Economists often situate the perfect market as a theoretical ideal, and they do so to good effect in many cases. In fact, one of the core axioms in the field is that perfectly competitive markets are efficient in the sense that no reallocation of resources would make someone better off without leaving someone else worse off.[15] By assuming away the complexity of real-world markets, economists can isolate certain variables and study the interrelationships among them. They also set up a standard against which to judge economic performance.

The "free-market" ideal can distort economic analysis in subtle ways, however, even when positioned as an assumption, rather than as a description of reality. It implies that imperfect markets are the puzzle to be explained and perfect markets the natural order, and this can produce a bias in the research agenda. Scholars may seek to explain collusion, for example, more than to explain competition. Or more broadly, they may seek to explain deviations from market behavior more than market behavior itself. And the perfect market ideal implies policy choices that juxtapose free markets versus government intervention, thereby obscuring the very real possibilities of government action that enhances markets or government non-action (or removal of action) that undermines markets. (See Table 1.2 from Chapter 1)

Furthermore, the "free-market" lens positions the perfectly competitive market as the alternative to government action, rather than the real-world market thoroughly sullied with collusion, fraud, confusion, incompetence, and power imbalances. This can give policy analysis an unwarranted bias against government action, as discussed in greater detail under "Policy" later in this chapter. In addition, it can lead analysts to miss the ways in which private-sector practices and norms might affect policy outcomes. For example, the removal of government price regulation might lead to competition in one country but collusion in another.

Likewise, the free-market ideal implies that there are more ways to deviate from the ideal than to approximate it. As Paul Krugman has quipped, "All perfect markets are perfect in the same way: all imperfect markets imperfect in their own different way."[16] Of course, Krugman is right that there is only one perfectly competitive market (equilibrium) in the realm of theory. But in the real world there are many different ways to move from the real-world status quo toward more developed markets. In fact, as stressed in Chapters 1 and 2, we confront many choices along dimensions that defy categorization as more or less market oriented, such as pro-competitive versus laissez-faire antitrust policy, or stringent versus permissive patent protection.

In policy debates, many economists favor market liberalization. But given the argument presented thus far, this begets a critical question: What does market liberalization really mean? Some economists express a preference for free markets or for market liberalization as if it were obvious what they mean by this. But do they mean market reform in the sense of removing constraints on markets (market liberalization narrowly defined), or do they include market reform in the sense of improving market governance, even when that means more regulation (market liberalization more broadly defined)? As stressed earlier, the conventional terminology of these debates contributes to the confusion. If we replace the term *market liberalization* with *market development*, that makes it more evident that governments have to craft markets to optimize their performance, rather than to just get out of the way. As noted at the outset of this volume, scholars have come further in refining this insight with respect to developing countries and transition economies than to developed ones. As Dani Rodrick argues,

> Economists and policy makers learned this the hard way during the 1980s–90s frenzy over market liberalization. Freeing up prices and removing market restrictions, many thought, would be enough for markets to work and allocate resources efficiently. But all models of market economics presume the existence of various social, legal, and political institutions. . . . Where those institutional underpinnings are nonexistent or weak, as in much of the developing world, freeing up markets not only fails to deliver the expected results, but also can backfire. . . .[17]

I concur with Rodrick's point, but I would add that the same logic applies to advanced industrial countries; that is, the rich countries must develop effective market institutions or they too may face dire consequences, as the global financial crisis powerfully demonstrated.

Certainly not all economists fall into these traps, but mainstream models tend to overestimate the benefits of liberalization; to define market reform narrowly, as the removal of constraints rather than the strengthening of market infrastructure; and to underestimate the enormity of the marketcraft challenge.

Economists typically evaluate policy choices with reference to the costs of "market failure" and "government failure." The common list of market failures includes information asymmetry (sellers may know more than buyers), positive externalities (public goods, such as parks), negative externalities (public bads, such as pollution), and monopoly. This is a helpful way of looking at how government action can remedy specific problems, and assessing when action may or may not be helpful. In fact, the case for the government role in making markets work presented in Chapter 2 could very easily be expressed in the language of market failure and response (Table 2.1). But the market failure frame can also be misleading, for it implies that failure is an anomaly that needs to be corrected, rather than the norm. It suggests that it is possible for the market to not fail, and therefore that government action is a second-best solution, rather than a prerequisite for modern markets to function in the first place.[18] And it evokes an image of a one-by-one matching of government response to market failure, rather than a more holistic process of market design.[19] More fundamentally, the

language of market failure positions the government in a corrective role, repair-
ing market defects, rather than a generative role, building market infrastructure.
To study market institutions, we may be better off with a framework that centers
on market governance or market design, rather than one of market failure and
government response.

Many economists also stress government failure: how governments fail to
regulate markets efficiently or effectively.[20] But here again, the conceptual lens
can beget an analytical bias, focusing on failures of government intervention
into markets, rather than on failures of the government design of markets. In particular, economists tend to ignore a critical category of government failure: the
failure to develop markets. This failure may be less visible because it involves the
counterfactual of what the government could have done but did not, yet it has
major welfare implications. The market failure versus government failure dichotomy implies that failure is attributable to the market *or* the government, but not
both. This framing neglects the important category of government-market failure: the underdevelopment of market infrastructure or the failure of market
design. For example, the case studies of financial crises in this volume demonstrate that governments can fail at "deregulation" just as much as they can fail
at regulation. And that is because regulatory reform is a form of government
action—and not the removal of regulation—and therefore there are many ways
to design it, many ways to get it right, and many ways to get it wrong.

More fundamentally, by assuming that markets are self-generating and self-
sustaining, standard economic models assume away market governance.[21] The
subfield of economic sociology—as well as subfields in other disciplines, such as
comparative political economy and economic anthropology—focuses on filling
the gap. The critical question for the analyst is whether one gains more by assuming away the institutional complexity of real-world markets or by embracing it.
And the short answer, not surprisingly, is that it depends on what the analyst is
seeking to do. If an economist is trying to figure out how government spending
affects unemployment, for example, then he or she would be right to begin with
a simple model, and only to begin relaxing assumptions after that.

Nonetheless, economic sociologists have demonstrated how the social structure of markets can be essential—not incidental—to understanding the very
market outcomes that interest economists. Harrison White, for example, argues
that firms do not set price and quality in response to consumer demand so much
as they situate niches relative to their competitors.[22] In his seminal essay on
the social embeddedness of markets, as noted in Chapter 4, Mark Granovetter
contends that one cannot understand the preference of Japanese firms for subcontracting the manufacture of core subsystems, such as transmissions, over
vertical integration without understanding how the assembly firms and supply
firms are integrated into social networks that foster trust and thereby facilitate

collaboration and deter opportunism.[23] Or Neil Fligstein argues that an understanding of the social structure of a particular product market can explain corporate behavior that defies the standard assumption of profit maximization. Companies may leverage ties with suppliers or the government to achieve market stability (and ensure survival) rather than to maximize returns.[24] Likewise, as noted in Chapter 3, economic sociologists argue that social rules or cognitive frames explain why US firms downsize more than would be economically rational.

Over the past few decades, the field of economics has moved in many fruitful new directions that transcend the assumption of perfect markets. The subfield of behavioral economics has built on insights from psychology to explore how individuals often act in ways that deviate from the rational maximization of utility.[25] The subfield of market design, as noted in Chapter 2, has developed increasingly sophisticated models of how to fabricate markets where they do not spontaneously arise.[26] And leading figures in the discipline have developed more sophisticated arguments favoring government industrial policies under certain conditions.[27]

Not surprisingly, the subfield of institutional economics has provided a particularly powerful way to understand market institutions and to analyze their development. This subfield leverages the concept of transaction costs to model various institutions as contracts, and to develop specific hypotheses about the development and reform of these institutions. Yet institutional economics shares with standard economics its reliance on the perfect market as a reference point. Institutional economists stress that there is no such thing as a perfect market, but they conceive of transaction costs as deviations from this ideal—as the friction that impedes seamless markets. They subdivide transaction costs into information costs and enforcement costs. And they depict institutions as solutions to transaction cost problems. This opens some versions of this work to the critique that the analysis is functionalist: that is, that it assumes that institutional solutions follow from transaction cost problems and therefore produce better economic governance over time.[28] Douglass North demonstrates how institutional economists can transcend this functionalism with a more open-ended model of institutional change that recognizes a role for politics and ideology.[29]

Nonetheless, we need to keep in mind that real-world history proceeded in the other direction: not from perfect markets to institutions, but from social institutions to market institutions. North writes:

> How do we account for substitutes for price-making markets of which families, firms, guilds, manors, trade unions, cooperatives, etc., are *organizing* institutions which allocate resources in place of markets. Most fundamental of all, how do we explain governments? . . . It is

the contention of this essay that transaction cost analysis is a promising analytical framework to explore non-market forms of economic organization.[30]

There is something slightly perverse about depicting the family as a substitute for price-making markets, or a solution to a transaction cost problem. The family certainly fulfills economic functions, and it gradually took on more market functions as society developed more elaborate and more productive market institutions. But the family as a social institution, including procreation and child care, comes first, both historically and logically.

Institutional economics, like economic sociology, offers a remarkably productive paradigm for analyzing market institutions, but it can lead us astray if we do not keep the underlying assumptions in mind. This framing might lead us to view the personal networks described by Granovetter, for example, as instruments of market rationality, rather than as social relationships that only serve a secondary function in the marketplace.[31] Or it might imply that the national governance models described by Hall and Soskice are the product of rational adaptations by firms, rather than a more contingent sequence of historical events, political conflicts, government policies, and business strategies.[32]

Political Science

Political scientists often follow the lead of economists in situating the free market as a reference point when studying the politics of international trade or domestic regulation. Economists may be justified in treating a hypothetical perfect market as a default to assess the welfare effects of policy action. And political scientists may reasonably treat it as a benchmark to assess how real-world policy diverges from that position, and then to explain how politics explains the divergence. Yet if political scientists view government regulation primarily as a barrier to trade and an impediment to competition—and not as a foundation *for* markets—they too risk introducing a bias into their analysis. Specifically, this framing can lead them to focus too much on those types of regulation that best fit this framing; to misidentify actors' policy preferences; to misconceive of market reform as movement toward a single "free market" equilibrium; or to study government regulation without sufficient attention to private-sector market governance.

In practice, political scientists have focused disproportionately on precisely those types of regulation that best fit the government-versus-market lens: namely, tariffs and quotas for international markets, and price and entry regulations for domestic markets. They have devoted relatively less attention to the broader array of market governance mechanisms listed in Table 1.4

(in Chapter 1). Much of the literature on political economy still reflects its roots in debates on free trade versus protectionism that date back to Adam Smith and beyond. The subfield of international political economy has focused particularly on the conditions under which countries agree to lower trade barriers. Some scholars have leveraged the economic literature on the gains from trade to construct game-theoretic models to assess why governments might agree to cooperate in trade negotiations.[33] Others have developed more elaborate models of domestic politics, illustrating how a country's industrial structure, for example, might affect its trade policy preferences.[34] Over time, scholars have devised more sophisticated analyses that come closer to approximating the real-world preferences of these actors and the actual array of choices they face.[35]

As stressed in Chapter 2, the assumption that government regulation impedes trade, and therefore reductions in regulation would liberate trade, fits tariffs and quotas better than other forms of market governance. This framing becomes less appropriate as international negotiations move from tariffs to non-tariff barriers. Yet the very language of non-tariff *barriers* implies government rules that impede trade, such as customs procedures, rather than the *lack* of government rules that foster trade, such as antitrust regulations. But of course effective antitrust regulations can facilitate trade, so their inadequacy constitutes a "non-tariff barrier," even if the choice of this term may obscure the point. The politics of structural reforms that facilitate trade and investment differ from the politics of tariffs and quotas because interest group preferences on these issues transcend their trade implications. As Cornelia Woll notes, traditional trade models are more appropriate for tariff negotiations than for newer trade issues such as regulatory harmonization. For the latter, it is less appropriate to deduce industry preferences based on economic models of the distributional effects of trade liberalization.[36] The analytical framework introduced in this volume can offer some insight here. Specifically, government regulation can facilitate trade as well as impede it, and it can influence outcomes in ways that cannot be captured by the free trade-versus-protectionism dichotomy. Therefore, the actors involved in policy debates over structural reform need to engage in complex assessments of the relationship between government action, market access, and other objectives.

Similarly, political scientists and economists studying the politics of domestic economic regulation have focused disproportionately on price and entry regulation, which also fits the government-versus-markets frame better than other facets of market governance. Political scientists Samuel Huntington and Marvin Bernstein developed models of regulatory capture in the 1950s, and Chicago School economist George Stigler followed with his seminal article on the economic theory of regulation in 1971.[37] Stigler asserts that a small group with high stakes in a given policy, such as a regulated industry, will press its views more effectively than a larger group with smaller stakes per capita, such as consumers. Thus the regulated industry tends to "capture" the agency that regulates it, obtaining price and entry regulations that insulate it from competition. The theory of regulation accounted reasonably well for some of the patterns of price and entry regulation in the United States through the mid-1970s, but it could not explain the market reforms ("deregulation") that followed. Theodore Keeler refined the theory in light of these reforms, arguing that rational regulators respond to both special-interest and public-interest pressures and balance the two to maximize support.[38] And Samuel Peltzman argued that regulators shifted toward market reforms as the economic benefits (rents) of price and entry regulation for the regulated industries diminished.[39] Yet these scholars define regulatory capture in the limited sense of government agencies preserving price and entry controls to protect the regulated industry (pro-regulation capture). They neglect the possibilities of other forms of regulatory capture, such as capture by interests favoring market reform (pro-market capture), or capture by interests opposing regulation because they benefit from a private governance regime that favors them (anti-regulation capture).[40]

Political scientists also sometimes misidentify policy preferences by assuming that protection and regulation reflect narrow vested interests (rent-seeking), whereas the removal of those barriers reflects more diffuse interests. They build on standard economic models that assert that trade barriers and price/entry regulations undermine consumer welfare.[41] But political scientists can get in trouble if they allow the economic theory to sway their interpretation of the politics. For example, the advocates of protection or regulation may sincerely believe that they are promoting the broader public interest, or they may be promoting these policies to appeal to a diffuse constituency rather than a narrow one.[42] Likewise, the advocates of removing trade barriers or price/entry regulations may be catering to narrow constituencies. This becomes more evident once we recognize that there is not one way to liberalize markets, but many. Political leaders pursuing market reform may not be serving the broader public good, but rather the narrow interest of specific constituencies that advocate a particular mode of market governance that favors them.

The political science literature has moved in some promising new directions since the heyday of the theory of regulation in the 1970s and 1980s. First, scholars have stressed that market reform entails "reregulation": the expansion of regulatory capacity and the proliferation of rules.[43] Second, they have turned their attention more to issues of market governance (Table 1.4), such as corporate governance.[44] And third, they have directly critiqued the theory of regulation. They have argued, for example, that regulation does not always reflect narrow political interests, but also broader public interests or ideas about what would best serve the public welfare.[45]

In sum, political scientists have conducted more research on the politics of constraints on markets (tariffs and quotas, and price and entry regulations) than on the politics of crafting markets. To put this in terms of Table 1.2, they have focused more on the free trade-versus-protection axis than on the developed-versus-underdeveloped markets axis. I simply propose that political scientists should devote more attention to the politics of marketcraft. They should examine the full range of market-oriented governance mechanisms, and the different political pressures shaping them: not just the removal of tariffs, but also the enhancement of patent protection, and not just the removal of price controls, but also the tightening of antitrust enforcement.

Likewise, if analysts view market reform primarily as a negative action—the removal of government barriers to market activity—then they may mistake market reform for a movement toward a single equilibrium—free markets—rather than toward a wider variety of market governance structures. Crouch and Streeck, for example, claim that "[a] deregulated international economy subdivided into deregulated national economics would be an institutional monoculture."[46] In doing so, they underestimate the multiplicity of ways to enhance markets, the technical complexity of making markets, and the diversity of interests supporting different varieties of market reform.[47] The market-institutional perspective advocated here stresses that market reform is a highly complex process precisely because it requires building new institutions and not simply removing barriers. The standard government-versus-markets rhetoric is particularly misleading on this point because it makes it seem as though market reform should be easy: just get the government out of the way and markets will flourish. But this misses a critical part of the story: it is not easy to enhance market systems or to make them more competitive. In other words, the challenge of market reform is functional as well as political, and the political difficulty is compounded by the functional complexity.

Ultimately, political scientists need to develop a deeper archaeology of the interests in debates over market governance. Much work in political science defines interests in economic terms: capital wants lower wages and labor wants higher wages; producers want higher prices and consumers want lower prices, and so on.[48] Gourevitch and Shinn suggest one way to refine and update the analysis of economic cleavages in their study of the politics of corporate governance. They demonstrate that the salient cleavages transcend the dichotomy of management versus shareholders to include other stakeholders such as workers, customers, the local community, financial institutions, subcontractors, and other business partners. They model the interaction as a three-way contest among shareholders, managers, and workers, depicting three possible alliances (manager-shareholder, manager-worker, and shareholder-worker) that support different systems of corporate governance. They concede that the country cases do not map perfectly onto these ideal types, yet the typology nonetheless helps move the analysis beyond a cruder characterization of the interests and alliances involved.[49]

Likewise, we found that the underlying cleavage on many issues defies the dichotomy of pro-market versus pro-regulation, as discussed in Chapter 2 and summarized in Table 2.2. For regulatory reform, for example, the core cleavage often poses incumbents against challengers. The introduction of competition typically requires regulatory advantages (asymmetrical regulation) to enable challengers to compete with the incumbent. Thus regulatory battles pose an incumbent that wants to reduce pro-competitive regulation against challengers that want to increase it. And regulators have to keep recalibrating this regulatory balance as the market evolves.

Nonetheless, the irony is that political actors themselves often frame these debates *as if* they were making a choice between government and market, and this powerfully shapes both the policy process and reform outcomes. In the United States, for example, Republicans may oppose government regulation even when it fosters markets, and Democrats may oppose markets even in the service of causes they support, such as environmental protection. So the astute political analyst has to assess the underlying cleavages of interest plus the way partisans frame these interests. The juxtaposition of multiple cleavages—such as Democrats versus Republicans, pro-government versus pro-market, and pro-challenger versus pro-incumbent—produces some strange political dynamics. In Chapter 3, for example, we found divisions *within* each of the two major parties on issues such as financial regulation or net neutrality that defy the government-versus-markets dichotomy.

Political scientists also tend to have a blind spot for private governance. They focus on the public side of market governance—laws and regulations—but not the private-sector dynamics that underpin the real-world relationships among firms and other market actors.[50] Yet we cannot understand market governance without examining *both* government policies and corporate practices, and political scientists have much to offer in this endeavor.[51] As Peter Gourevitch notes, macro politics shapes micro governance; that is, political dynamics shape regulatory policies, and these policies in turn affect private-sector governance, such as inter-firm networks or corporate governance structures.[52] Likewise, the sociologist Neil Fligstein stresses the political nature of micro-level conflicts, such as contests for control within and among firms.[53] Political scientists could usefully contribute to the study of the politics of inter-firm and intra-firm relations, because some of the core concepts of political science, such as alliances and veto points, could be usefully applied at the sectoral or firm level.

Market reform often means replacing one mode of market governance with another.[54] This includes not only switching from one type of government regulation to another, but also replacing government regulation with private-sector governance and vice versa.[55] This interaction can take many different forms. In Japan, government policies to promote international trade and investment or domestic competition have often been accompanied by private-sector responses to preserve some form of insulation from the full force of competition. In the 1960s, for example, the government removed capital controls, and corporations responded by substantially increasing their cross-shareholdings to protect themselves from foreign takeovers. In the 1970s, the government moved forward with trade liberalization, and some industries replaced tariffs and quotas with private-sector substitutes, including preferential procurement practices, exclusive dealerships, and cartels.[56] In the 1980s, the government implemented sector-specific regulatory reform ("deregulation"), yet this sometimes failed to spur competition or was replaced by collusion among producers. And in the first decade of the 2000s, as noted in Chapter 4, the government introduced reforms to facilitate foreign mergers with and acquisitions of Japanese companies, yet it enacted corporate law reforms to facilitate corporate takeover defenses and issued guidelines to clarify what defense strategies would be legal and appropriate, and companies rushed to prepare defenses to insulate themselves from foreign takeovers.

For a different kind of example, the evolution of labor markets in the United States and Japan since 1980 (presented in Chapters 3 and 4) also illustrates this point. We might characterize the broad trends as more competition without policy change in the United States and policy change without more competition in Japan.[57] This demonstrates how government and private-sector reforms do not necessarily coincide. The US government has not made major changes to labor law, but adjustments in policy implementation and corporate practices have combined to produce more competitive labor markets. The Japanese government has enacted considerable policy reforms, yet corporations have adjusted their labor practices relatively cautiously. Political scientists must examine both government regulation and private-sector practices, and the interaction of the two, to understand how market governance evolves.

Markets as Institutions

As stressed throughout this volume, a well-developed scholarly literature across multiple disciplines views markets as institutions, and the analysis here builds upon these foundations. This volume does not challenge this literature so much as celebrate it, while stressing how much conventional discourse and real-world policy ignore its lessons. Yet scholars of market institutions have not always followed the implications of their own analysis to their full logical conclusions.

Thus a secondary goal of this volume has been to explore the ramifications of this perspective further.

We can see some of the tensions within a market-institutional perspective in the work of Karl Polanyi himself, who so powerfully articulated the view that traditional markets were inherently embedded in society and that governments actively constructed the self-regulating markets of the nineteenth century. As Block and Somers note, Polanyi's work reveals a tension between the assertion that markets can become disembedded from society and the idea that markets are *always embedded* in society.[58] On the one hand, Polanyi argues that markets that were embedded in feudal society became disembedded from society in the nineteenth century. This drove the commodification of the fictitious commodities, labor, land, and money, and culminated in the self-regulating market. In certain passages, Polanyi seems to view disembedding as a reality, or at least a grave potentiality. For example,

> A self-regulating market demands nothing less than the institutional separation of society into an economic and political sphere. . . . Normally, the economic order is merely a function of the social, in which it is contained. Neither under tribal, nor feudal, nor mercantile conditions was there, as we have shown, a separate economic system in society. Nineteenth century society, in which economic activity was isolated and imputed to a distinctive economic motive, was, indeed, a singular departure.[59]

On the other hand, Polanyi begins the book by proclaiming that the self-adjusting market was "a stark utopia."[60] And his discussion of how reciprocity and redistribution govern primitive economies suggests how markets might be embedded in society in all periods, just in different ways. And his description of the rise of the liberal creed in the nineteenth century demonstrates how the self-regulating market itself is embedded in society in the sense that it is propelled by a particular social class with a distinctive ideology; that is, markets are themselves cultural products, governed by the norms and behaviors of a specific time and place.[61] This was true in the past, and it is equally true today.[62]

Block and Somers contend that this tension reflects the development of Polanyi's own thought, which he was unable to resolve in *The Great Transformation* because he wanted to publish quickly given the real-world importance of the argument for the debates to ensue at the end of World War II. Polanyi was heavily influenced by Marx in his early years, and this is the Polanyi that stresses how nineteenth-century markets were disembedded—or in the process of disembedding—from society. But Polanyi came to see that all market systems are embedded in society, especially as he immersed himself in the study of primitive and remote societies, and it is this later Polanyi that evokes the always-embedded market.[63] There remains an unresolved tension, however, for the logic of this volume would suggest that market systems were not really disembedding from society in the nineteenth century, but rather re-embedding. That is, the market system went from a culture embedded in feudal practices and relationships to one embedded in market practices and relationships. The subfield of economic sociology has been most influenced by the "always embedded" side of Polanyi's work. Polanyi motivated later scholars to study moves toward the market as the cultivation of a market culture, and not simply the abandonment of a traditional culture, and to study the variation in market cultures across nations, industrial sectors, and firms.

The "Varieties of Capitalism" school championed by Peter Hall and David Soskice combines insights from institutional economics with elements from economic sociology and political science. The core logic most closely reflects institutional economics, as countries develop distinctive institutions to address coordination problems in labor, finance, and product markets. As noted in Chapter 3, Hall and Soskice begin with the dichotomy between liberal market economies such as the United States and Britain, and coordinated market economies such as Germany and Japan. This framework has spawned a major stream of research in the subfield of comparative political economy, and has fostered greater attention to the kinds of market institutions highlighted in this volume. Yet even Hall and Soskice view LMEs as less institutionalized than CMEs. In fact, they contend that it is easier for a CME to become an LME than for an LME to become a CME.[64] The evidence from Chapter 4 suggests the opposite: It is at least as daunting for a CME to be become an LME, perhaps more so. One can see why Hall and Soskice might view the CME model as more institutionalized than the LME model: after all, it is difficult to generate the levels of trust and the mechanisms of coordination to sustain a German-style sector-wide apprenticeship system or a Japanese-style subcontracting system. But I would contend that it is an equally immense challenge to develop the laws, practices, and norms that sustain a liberal market system.[65]

Similarly, Mari Sako argues that moves from LME to CME are likely to require a large mobilization of resources for collective action, whereas shifts from CME to LME—which she refers to as the "dismantling" of the institutions of coordination—may occur gradually via dissipation or erosion.[66] Chapter 4 demonstrates, however, that Japan's effort to move toward the LME model included not one but multiple large-scale efforts at coordinated institutional development, including the financial, accounting, and labor "big bangs" and a carefully orchestrated sequence of corporate law reforms. And even that was not enough to shift Japan to the LME model.

Skeptics of this argument might counter that a liberal market system is more natural or less institutionalized by building on Adam Smith's maxim that people have a natural propensity to truck, barter, and exchange.[67] But which is more natural: market behavior or social behavior? I maintain that analysts should not begin with any preconceived notion of a natural or default position, but rather should assume that *all* outcomes require explanation. For the sake of argument, however, let us consider the case that the more market-like behavior in liberal market systems is actually the *less* natural position that requires *more* explanation. Here we would build not on Smith but on Weber and Polanyi, who contend that people are motivated more by social (or ideal) goals than material ones, and that material goals are largely a subset of social ones; that is, people desire material goods beyond subsistence primarily for their social value.[68]

I would not go so far as to posit that people do not have material goals or even a propensity to exchange. Yet if Weber and Polanyi are even partially right—that is, if people are motivated by social as well as material goals—then that suggests that market cultures have to be cultivated, and that they can vary across time and space. Applying this logic to the contemporary varieties of capitalism, let us simplify three of the features from the Hall and Soskice LME model into the following principles. First, a firm should hire and fire employees based on job performance and a financial calculus of the firm's needs, rather than based on personal relationships or normative commitments. Second, a firm should primarily serve its shareholders, not the broader range of stakeholders, including employees, customers, and the community. Third, a firm should compete with rivals, not collude with them. In each of these instances, one could make a strong case that the latter (social behavior) is the more natural behavior, and also the more original behavior moving through historical time. So that would mean that a society would need to develop practices and cultivate norms to shift behavior in the direction of the former (market behavior). And the implication would be that it would be easier to move from the former to the latter than vice versa.[69]

Markets and Freedom

Market liberals contend that markets constitute a realm of freedom; progressives counter that markets constrain freedom. The argument presented here rejects the crude version of the market liberal position because government action can enhance market freedom and government failure to act can constrain it. It also incorporates an element of the Marxian argument that real-world markets reflect power relationships and constrain freedom for many people, even in the absence of government action. Managers control workers, firms manipulate consumers, incumbents impede entrepreneurs, and so on. But it does not rule out a more sophisticated market liberal position (discussed further under "Lessons for Market Liberals" later in this chapter) that would favor institutions that support markets and market freedom to the greatest extent possible.

Milton Friedman argues that markets are constitutive of freedom because freedom to engage in voluntary exchange is an important element of freedom; and they are instrumental for freedom because they cultivate other forms of freedom. For example, individuals garner more contacts, capabilities, and information through their participation in the market, so this helps them to exercise political freedom.[70] This version of the market liberal position exaggerates the freedom of the market, and fails to grasp the coercion common in the real-life operation of the market. It overestimates the degree to which government activity constrains freedom, and misses the critical role that the government plays in cultivating market freedom. By viewing the market as a realm of freedom and government as a constraint, crude market liberals eschew the difficult but essential work of discerning when governments constrain markets and when governments empower them.[71] Likewise, they underestimate the degree to which the rules dictate the play: how market governance shapes market outcomes.[72]

In contrast, I contend that the degree to which governments foster or constrain freedom—including the freedom to participate in markets freely—is an empirical question. Freedom should be defined not solely as freedom *from* government, but also as freedom *to* participate in markets: the freedom to compete. This then allows us to assess the relationship between markets and freedom more effectively. In the case of limited liability, for example, the government's legal imposition of a law enhances markets. This is a constraint on freedom in the sense that the government restricts the rights of actors to pursue damages from company directors beyond prescribed limits. But it also generates the freedom to participate in more robust financial markets than would have been possible otherwise. To put this differently, limiting the government's role in crafting markets would deny the very entrepreneurs at the heart of the market liberal vision the freedom to participate in more dynamic markets. Government action enhances market freedoms in multiple ways: it gives entrepreneurs the freedom to challenge incumbents without being shut out by anticompetitive practices; it allows consumers to engage in the market without undue risk of fraud; and it enables individuals to participate in markets that otherwise would not exist.[73]

Robert Taylor presents a distinctive version of this argument, building on Philip Pettit's conception of freedom as "antipower." Taylor defines market freedom as non-domination in the context of economic exchange. He stresses that competition restrains market power and thereby enhances market freedom. Therefore the state is justified in securing the regulatory and institutional preconditions for effective competition, even when judging this action by its contribution to freedom. In concrete terms, Taylor contends that this justifies an aggressive antitrust policy.[74]

Polanyi concludes *The Great Transformation* with the issue of freedom, arguing that government regulation both extends and restricts freedom:

> The liberal idea of freedom thus degenerates into a mere advocacy of
> free enterprise—which is today reduced to a fiction by the hard reality
> of giant trusts and princely monopolies. This means the fullness of free-
> dom for those whose income, leisure, and security need no enhancing,
> and a mere pittance of liberty for the people who may in vain attempt to
> make use of their democratic rights to gain shelter from the power of the
> owners of property. . . . If regulation is the only means of spreading and
> strengthening freedom in a complex society, and yet to make use of this
> means is contrary to freedom per se, then such a society cannot be free.[75]

Polanyi acknowledges that power and compulsion are inherent in any society,
so he concludes that regulation is the only viable means of expanding freedom.

Karl Marx, of course, demonstrates vividly how market activity reflects power
relations. Workers are not exercising freedom in their exchange with employers,
for they have nothing to wager but their own labor. The market locks them into
a relationship of exploitation, reflecting preexisting inequalities of power and
wealth, rather than voluntary exchange. The market liberal idea claims to be universal, yet it reflects the interests of the bourgeoisie.

We do not have to adopt Marx's class analysis to accept the fundamental
insight that market relationships take place within a structure of power. This
suggests that private governance can constrain freedom as much as government
regulation does. Thus if the government fails to act, it favors existing power and
wealth by doing so. In other words, the market governance structure distributes
rents even in the absence of government "interference." The real-world market
is not neutral: private actors benefit from a given market design, and prefer one
form to another. There is no bright line between public and private governance,
conscious and spontaneous governance, coercive and free governance. Some
market liberals would counter that there is in fact a fundamental difference
between government coercion and market freedom. Government regulation is
coercion; private activity is voluntary. But these market liberals build on overly
simplistic conceptions of freedom and constraint.

Measuring Economic Freedom
and Market Governance

The ideology of free markets has also penetrated the ostensibly technical exercise of measuring economic freedom. Most indices of economic freedom

view government regulation as a constraint on markets more than as an enabler of markets. They code regulations—including antitrust, labor, and financial regulations—almost exclusively as negative indicators of freedom.[76] They largely ignore the vast array of regulations that empower markets, such as those outlined in Table 1.4 and surveyed in Chapter 2. Yet those regulations constitute the heart of market governance that is critical to fostering economic freedom. In essence, these indices incorporate a systematic bias that assumes that government regulations limit economic freedom without any serious effort to parcel out regulations that enhance freedom from those that restrict it. They simply rule out by definition the possibility that regulations might enhance markets and/or freedom.

Admittedly, libertarian think tanks sponsor two of the most prominent indices, so we should not be too surprised to find some bias in their measures. Nonetheless, scholars and journalists widely cite these indices, and sometimes even incorporate them into their own indices as if they objectively measured something called economic freedom. And policymakers routinely refer to these indices when assessing policy options.

The Heritage Foundation Index of Economic Freedom, for example, focuses on four categories: the rule of law, limited government, regulatory efficiency, and open markets. The *rule of law* includes property rights and freedom from corruption. It defines property rights as guaranteed protection of private property by government, enforcement of contracts quickly and efficiently by courts, punitive measures in the justice system for confiscation of private property, and no corruption or expropriation. So the index recognizes a positive role for government in this narrow sense. *Limited government* focuses on taxing and spending, coding them as negative irrespective of whether the spending enhances or limits freedom in practice. The authors themselves concede that this benchmark includes spending to protect property rights, which obtains a positive score under the rule-of-law category. Hence this spending shows up on both sides (positive and negative) of the economic freedom ledger. *Regulatory efficiency* breaks down into business freedom, labor freedom, and monetary freedom, and focuses exclusively on government regulations as constraints. So the index omits many regulations that enhance economic freedom, and codes others as negative. Finally, *open markets* breaks down into trade freedom, investment freedom, and financial freedom, and once again government regulations are coded as negative. The index even assigns a negative value to antitrust policy, which certainly can enhance markets and freedom.[77] The Fraser Institute's Economic Freedom of the World index is similarly skewed, although it focuses more on sound money and less on domestic regulation. Its category focused on domestic regulations includes credit market regulations, labor market regulations, and business regulations, which are all scored as constraints on freedom.[78]

Even less partisan sources reveal some biases and omissions in their indices of regulation. The World Bank's *Doing Business Report*, for example, tends to score government regulation as a hindrance to doing business more than as a positive force for business. It is more careful in its methodology than the Heritage Foundation and the Fraser Institute, and it includes measures that recognize government's positive role in supporting business, as well as its negative role in constraining it. It assigns a positive score, for example, for government regulations that protect minority investors and resolve insolvency. Nonetheless, the index gives the greatest weight to measures that position government regulation as an obstacle to the ease of doing business.[79]

The OECD Product Market Regulation Indicators provide an even more balanced assessment of government regulations that constrain and promote competition. The OECD divides the indicators in precisely that way: regulatory barriers to competition, on the one hand, and antitrust policy, on the other. It also includes assessments of the capacity, independence, and accountability of regulations. Yet even the OECD focuses disproportionately on government regulations as barriers to entrepreneurship, trade, and investment, and as administrative burdens on businesses.[80] Despite their limitations, the World Bank and OECD indices suggest how we could develop better measures for economic freedom or business climate. The measures would need to incorporate judgments about whether government regulations contribute to these goals or not, and give due weight to the positive role of government regulation and market governance. Indices of economic freedom should give positive scores for antitrust and pro-competitive regulations that give entrepreneurs greater ability to challenge incumbents and consumers greater choice in products and services. And indices of market governance should assign positive scores for effective labor and financial regulations.

Policy

As one form of recap of the argument, let us consider how conceptual lapses might contribute to specific policy errors. Many analysts and commentators evaluate economic policy issues through the lens of a dichotomy between governments and markets. They fail to differentiate those government actions that impede competition from those that promote it. They focus on removing obstacles to markets while missing options for government action to create, expand, or invigorate markets. They underestimate the range of market-oriented policy options. And they evaluate policy options with reference to the free market ideal, rather than to real-world markets. In short, they pay insufficient attention to marketcraft.

The conventional view of markets fails to appreciate the wider array of power relationships, private-sector practices, and social norms that define markets. Policy actions should not be weighed against an imagined free market, but against real-world publicly and privately governed markets. This means realistically assessing the inefficiencies and inadequacies of the status quo. Gregory Mankiw proposes a very different way to judge policy options:

> Economists should be sure to apply the principle "first, do no harm." This principle suggests that when people have voluntarily agreed upon an economic arrangement to their mutual benefit, that arrangement should be respected. . . . As a result, when a policy is complex, hard to evaluate and disruptive of private transactions, there is good reason to be skeptical of it.[81]

I concur with Mankiw that policymakers should consider the costs of government action, whether those be the logistical costs of enforcement or the dynamic costs of impeding competition. I would counter, however, that he overestimates the voluntary nature of market transactions, and he fails to recognize that government non-action could be a form of harm just as much as government action could be, for it might entrench private constraints on market freedom or fail to enable that freedom.

Let us now turn to some examples from Chapters 2–4 to illustrate more specifically how an insufficient appreciation for the institutional character of markets might lead policymakers astray. Table 5.2 breaks down the examples into types of conceptual lapses and policy errors to illustrate how the two may be linked. In the British telecommunications case, we found that the architects of reform assumed that pro-competitive regulation could be withdrawn once competition took hold. They underestimated the need for ongoing regulation to support competition. Even today, some policymakers in the United States and Japan assume that intermodal competition will eliminate the need for pro-competitive regulation in telecommunications.[82] Yet the record of the past 40 years suggests the opposite: incumbents will continue to engage in anticompetitive practices even as technology alters the terms of competition. And advances in transmission technology do not eliminate the need for regulation, but rather require perpetual readjustments to the regulatory regime.

In the US net neutrality debate, the FCC chair failed to classify Internet communications as a utility in 2002, believing that competition would be sufficient to protect consumers from abuses by service providers without common carriage regulation. And as the debate resurfaced in 2014, some Republicans judged the issue as a simple case of government versus market, leading them to view government regulation as a constraint on freedom, rather than as a mechanism to

Table 5.2 **Conceptual Lapses and Policy Failures: Some Possible Connections**

Conceptual Lapse	Policy Example
Overestimating the ability of market forces to sustain competition	British, US, Japanese telecommunications reform
Assuming that regulation constrains markets and freedom	The US net neutrality debate
Favoring caution (non-action) in antitrust enforcement	US Microsoft and Google cases
Assuming that stronger property rights support markets and innovation	US overextension of patent rights and overprotection of copyrights
Emulating specific policies without viewing market governance holistically	Japanese attempts to emulate the Silicon Valley innovation model and to spur the information revolution
Overestimating the benefits of regulatory reform ("deregulation") and other market reforms; evaluating reforms relative to free markets rather than to privately governed markets	Japanese regulatory reforms, corporate governance, and labor market reforms
Underestimating how reforms could undermine existing institutions	Japanese financial, corporate governance, and labor market reforms
Favoring market incentives without due attention to their design	US policies favoring stock options
Assuming that financial liberalization would bestow benefits without stronger prudential regulation	US savings and loan crisis, Japanese financial crisis, US financial crisis
Failing to view "deregulation" as market design	US electricity markets, especially California
Underestimating the costs of not regulating derivatives; misunderstanding the linkages among segments of the financial industry; ignoring misaligned incentives; placing too much faith in private-sector governance	US financial crisis

enhance access to the Internet and to enable Internet-related start-ups. Senator Ted Cruz even famously declared that net neutrality was "Obamacare for the Internet." Some Republicans eventually recognized the subtleties of the issue—as well as the popular support for the net neutrality position—and revised their position. Yet many continued to frame the debate in terms of government versus market, and to insist on minimizing regulation, rather than devising the most effective regulation to foster competition and market freedom.[83]

In antitrust, US regulators' propensity to view economies of scale as beneficial to consumers in the absence of incontrovertible evidence otherwise may have led them to move too cautiously in the Microsoft and Google cases. The argument for action rests on a complex economic analysis, but some antitrust experts contend that regulators must consider acting proactively to preserve the competition that fosters the innovation that is so critical in IT sectors.[84]

For intellectual property rights, many policymakers have viewed strong patent and copyright protection as elements of the basic protection of property rights that underpins "free" markets. This has contributed to the expansion of intellectual property rights to new realms, such as software and business methods, and the strengthening and extension of protection over time. But this perspective has impeded policymakers from recognizing how too much protection can impede innovation, one of the key goals of protection in the first place, and limit the dissemination of knowledge.

The US and Japan information revolution cases illustrate the holistic nature of market governance. The Silicon Valley model is more than simply the product of government policies: it is an innovation eco-system that integrates a broad range of national and local policies, universities, venture capital firms, human networks, distinctive business practices, and social norms. Thus the Japanese government's effort to identify particular policies that supported the model and then to emulate those policies was destined to fail because it could not replicate the broader ecosystem.

Likewise, Japanese advocates of regulatory reform and other neoliberal reforms overestimated the efficiency benefits of these measures because they viewed them in isolation, not looking deeper to assess how policy changes would interact with private-sector practices and norms. In the case of regulatory reform ("deregulation"), government reforms tended to give way to private-sector alternatives, such as collusion via industry associations. As noted in Chapter 4, statistical analyses fail to show the expected productivity benefits from regulatory reform.

Advocates also overestimated the benefits of Japan's reforms in other areas, such as corporate governance and labor reform, because they failed to see how these reforms would be filtered by corporate strategies. Japanese firms have only selectively adjusted their practices in response to policy reforms, adapting to market conditions without undermining valued institutions, including relationships with workers, banks, and other business partners. For example, they embraced new options for corporate reorganization such as spin-offs and M&A, but were more cautious about introducing US-style committee boards or outside directors. Likewise, they welcomed the ability to extend the dual labor system to a new tier of flexible workers, agency temps, but they were more selective in adopting performance-based pay systems or moving to a more flexible model of human resource management.[85]

The Japanese authorities also underestimated the degree to which reforms could undermine existing institutional strengths. They were right to reform some institutions, of course, such as a labor relations system that relied on systematic gender discrimination and an antitrust regime that tolerated collusion among firms. Nonetheless, government and corporate reforms may have undermined valued practices such as government-industry and management-labor collaboration; and may have increased economic inequality, jeopardized social solidarity, and eroded consumer confidence.[86]

The original arguments in favor of stock options in the United States reflected the presumption that they would align managers' incentives with those of shareholders. Yet the proponents failed to appreciate how stock options could produce perverse incentives. Stock options gave managers greater ability to boost their own pay without close shareholder scrutiny, and provided them an incentive to maximize returns to optimize their own ability to cash out the options, rather than to serve the long-term interests of shareholders. They rewarded managers for boosting the stock price, but did not punish them for destroying shareholder value in the long term. Stock options offer a nice example of how a non-action can distort market incentives and undermine competition, for by not requiring companies to expense stock options (until 2004) the US government gave them a regulatory subsidy and encouraged them to deploy stock options more than they would otherwise have done.[87] In essence, a measure that introduces market incentives is not beneficial per se: it has to get the incentives right.

Likewise, the various financial crises discussed in this volume—the US savings and loan crisis of the 1980s, the Japanese financial crisis of the 1990s, and the global financial crisis of 2008—share the common theme of market design failure. The combination of market reforms that intensified competition and gave financial institutions greater freedom to take risks—without complementary measures to strengthen supervision and control risks—fueled these crises. The California electricity case also involved a failure of market design, combining pro-competitive reform that did not fully account for the interaction between different market segments and the potential for market volatility to destabilize the system.

The US financial crisis represents the ultimate case of policy failure, given the multitude of failures and the enormous real-world impact. On the one hand, so many different aspects of market governance combined to produce the crisis, and the sheer technical detail of the case is so complex, that it is difficult to sort out the causal primacy among the factors. On the other hand, the framework introduced in this volume offers some insights into the underlying logic of some of the key errors. In fact, I would contend that greater attention to market design—as advocated by some experts prior to the crisis—could have prevented many of these errors. For example, we noted in Chapter 3 that the authorities chose not to regulate derivatives in the late 1990s, partly due to the contention by some government officials that they did not have the legal authority to regulate these instruments. But they also viewed derivatives as instruments within an isolated market of sophisticated investors. They underestimated the degree to which risks in one segment of the industry would spill across institutional boundaries. The authorities also failed to appreciate the degree to which the US mortgage-backed securities market had become plagued with misaligned incentives.[88] They had too much faith in private-sector self-regulation and in private-sector intermediaries, such as credit-rating agencies and financial analysts. And as we saw with the Greenspan testimony in Chapter 3, they had too much confidence in the ability of private financial institutions to protect their own shareholders.

The perspective introduced here also has implications for the post-crisis reforms. It suggests, for example, that the government should further increase reserve requirements to foster stability, and that the Systemic Risk Council is a particularly important element of the Dodd-Frank reforms because it prioritizes an overall assessment of risk and institutionalizes monitoring of this risk. And it highlights the need for a structural solution, along the lines of the Glass-Steagall Act, that would insulate federally insured deposit-taking institutions from the higher-risk activities of US investment banks.

In sum, we must strive to eliminate the analytical errors that contribute to policy failures. Most critically, this means weighing any government policy option against the real-world status quo, rather than an idealized free market. It suggests carefully separating out policy measures that enhance markets from those that undermine them, and estimating how a regulatory change could alter market dynamics over time. And it means appreciating the interconnections among the various government regulations and private-sector practices. The argument presented in this book stresses that policymakers should assess who actually governs markets, by what means, and in whose favor—and not simply frame choices in terms of whether or not to intervene in markets assumed to operate spontaneously.

Let me be clear: government regulation imposes substantial costs; it can constrain markets; and excessive government red tape is a very real problem. I do not mean to suggest that regulation is always beneficial, or that more is better. I simply contend that government regulation should be judged against real-world market governance in the absence of that regulation, with all of its own inequities, distortions, and costs. I propose that better analysis provides the starting point for better market governance, and that this would serve *both* progressives and market liberals.

Lessons for Progressives

For progressives, the core lesson is that since markets are always governed, the government should actively strive to improve that governance. The need for government to create and sustain markets powerfully undercuts the market liberal position against government, and forms the logical core of the case for an active government role in the economy. It exposes the contradictions of the conventional libertarian view that claims to advocate less government and more market, because it demonstrates that one cannot empower markets without government. Libertarians may challenge government's role in social regulation or welfare policy, but they cannot oppose the government's role in fostering markets without compromising their claim to champion markets.

For progressives, undercutting the crude version of the market liberal argument becomes the entry point for making the broader case for active government in other areas of marketcraft as well. If there are multiple ways to design a market, and one is not clearly more efficient than another, then the government could reasonably consider goals other than efficiency in choosing among them. For example, the government might structure markets to promote technological innovation, to conserve resources, or even to constrain the political power of big business. And if markets are neither natural nor neutral, then progressives have a powerful rebuttal to the argument that market outcomes reflect market value. They can counter that the democratic process should determine what society values, not market outcomes that emanate from a marketplace that happens to be governed in a particular way that favors certain interest groups over others. If progressives can demonstrate that markets are structured by institutions that reflect political choices, then they will be well positioned to argue that those choices could be made differently.

Progressives might also stress, as noted earlier, that the real-world alternative to government action is not the perfect market, but a market sullied with private-sector inefficiency, fraud, and imbalances in power and resources. So the astute progressive would want to thoroughly assess the real-world public and private governance of markets to identify inefficiencies and power imbalances and propose ways to rectify them. Progressives could argue that it would be entirely appropriate to redesign market governance to promote social goals, including greater equality of opportunity and more equitable distribution of wealth; that is, market governance could be improved to achieve greater economic equality not via redistribution, but rather via market governance that would enhance equal opportunity.

What might this look like in practice? Ironically, the first step would entail a progressive version of "deregulation": the removal of specific features of market governance that favor the powerful and the wealthy and thereby undermine both equal opportunity and economic equality. For example, the government might curtail market governance that distributes upward, such as regulations that protect incumbents, enrich executives, or disempower workers. Enlightened progressives and market liberals should be able to agree on these measures.

Marketcraft offers progressives a broad toolkit of policy options beyond the standard set of redistributive policies. In the United States, for example, they might propose improving labor representation within corporations and strengthening labor's ability to bargain with employers. They could advocate reforms to shift from the dysfunctional form of shareholder sovereignty described in Chapter 3 to a more balanced model that would maximize returns for shareholders, workers, and business partners. This could mean revising corporate law to expand the fiduciary duties of managers or to require firms to appoint stakeholders such as employee representatives to their boards. Progressives could seek to shift the power balance between employers and employees by revising labor laws and practices to facilitate labor union formation and expansion. And they could favor measures to constrain financialization, such as imposing a financial transactions tax.[89]

There is an irony here, for these reforms would mean shifting the United States selectively in the direction of Japan. I am certainly not proposing that the United States attempt a wholesale conversion to the Japanese model. That would not be feasible or desirable, and the very suggestion would contradict my own argument about the complementarity among different elements of a market system. But shifting corporate governance toward a stakeholder model, for example, would imply a partial move toward the Japanese model. The US government, industry, and individuals could strive to foster marketcraft that would deliver both more equal opportunity and superior economic performance.

While market liberals may oppose government too mechanically, some progressives dismiss market solutions to policy problems too readily. If progressives view markets as a means and not as a goal, then they should be open to the possibility of tapping market design as a powerful mechanism to achieve their goals on a broad range of issues. This would also be a savvy political strategy because they are more likely to forge winning coalitions if they do not reject market-based solutions out of hand, and if they are sensitive to the costs of their proposed solutions. More importantly, however, this makes sense because progressives should want to achieve their policy goals in the most efficient manner possible: to get the most environmental protection for a given level of cost, for example. Perhaps they should not seek to tame markets so much as to channel them for the public good.

Lessons for Market Liberals

For market liberals, the lesson is that if one appreciates the magic of markets, then one should want them to be governed well. The view presented here challenges a simplistic view that favors markets over governments. The "free market" default is an inadequate shorthand that obscures what it really takes to make markets thrive, and what is in the best interest of entrepreneurs, firms, and the economy. Yet the argument is consistent with a more sophisticated market liberal position: a pro-market stance that appreciates the necessity and the complexity of market governance. Sophisticated market liberals should embrace governance that fosters broader, deeper, and more competitive markets. They should aspire not to "free" markets, but to markets crafted optimally to promote competition and economic freedom. To adopt this position, they would have to undertake the difficult task of defining what a pro-market governance regime would really mean, and to specify which policies and institutions are necessary to support it. They would have to determine how to design markets to get incentives right. And they would have to recognize that economic freedom means the empowerment of markets and the expansion of market opportunities, rather than simply the removal of constraints.[90] In essence, they would have to recognize that good governance, not "free markets," best promotes economic freedom.

In practical terms, as noted earlier, market liberals should attack regulations that favor the powerful and the wealthy. They might challenge firms' ability to exercise monopsony in labor markets (through no-compete clauses, for example), or professional licensing requirements that protect incumbents rather than preserving safety or quality standards. They might advocate more aggressive antitrust enforcement or net neutrality regulation designed to give start-ups more opportunity to challenge incumbents. They might press for more limited patent and copyright protections to promote competition, innovation, and the diffusion of ideas. And they might strive for simpler and less intrusive approaches to financial regulation that would still ensure sound financial markets, such as higher reserve requirements, or firewalls between federally insured deposit-taking financial institutions and those engaged in higher-risk investment activities.

The crude market liberal position does not even function well as a self-serving ideology for those who benefit from "free markets," whether we define the beneficiaries as the capitalist class or some narrower subgroup, such as Wall Street investment bankers. One might quip that some capitalists suffer from their own peculiar form of false consciousness: they espouse a doctrine, laissez-faire, that would undermine the market economy.[91] Market liberals should advocate better market governance as a political strategy as well, for market failures, financial crises, and rising economic inequality are fodder for those who want to contain markets—as demonstrated dramatically with Britain's "Brexit" vote and Donald Trump's victory in the presidential election of 2016.

Market liberals and progressives should be able to agree that markets should be governed well. They spar on issues such as financial regulation or net neutrality where their core goals diverge little, due to ideological blinders and partisan competition. They should both want greater state capacity and autonomy from particular interests as prerequisites for good market governance. Then they could channel their partisan fury on other issues, such as social regulation and welfare policy.

Marketcraft and the Public Good

This book has focused on market governance, not social regulation or welfare policy. This makes sense for analytical purposes, for I have sought to demonstrate that modern markets require good governance for their own sake. Governments certainly need to regulate markets to protect people and nature and to support those in need—but those are subjects for another book. Yet the analytical distinction between market governance, on the one hand, and social regulation and welfare policy, on the other, sidesteps a critical point: market governance itself has huge welfare implications. It affects all facets of economic and social performance: economic growth, technological innovation, economic opportunity, economic security, the distribution of wealth, environmental protection, health, safety, and more. Moreover, the marketcraft realm is growing as a share of what governments do, and as a core element in how governments enhance or undermine the welfare of their people. Some of the most rapidly growing sectors in the economy—information technology, finance, and services more broadly—are also those most powerfully shaped by marketcraft.[92] And some of the core items on the marketcraft agenda—financial regulation, telecommunications reform, and intellectual property rights—are among the most consequential economic policy issues today.

So to conclude, let us briefly review some of the implications of marketcraft for the public good. It can be difficult to determine whether a particular facet of market governance has a negative or positive effect on a particular dimension of welfare, much less to measure this effect with any accuracy. Nonetheless, the cases reviewed in this volume provide some initial evidence. Chapter 3, for example, demonstrated that US market governance shaped an information technology revolution that extended human capabilities and generated enormous wealth. The breakup of AT&T accelerated the IT revolution by generating competition in telecommunications, thereby lowering transmission costs and driving innovation, and by creating a new class of aggressive IT users in the form of the Baby Bells.[93] Likewise, Chapter 4 reviewed how Japan's distinctive governance of labor, finance, and product markets fueled the economic "miracle" of the postwar era.

In contrast, the US-led global financial crisis provides the extreme example of marketcraft gone wrong. In the United States, as in Japan, financial reforms set the stage for a massive crisis. This raises the question of whether financial reform delivers efficiency benefits that justify greater vulnerability to crisis. Financial reform can spur innovation that delivers more efficient allocation of resources and better management of risks, yet it can also facilitate market manipulation, undermine market confidence, increase market volatility, and contribute to financial crises.[94] Yet there is not a purely zero-sum relationship between efficiency and stability: better regulation can produce a better balance.

Financial and corporate governance reforms have also fueled financialization and economic inequality in the United States, Japan, and other advanced industrial economies. Economic inequality is driven not only by the government's failure to *redistribute* resources more aggressively, but by market governance that *distributes* resources unevenly in the first place. Shi-Ling Hsu argues that US legal rules and institutions have increased economic inequality due to an inherent bias toward increasing the returns to capital over economic growth for all. Hsu cites several specific examples to drive home this point: financial regulation, not surprisingly, but also oil and gas subsidies, grandfathering (regulatory relief for incumbents), and electric utility regulation.[95]

An overzealous antitrust policy can reduce consumer welfare by preventing companies from achieving economies of scale, but an overly cautious one can undermine it by limiting competition. And vigorous competition has been shown to have a wide range of welfare benefits, including higher growth, productivity, innovation, and economic equality and opportunity.[96] In the United States, market concentration has gradually increased over the past several decades in many sectors, such as airlines, as antitrust enforcement weakened after 1980. And the rising industries of information technology were particularly vulnerable to network effects. This market power translates into a concentration of political influence as well. In Japan, weak antitrust enforcement permitted some of the collaborative behavior that supported the postwar model, but government efforts to increase competition since 1990 have not fundamentally transformed the country's industrial structure.

Sector-specific regulatory reform has had very different welfare effects, depending on the sector and the specific market design. Telecommunications reform is the clearest success story because it has lowered prices dramatically and spurred innovation. The United States moved early, but competition has stalled in recent years, with higher broadband rates and lower access than many other advanced economies. Japan moved later, but pro-competitive regulation has paid off with lower broadband rates and higher access. Electricity markets have delivered efficiency benefits in the United States, but also greater vulnerability to crisis, such as the devastating California crisis of 2000–2001. O'Neill and Helman judge that the benefits of electricity markets outweigh the costs *if* the government is able to craft an appropriate market design.[97]

Intellectual property rights play an increasingly critical role in shaping market dynamics in the information age, as stressed in Chapter 2. They can give inventors a powerful incentive to innovate.[98] Yet scholars increasingly conclude that the US regime overprotects, thereby reducing innovation, impeding the dissemination of information, and restricting public access to some of the benefits of new technology. Patents can constrain innovation by making it too costly or cumbersome for entrepreneurs to build on the work of others.[99] In Chapter 3, we found that the patent "thicket" has impeded firms from building innovations on a base of existing patents, and the proliferation of patent "trolls" has curtailed innovation and undermined consumer welfare. And the US copyright regime increasingly hampers the diffusion of knowledge in the digital era.[100]

In essence, marketcraft can deliver critical public goods, as in the case of the IT revolution, or foster rampant rent-seeking, as in the case of the financial crisis. It can serve as enlightened industrial policy or as politically motivated protectionism. We can craft markets so they distribute returns more fairly, rather than directing rents disproportionately to those in the very highest wealth brackets, as they do in the United States today. We can design financial markets so they bestow fewer rents to the intermediaries, better returns for savers, and less volatility for society at large. We can structure markets to enhance equality of opportunity, in practice and not only in rhetoric. We can reform intellectual property protection to promote greater innovation and broader dissemination of knowledge. And we can promote competition more consistently and effectively, recognizing that laissez-faire is not likely to produce competitive markets in many sectors.

In this book, I have sought first and foremost to demonstrate how the language and the framing of "free markets" undermines scholarly analysis and policy prescription. Markets are crafted, so pretending that they are nothing more than spontaneous forms of order that emerge from individual free choices obscures the policy decisions that underlie these choices, whether they are acknowledged and understood or not. Markets should be viewed as means and not goals in themselves, and the goals should be determined via the democratic process, not by "leaving" choices to the markets themselves. I have also demonstrated how the government-versus-market framing can foster policy errors and how greater attention to marketcraft could produce better policy outcomes, and I have offered specific examples to support these claims. This conceptual framework could then be applied to develop a more detailed set of policy prescriptions in further research.

The stakes in the game of marketcraft could not be higher. This book has emphasized that governments, firms, and individuals make markets work. The "free market" myth obscures our own agency in crafting markets for our own purposes. We can craft better markets, but to do so we must recognize that markets are human constructs, not natural phenomena that flourish in the absence of governance. We are not limited to a choice between "leaving" markets as they are—riddled with imbalances of power, inefficiencies, and fraud—or stifling them with regulation. We can craft governance to empower markets and to direct them toward the public good. Governments play the central role in crafting markets, so we should want them to do so effectively. This requires a sophisticated understanding of the myriad ways in which governments and private-sector institutions affect market performance. If we pretend that markets govern themselves, however, we relinquish the analytical capacity to find answers to the complex problems of advanced economies.

NOTES

Chapter 1

1. This chapter builds on Vogel 2007 and Barma and Vogel 2008.
2. North 1990, 3.
3. I use the term "market liberals" to refer to those who advocate free markets with limited government, including classical liberals such as Adam Smith and more recent theorists such as Ludwig von Mises, Friedrich Hayek, and Milton Friedman (Smith 1976; Von Mises 2011; Hayek 1944; Friedman 1962; Friedman and Friedman 1980). I call them "market liberals" to distinguish them from "liberals" as the term is used in US politics, meaning progressives who support active government, including social welfare programs.
4. North 1986; Williamson 2000. Anthologies include Williamson and Master, eds. 1995; Menard 2004; Menard and Shirley, eds. 2005.
5. Granovetter 1985; Fligstein 2001. Anthologies include Biggart, ed. 2002; Dobbin, ed. 2004; Smelser and Swedberg, eds. 2005; and Nee and Swedberg, eds. 2005.
6. I employ this term broadly to mean that markets are inherently part of society and therefore inseparable from it, following Polanyi 1944, not more narrowly to mean that markets are submerged in interpersonal networks, following Granovetter 1985. See Krippner 2001 for a critique of Granovetter's use of the term.
7. Barma and Vogel 2008, 1–9, define the "market-institutional" perspective as one in which markets are viewed as institutions situated in a particular social and political context. This broad camp includes most of institutional economics, economic sociology, comparative political economy, and economic history, plus much of the work in law and economics, law and society, business administration, economic geography, economic anthropology, and more.
8. See, for example, Polanyi 1944 and North 1981 on the historical evolution of markets; Cohen, Schwartz, and Zysman, eds. 1998 and Stiglitz 2002, 133–165, on post-communist transition, and Chaudhry 1993, World Bank 2002, and Rodrick 2007, especially 16–21, on development.
9. The free-market presumption and the government-versus-market dichotomy are ubiquitous in popular discourse, but Greenspan (2007, 15–16) and Forbes (2012, xi) offer typical examples from two influential opinion leaders. Wolf (1988, 1) depicts government versus market as "the cardinal economic choice." Yergin and Stanislaw (1998) and Tanzi (2011) juxtapose governments versus markets in the very titles of their books.
10. See Graeber 2011 on the history of credit.
11. North 1981, 34–37.
12. Polanyi 1944, 141.
13. See Barma and Vogel 2008 on the debates over shock therapy (10–11, 355–423), the Washington consensus (11–13, 425–427), and deregulation (9–10, 329–354).
14. Lindblom 1977, 107–114.
15. Vogel 1996.

16. Crouch and Streeck 1997; Hall and Soskice, eds. 2001.
17. Hodgson 2015, 76–79.
18. Coase 1960.
19. Coase himself did not go this far (McCloskey 1998; Cassidy 2013).
20. Moss 2002, 49–52, 436 (fn 42).
21. Bevir 2013.
22. Fligstein (2001) stresses this dual strategy whereby firms strive to exert control both within the private marketplace and by lobbying government.
23. See Hodgson 2015, 138–139, for a definition that is more thorough but less succinct.
24. Roth (2015, 8–12) describes well-designed markets as thick (many participants), uncongested (not requiring too much time to consummate deals), safe (reliable), and simple.

Chapter 2

1. Véron, Autret, and Galichon 2006, 8–9.
2. Bakan 2004, 153.
3. Moss 2002, 56.
4. Moss 2002, 54–69.
5. Rajan and Zingales 2003, 45–46. Historical comparisons across US states provide some evidence supporting limited liability's contribution to economic performance. For example, states tended to experience increased rates of incorporation after adopting limited liability. Economic historians find that limited liability was particularly important as the United States shifted to heavy industrialization (Moss 2002, 69–70).
6. Smith 1976, vol. 2, 264–265.
7. Ciepley 2013, 143.
8. Ramanna 2015, 151–153.
9. Véron, Autret, and Galichon 2006, 57–60.
10. Véron, Autret, and Galichon 2006, 63–64.
11. Véron, Autret, and Galichon 2006, 77.
12. Ramanna 2015, 65–66.
13. Véron, Autret, and Galichon 2006, 104–107.
14. Véron, Autret, and Galichon 2006, 16–18, 89–91.
15. Ramanna 2015, 143–148.
16. Bradshaw and Sloan 2002. The Analyst's Accounting Observer reported that over 90% of S&P firms reported non-GAAP results in 2015; and that non-GAAP income showed a 6% average increase over the previous year, compared to an average *decline* of almost 11% for GAAP income (*New York Times*, April 24, 2016, S1).
17. Macey 2007, 43–44.
18. In the financial sector, regulatory competition can foster races to the bottom, whereby financial institutions seek more permissive jurisdictions, or races to the top, whereby investors seek to allocate funds in jurisdictions with more effective regulatory regimes. See D. Vogel 1995 on these two logics, and Vogel 1997 on competition in regulatory subsidy versus competition in regulatory laxity.
19. Black 2001, 782.
20. Pistor 2013, 321.
21. Black 2001, summary table with a list of core institutions 817–819, and detailed analysis 781–819. Black distinguishes between "direct self-dealing," in which insiders engage in transactions to enrich themselves or their allies, and "indirect self-dealing" (insider trading), in which insiders use information about the company to trade shares (804).
22. Black 2001, especially 786–789.
23. Gourevitch and Shinn (2005, 27–51) provide a succinct summary of the scholarly literature that focuses on the question of whether managers ("agents") serve shareholders ("principals"), with the operating assumption that their primary concern should be to maximize returns for shareholders.
24. Hall and Soskice, eds. 2001.

25. Fannion (2014) demonstrates how the particularities of German corporate law contributed to the tight organizational links between firms and banks characteristic of the German model.
26. Fligstein 2001, 147–169, 184–185.
27. Véron, Autret, and Galichon 2006, 136–139.
28. Jensen and Murphy 1990. Yet as Véron, Autret, and Galichon (2006, 76, 112–113) stress, shareholders ultimately pay for the cost of options.
29. Bebchuck and Fried 2004.
30. Bhagat and Black 2002; Hermalin and Weisbach 2003, 12–13.
31. "Poison pills" refer to a range of legal mechanisms that protect firms from hostile takeovers, such as granting rights for incumbent shareholders to purchase stock at a steep discount when an outside buyer accumulates a threshold level of shares without the approval of managers.
32. Deakin and Wilkinson 1998, 17.
33. Posner 1984; Epstein 1984 (cited in Deakin and Wilkinson 1998).
34. Deakin and Wilkinson 1998, 35.
35. Deakin and Wilkinson 1998.
36. Smith 1976, vol. 1, 144.
37. Hovenkamp 2005, 20–25.
38. Renda et al. (2007, 28) report that private claims represent less than 10% of antitrust litigation in the European Union, compared to more than 90% in the United States.
39. Bergman et al. (2010) find that the European Union has been tougher than the United States in merger cases, leading to lower market shares.
40. Antitrust Source 2012, 10.
41. Posner 1979; Landes and Posner 1981; Hovenkamp 2005, 25–30. Influential works include Stigler 1964; Williamson 1968; Demsetz 1974; Bork 1978; Easterbrook 1984.
42. Hovenkamp 2005, 35–38.
43. Wilks 2010.
44. Hovenkamp 2005, 38–39.
45. Kenney and Zysman 2016, 68.
46. Rubinfeld 1998, 869.
47. This section builds on Vogel 2007, 34–35.
48. As Stern (2003) notes, the Littlechild 1983 report suggested that sufficient competition would emerge within five years or so and that price-cap regulation could be abolished after that. Yet competition was slower to emerge than Littlechild expected, and the need for regulation never disappeared.
49. O'Neill and Helman 2007, 129–130, 133–143.
50. Vogel 1996, 124–125.
51. Vogel 1996, especially 58–60, 256–260.
52. Scott Morton and Shapiro 2014, 464.
53. Reback 2009, 141.
54. North 1981, 5–6, 16.
55. Reback 2009, 142.
56. Reback 2009, 150–152. In Europe, in contrast, exclusion payments are illegal per se.
57. McMillan 2002, 115–117.
58. Reback 2009, 100–101.
59. McMillan 2002, 105.
60. The subfield of market design within the discipline of economics focuses particularly on how to design complex markets, such as auctions, but also matching systems for internships, jobs, or schools. See Roth 2015 for an accessible review.
61. Guala 2001.
62. McMillan 2002, 80–85.
63. McMillan 2002, 182–188.
64. McKenzie 2007.
65. Palmer 2015, 89–112.

66. Scheffler and Glied 2016; Scheffler et al. 2016.
67. *New York Times* (February 7, 2017), A1.
68. Newman and Zysman 2006.

Chapter 3

1. The United States is at or near the top in regulatory complexity, with Japan closer to the average or below, according to the Global Regulation Database (2017) index of regulatory complexity, which is based on the number of regulatory laws and the number of words in each law.
   For bank regulation, for example, the United States is in the highest group for both number of
   laws and complexity of laws (along with Britain and France), and Japan is in the lower range
   for number of laws and the average range for complexity. For Internet regulation, the United
   States is in the top group for both dimensions (along with Australia), and Japan ranks low for
   number of laws and average for complexity. As of 2016, the US Federal Register had 31,184
   documents and 97,069 pages; and the Code of Federal Regulations had 242 volumes with
   185,053 pages (Office of the Federal Register 2017). The Mercatus Center (2017) estimates
   that the Code of Federal Regulations includes 36,508,955 "restrictions" as of 2016, as measured by words that indicate an obligation to comply.
2. Regulatory Studies Center, George Washington University 2016; Mercatus Center 2017.
3. Prasad (2012, 6–7, 175–177, 243) contends that the United States is not really a liberal market economy because it embraces heavy regulation. But if we define a liberal market economy
   as one characterized by competitive capital, labor, and product markets, then the argument
   presented here would predict that an LME would require heavier market regulation.
4. See Vogel 2006, 12–13, 157–158, 198–201, on sectoral variations.
5. Kagan (2001, x) describes the US legal and regulatory regime as characterized by "more
   detailed and prescriptive legal rules, more litigation, more costly forms of legal contestation,
   more fearsome legal penalties, more political conflict, and higher levels of legal malleability
   and uncertainty." He argues (2001, 34–58) that adversarial legalism increased after 1960 as
   reformers sought to drive social change through a fragmented political system characterized
   by distrust of central government authority. Kagan (2010) explores explanations for US legal
   complexity, including the fragmented political structure.
6. Wilensky 2002 and 2012.
7. D. Vogel 1989; Lehne 2001, 115–133.
8. Wilensky 2002 and 2012.
9. Block 2007, 12–13; Prasad 2012, 6–7.
10. Hall and Soskice 2001, 27–33.
11. Prasad 2012, 197.
12. Zysman 1983, 269–72.
13. Cioffi 2004, 255–260.
14. Fligstein 1990, 29–31, 191–294; Fligstein 2001, 130–31, 183–184.
15. Freeman 2007, 7–19; Wilenksy 2012, 178–180.
16. Rosenbloom and Sundstrom (2009, 9–12) argue that the geographic division between the
    slave South and the free North fostered a distinctive American conception of "free" labor in
    the North, subsequently reinforced by the courts in the early eighteenth century, which con-
    tributed to enduring norms of low labor attachment and high mobility.
17. Wilensky 2012, 219.
18. Eisner 2011, 95–97.
19. Western and Rosenfeld 2011. The authors explain: "Unions are pillars of the moral economy
    in modern labor markets. Across countries and over time, unions widely promoted norms
    of equity that claimed the fairness of a standard rate for low-pay workers and the injustice of
    unchecked earnings for managers and owners" (517–518).
20. Hall and Soskice 2001, 21–33.
21. Mowery and Rosenberg 1993.
22. Coriat and Weinstein 2012, 279.
23. The following three sections build on Vogel 2006, 63–69 and 143–146.
24. Vogel 1996, 1–61.

25. King and Wood 1999.
26. Vogel 2001.
27. Eichengreen 2015, 66–77. Also see Krippner 2011 on financial reforms (58–85) and subsequent financialization (27–57).
28. This section builds on Vogel 1996, 223–228; and Vogel 2006, 66–68.
29. Krippner 2011, 27–57.
30. Philippon 2015. Philippon measures the unit cost of financial intermediation as the ratio of the income of financial intermediaries to the quantity of intermediated assets.
31. Philippon 2012.
32. Fligstein 2001, 156.
33. Lazonick and O'Sullivan 2000, 17.
34. Fligstein 2001, 152–153.
35. Fligstein 2001, 148.
36. Jensen and Murphy (1990); discussed in Lazonick and O'Sullivan 2000, 15–16.
37. Chief executive officer compensation grew 1,271% from 1978 to 2000, and more than 200% from 1995 to 2000 alone (Mishel and Davis 2015). The stock options and long-term incentive plan shares of CEO compensation grew from 7% and 19%, respectively, in the 1980s to 15% and 32% in the 1990s and 23% and 37% 2000–2005 (Frydman and Jenter 2010).
38. Fligstein 2001, 185–189. According to Thomson Reuters 2016, from 1978 through 1990 the United States had 541 hostile takeover attempts (175 successful), and Japan had 2 (1 successful). From 1991 through 2015, the United States had 385 (82 successful) and Japan had 20 (9 successful).
39. O'Sullivan 2000, 161–175; Fligstein 2001, 147–169.
40. Cioffi 2004, 265–271.
41. The Dodd-Frank Bill of 2010, discussed in the financial crisis section of this chapter, also included corporate governance reforms.
42. Belloc 2012.
43. Companies have been permitted to buy back shares on the open market with virtually no regulatory limits since 1982. The 449 companies in the S&P index that were publicly listed from 2003 through 2012 used 54% of their earnings, $2.4 trillion, to buy back stock (Lazonick 2014).
44. Lazonick 2013. MSCI Environmental, Social and Governance (ESG) Research found a negative relationship between CEO pay and corporate performance in the United States 2006–2016 (*Economist*, September 17, 2016, Special Report 15–16).
45. *New York Times* (September 13, 2015), B1.
46. Hacker 2006.
47. Wilensky 2012, 157–158.
48. Golden, Wallerstein, and Lange 1999, 201, 221–225.
49. Western 1995, 187.
50. Western and Rosenfeld 2011. The authors (2011, 514) estimate that union decline explains one-third of the increase in wage inequality from 1973 to 2007 for men and one-fifth for women.
51. Cohen 2000, 133–134; Western 1995, 186.
52. Levitt and Conrow 1993; Logan 2002.
53. Hacker and Pierson 2010, 58–60; Bronfenbrenner 2009. Kagan (2001, 54) notes that 30,000–45,000 unfair labor practice cases are filed with the NLRB each year, compared to 500–1,000 cases for labor commissions in Japan.
54. Dark 2008–2009. The Obama campaign had promised to move forward with the Employee Free Choice Act, but the proposal faltered as labor's clout faded (Hacker and Pierson 2010, 278–279).
55. Useem 1996.
56. Jackson 2005, 424.
57. Vogel 2006, 119, for Japan; Lazonick and O'Sullivan 2000, 21, for the United States.
58. This paragraph builds on Vogel 2006, 208–209. Budros (1997 and 1999) and McKinley, Zhao, and Rust (2000) survey representative studies. Baumol, Blinder, and Wolff (2003) find

that downsizing does not improve productivity and lowers stock prices, but it raises profits (by depressing wages).

59. Wilensky 2012, 169.
60. Budros 1997 and 1999.
61. McKinley, Zhao, and Rust 2000.
62. Department of Labor, Bureau of Labor Statistics (2017).
63. Hacker and Pierson 2010.
64. *New York Times* (September 4, 2017), B1.
65. The scholarly foundations of the Chicago School date back to the 1950s and 1960s (Posner 1979).
66. Hovenkamp 2005, 2.
67. Reback 2009, 45–47.
68. Reback 2009, 163.
69. Dau-Schmidt et al. (2000) report 161 Department of Justice antitrust cases 1975–1979; 127 cases 1980–1984; and 83 cases 1985–1989.
70. Fligstein 2001, 147–169.
71. Hovenkamp 2005, 5–7.
72. Reback 2009, 159–160.
73. Reback 2009, 236–237.
74. Google had 75% market share in the United States and 71% of the world market as of 2016, according to IBISWorld.
75. *New York Times* (January 4, 2013), A1.
76. *Economist* (July 1, 2017), 55–56.
77. Council of Economic Advisers 2016B, 4. This scoring is based on the revenue share earned by the top 10 largest firms in the sector. The study also notes other trends suggestive of decreased competition: increased rents accruing to a few firms, lower levels of firm entry, and reduced labor mobility.
78. Kwoka 2015, 153–160.
79. Eisner 2010, 526–529.
80. Kahn 2002, 36–42.
81. US market share for 2017 according to IBISWorld (2017): American 23.1%, Delta 21.2%, United 16.6%, Southwest 14.6%.
82. O'Neill and Helman 2007, 143–147. Weare (2003, 2–4) offers a conservative estimate of the cost of the crisis at $40–45 billion, including higher energy prices, the costs of blackouts, and reductions in economic growth. And he stresses that the crisis also devastated the regulatory and market institutions of the electricity sector.
83. Interview with FERC official, April 2015; O'Neill 2014.
84. Vogel 1996, 218–223.
85. See Yoo 2008 on the welfare effects of the AT&T breakup.
86. New America Foundation 2015.
87. Ammori 2014, 72–73.
88. Crawford 2013.
89. Interviews with representatives of public-interest groups involved in the net neutrality debate, Washington, DC, April 2015.
90. *New York Times* (February 27, 2015, B1, and March 13, 2015, B1).
91. *New York Times* (February 6, 2017), A14.
92. Freyer 2010. The United States had 31,745 private antitrust suits from 1945 to 1988, compared to 15 in Japan during the same period (Schaede 2000, 110).
93. Vietor (1994, 320–321) argues that US incumbents responded to "deregulation" not by outright collusion but by devising market strategies to impede new entry, including market segmentation and manipulation of distribution channels.
94. Coriat and Weinstein 2012, 284–289.
95. Coriat and Weinstein 2012, 281–282.
96. Reback 2009, 143–145; Coriat and Weinstein 2012, 287–289. See Council of Economic Advisers 2016A for a succinct review of the literature and evidence.
97. Shapiro 2000.

98. Non-practicing entities' share of all patent lawsuits in the United States increased from 20% in 2006 to 67% in 2013 (Scott Morton and Shapiro 2014, 466).
99. Rader, Chien, and Hricik 2013. Scott Morton and Shapiro (2014, 482) conclude that patent trolls discourage innovation and harm consumers.
100. *Forbes* (March 15, 2013).
101. *New York Times* (June 5, 2013), B1.
102. Council of Economic Advisers 2016A, 5–7.
103. Reback 2009, 101–102.
104. Reback 2009, 107–138.
105. Weber 2005.
106. Hovenkamp (2005, 250–252) argues that copyright policy is particularly vulnerable to political capture.
107. Weber 2006, 221.
108. Kemp 2006.
109. Newman and Zysman 2006, 29–32.
110. Mazzucato (2014, 73–112) stresses that the US government funded much of the research that drove the information revolution.
111. Newman and Zysman 2006, 393. There have been some signs of "Moore's Law" slowing in the 2010s (*Economist*, March 12, 2016, Technology Quarterly).
112. Reback 2009, 247–249.
113. Borrus 1988.
114. Borrus and Zysman 1997.
115. Zysman 2006, 26–29.
116. Vogel 1996.
117. Cohen, DeLong, and Zysman 2000.
118. Newman and Zysman 2006, 398; Mazzucato 2014, 74–79.
119. Kenney 2003, 71–73, 81–84.
120. Cohen, DeLong, and Zysman 2000.
121. Newman and Zysman 2006, 399.
122. Mazzucato 2014, 73–112.
123. Saxenian 1994, 29–57.
124. Kenney 2003, 77–81.
125. US-based firms held 98% world market share for computer operating systems (2017), 86% for business intelligence and analytics tools software (2015), and 98% for desktop search engines (2016), according to Statista (2017).
126. T. Friedman 1999, 81.
127. Roth 2015, 7.
128. Bar 2001, 41.
129. Newman and Zysman 2006, 400–401.
130. Newman and Zysman 2006, 401.
131. Stiglitz 2010, 1–26; Johnson and Kwak 2010; National Commission on the Causes of the Financial and Economic Crisis in the United States 2011; Eichengreen 2015.
132. Reinhart and Rogoff 2009.
133. This is analogous to the debate about the Bank of Japan and Japan's bubble of the 1980s (Grimes 2002, 136–143; Vogel 2006, 23–25).
134. Greenspan 2007, 200–202.
135. Rajan 2005; also Baker 2004; Shiller 2007; Roubini 2008.
136. Wallison 2011.
137. Stiglitz 2015, 58.
138. Eichengreen 2015, 80–83.
139. Lindblom's argument (1977, 170–188) that business has a privileged role due to the government's reliance on business for economic performance would apply particularly well to the financial sector. Also see Kwak 2014 on cultural capture.
140. Lavelle (2013, 7) stresses that fragmented regulation facilitates regulatory arbitrage in the United States.
141. Litt et al. 1990.

142. See Campbell (2010) on the role of neoliberal ideology in regulatory failures; Eichengreen (2015, 72–73) on ideological influences on US financial regulation; Fligstein and Roehrkasse (2016, 625–626) on theories that presume that competitive markets will curb illegal behavior.
143. Commodity Futures Trading Commission 1998.
144. Levitt 1998.
145. Eichengreen 2015, 74–75.
146. See Carney 2012 on why the regulatory change had this effect, plus a rebuttal of the popular perception that it allowed investment banks to boost their leverage ratios.
147. Fligstein and Roehrkasse 2016.
148. A Securities and Exchange Commission study (2009) concluded that fair-value accounting has difficulty valuing assets accurately in highly volatile markets, such as those around the time of a bust or boom, or illiquid markets.
149. Greenspan 2008.
150. Kelleher, Hall, and Bradley 2012, 13–58.
151. Baily and Klein 2014.
152. *New York Times* (February 4, 2017), A1.

Chapter 4

1. Tyson and Zysman 1989, xiii.
2. This chapter builds on Vogel 2006, especially 4–10 and 78–105.
3. Eckstein (1975) argues that a "crucial case" presents near ideal conditions for confirmation of a hypothesis. It can be used to disconfirm a hypothesis, for if a hypothesis cannot hold true in such a case, then it can be reasonably rejected. For our purposes, the hypothesis in question is that enhancing competition ("liberalization") requires reducing regulation, not expanding it. Since Japan already has effective rule of law and strong protection of property rights—unlike developing countries and transition economies—and yet it has less competitive financial, labor, and product markets than liberal market economies, then it should offer optimal conditions for confirmation of the hypothesis.
4. Postwar Japan thus fits Evan's (1995, 12) model of "embedded autonomy": a state bureaucracy with strong ties to the private sector that retained some autonomy from particularistic demands. Representative works within the extensive literature on Japan's postwar political economy and industrial policy include Johnson 1982; Samuels 1987; and Okimoto 1989. See Vogel 1994 and Vogel 1996, 51–54 and 265–269, for a more detailed assessment of the nature of the Japanese state in the postwar era.
5. Vogel 1996, 51–54.
6. See Witt 2006 on government-industry networks.
7. Hall and Soskice 2001.
8. Hirschman 1970.
9. Zysman 1983, 234–251.
10. The Japanese originally differentiated the horizontal groups from other types of corporate networks (*keiretsu*), referring to them as industrial groups (*kigyou shuudan*).
11. Schaede 2000, 72–97.
12. Some experts argue that enforcement did not have much deterrent effect because fines were designed to generate revenue rather than to deter anticompetitive behavior, and amounts were calculated automatically so they did not reflect the severity of the collusion (Shishido 2014A, 42).
13. Schaede 2000, 110.
14. Gerlach 1992; Lincoln and Gerlach 2004.
15. Mazzucato 2014, 37–39.
16. Granstrand 2006, 273.
17. Vogel (2006, 14–15 and 157–204) analyzes these foundations in terms of three "circles of rationality"—(1) a simple cost-benefit analysis, (2) an institutional perspective, and (3) a broader sociological perspective—and then explores the dynamics empirically via case studies and quantitative analysis.

18. Aoki 1988. Alternatively, Shishido (2014A) models the Japanese corporate governance system in the "law and economics" tradition, which shares the basic analytical framework of institutional economics but focuses greater attention on legal foundations.
19. Dore 1987, especially 169–192.
20. Williamson 1985, 30–32, 85–102.
21. Granovetter 1985. Dore (1987, 172–174, 179–180) also addresses Williamson's argument directly; Hirschman (1992, 85–87) adjudicates the debate, siding with Granovetter; and Williamson (1996, 229–231) offers a rebuttal.
22. Aoki 1994. Hall and Soskice (2001) also stress these complementarities, as noted in Chapter 3.
23. Streeck 2009.
24. Wilensky 2002, 430–636.
25. Pempel 1978; Pempel and Tsunekawa 1979; Wilensky 2002.
26. Johnson 1982; Zysman 1983.
27. Womack, Jones, and Roos 1990; Fujimoto 2007.
28. Discussed in greater detail in Vogel 1996, 51–58.
29. An earlier version of this table appeared in Vogel 2006, 6.
30. Vogel 2006, especially 51–114.
31. Schaede 2008, 1–2.
32. This period is covered in more detail in Vogel 1996, 167–95.
33. I date reform legislation by the year of passage, not enactment. Most of the Big Bang reforms were enacted in 1998.
34. See Toya 2003 on the politics of Japan's financial "Big Bang."
35. Weinstein 2001.
36. Jurisdiction over accounting standards shifted from the MOF to the Financial Supervisory Agency in 1998 and to the FSA in 2000.
37. Kinney 2001.
38. Park 2011, 25–52.
39. Schaede 2008, 41–42.
40. Hardie et al. 2013, 721.
41. See Vogel 2006, 126–134 and 157–204, for a more detailed assessment.
42. See Tiberghien 2007, 149–151, and Schaede 2008, 34–35, for summary tables of the major reforms.
43. See Vogel 2006, 207–211, on the literature and evidence on the costs and benefits of these practices.
44. Lincoln and Gerlach 2004, 331.
45. The government coupled this reform with the Employment Contract Succession Law (*roudoukeiyaku shoukeihou*), which requires companies to consult with workers and unions before a reorganization and encourages companies to transfer existing employment contracts to the newly created divisions. It also added a resolution stating that precedents rule that companies cannot lay off workers if the sole reason for the dismissal is corporate realignment.
46. Schaede 2008, 99–100.
47. Interview, Berkeley, CA, May 27, 2015. Ministry of Economy, Trade and Industry 2005, and follow-up report 2008. Shishido (2014A, 37) suggests that US firms use "poison pills" (takeover defense schemes) to enhance negotiation leverage rather than to block hostile bids, whereas Japanese firms are able to combine their poison pills with cross-shareholdings to prevent hostile takeovers.
48. Buchanan, Chai, and Deakin 2012, 153–239.
49. Schaede 2008, 40–41.
50. Bank shareholding decreased from 15% of the total in 1987 to 4% in 2015, while foreign shareholding increased from 5% to 30% (Ministry of Economy, Trade and Industry 2014A, 48; Tokyo Stock Exchange 2016A, 4).
51. American Chamber of Commerce in Japan 2008. The Asian Corporate Governance Association (ACGA) published a corporate governance "white paper" in the same year (ACGA 2008), stressing that Japanese companies should be required to have independent

directors and to improve shareholder rights by making shareholder meetings more open and shareholder voting more accessible. Takaaki Eguchi, a former executive with a multinational investment management firm, reports, however, that the ACCJ and ACGA do not necessarily represent the voice of the investment community in Japan. The corporate governance professionals, such as proxy voting advisors, strongly advocate corporate governance reforms, but most investment professionals do not speak out on issues such as requirements for independent directors because they doubt that such formal standards will help (interview, Tokyo, May 28, 2014).

52. *Nikkei Bijinesu* (October 18, 2013). The DPJ merged with the Japan Innovation Party (*Ishin no Tou*) and Vision of Reform (*Kaikaku Kesshuu no Kai*) in March 2016, and renamed itself the Democratic Party (*Minshintou*).

53. Financial Services Agency 2014. As of December 2016, 214 institutions had formally accepted the code (Financial Services Agency, 2017).

54. Interview with Ryozo Himino, deputy director general, Corporate Accounting and Disclosure Division, FSA, Tokyo, May 27, 2014.

55. Interview, Tokyo, May 29, 2014. Nicholas Benes, the representative director of the Board Director Training Institute of Japan and a zealous advocate of corporate governance reform in Japan, advised Shiozaki on the corporate governance code and the "comply and explain" approach in particular (Benes 2016).

56. As of July 2016, 3,164 companies had submitted corporate governance reports with a "comply or explain" statement adhering to the code (Tokyo Stock Exchange, 2016B).

57. *The Oriental Economist* (April 2015), 8–10.

58. David Makman, attorney at law, presentation at the University of California, Berkeley, March 19, 2014.

59. Tokyo Stock Exchange (2017), 61–62. 637 companies (18.2%) had opted for the new audit committee with supervisory functions.

60. The Tokyo Stock Exchange reports that 95.8% of listed companies had at least one outside director as of 2016, up from 64.4% in 2014 and 54.7% in 2012; 88.9% had outside directors who qualified as "independent" by TSE listing rules in 2016, 46.7 in 2014, and 34.4% in 2012. Listed companies had an average of 1.75 independent directors as of 2016 (Tokyo Stock Exchange 2017, 75 and 77). In contrast, US companies in the S&P 500 have an average of 9.1 independent directors and 1.7 non-independent directors (Spencer Stuart 2017, 14).

61. Chapter 3 reports the Thomson One hostile takeover totals for the United States and Japan, but these numbers vary considerably depending on the definition of "hostile" (see Culpepper 2011, 46).

62. Miura 2012, 131.

63. *Ekonomisuto* (March 22, 2005), 37.

64. Miura 2012, 69.

65. Interview with Keiichiro Hamaguchi, former MHLW official and senior research director, Japan Institute for Labor Policy and Training (JILPT), Tokyo, May 28, 2014.

66. Interview Berkeley, CA, May 27, 2015.

67. Levy, Miura, and Park (2006) argue that Japan's failure to provide a social safety net is the greatest factor impeding liberal market reform.

68. The share of non-regular workers in the workforce rose steadily from 19.1% in 1989 to 24.9% in 1999, 32.6% in 2005, 37.5% in 2015, and 37.6% in 2016 (Ministry of Health, Labor, and Welfare 2016, Ministry of Internal Affairs and Communications, 2017A).

69. Miura 2012, 76–78.

70. *Toyo Keizai* (May 24, 2014), 50–63.

71. See Vogel 1996 (203–205) on the elaborate terminology governing different levels of regulation in Japan.

72. Interview with Hiromitsu Ohtsuka, senior deputy director, Labor Relations Law Division, Labor Standards Bureau, MHLW, Tokyo, August 2016.

73. Interview, Tokyo, September 19, 2017.

74. Interview with Yoshio Nakamura, vice chairman, director general, and representative director, Keidanren, Tokyo, August 6, 2013.

75. Saito 2010, 3, reports that Japanese executives earned 67% of their income from fixed salary, 18% from performance-based pay, and 15% from stock options, whereas US and European executives earned a smaller share from fixed salary (12% and 25%, respectively) and a larger share from performance-based pay (18% and 36%) and stock options (70% and 39%). The average Japanese CEO of companies with revenues over 1 trillion yen earned 140 million yen (about $1.2 million) in 2016, compared to 13.1 billion yen for a US CEO and 600 million yen for a German CEO (*Nihon Keizai Shimbun*, July 13, 2017, 14).

76. Kambayashi and Kato (2012, 29) report that mid-career hires in Japan increased from 1982 to 1997, but remained far below US levels. For the 30–34 age cohort, for example, mid-career hires represented 15.47% of the population in 1982 (versus US 38.15%) and 20.35% in 1997 (versus US 35.92%).

77. Kambayashi and Kato (2012) find that 10-year job retention rates for core employees remained remarkably stable at around 70% from 1982 through 2007, while the comparable rates in the United States actually dropped from over 50% to below 40%.

78. These patterns are documented in more detail in Vogel 2006, 115–126, 157–204.

79. Vogel 2006, 56–58, 61–63; Freyer 2006, 203–212.

80. From 1997 through 2002, 46 new holding companies were formed; from 2003 through 2014, 437 more were added (Ministry of Economy, Trade, and Industry 2015).

81. The JFTC was merged into the Ministry of Public Management, Home Affairs, of Posts and Telecommunications (MPHPT) under the administrative reform of 2000, and then separated out again in 2003. The MPHPT was renamed the Ministry of Internal Affairs and Communications (MIC) in 2004.

82. Interview with Yoshio Nakamura, senior managing director, Nippon Keidanren, Tokyo, July 20, 2004.

83. *Nihon Keizai Shimbun* (May 2, 2005), 11.

84. Schaede 2008, 44; interviews with JFTC officials, Tokyo, May 29, 2014.

85. Katz 2003, 243–244; JFTC data.

86. Interviews with a former FTC economist and a former DOJ lawyer, Washington, DC, April 2015.

87. Cross-held shares declined from more than 50% of the overall stock market in Japan in 1989 to a postwar low of 16.3% in fiscal 2014 (*Nikkei Asian Review*, July 23, 2015).

88. Further details in Vogel 2006, 140–143, 157–204.

89. Schaede 2008, 153–162.

90. This section builds on Vogel 1996, 137–166 and 196–213.

91. MPT merged into a new ministry in 2001, which was later renamed the Ministry of Internal Affairs and Communications (MIC).

92. The MoT was folded into the Ministry of Land, Infrastructure, and Transport in 2001 (renamed the Ministry of Land, Infrastructure, Transport and Tourism in 2008).

93. Interview with Akihiro Tada, deputy commissioner, Agency for Natural Resources and Energy, METI, Tokyo, August 12, 2016.

94. Ministry of Internal Affairs and Communications, Administrative Evaluation Bureau, 2016, 1–3.

95. Schaede 2000, 164–190.

96. Hoshi and Kashyap 2011, 21–22. The Japanese government's deregulation index, which examines the stringency as well as the number of regulations, shows that regulation declined over this period in the manufacturing sector, while it declined in the first five years but then reversed (increased) in the latter five years in other sectors (Hoshi and Kashyap 2011, 20–21).

97. Hamada 1996.

98. Schaede 2008, 211.

99. Takenaka 2009, 390.

100. Sakakibara and Branstetter 2001. Although some studies have found a positive association between the strengthening of patent rights in high-income countries since 1990 and domestic innovation processes, experts debate whether the expansion and strengthening of patent protections have had any visible effects on business innovation (Motohashi 2003; Lippoldt 2009).

101. Motohashi 2003; Kani and Motohashi 2011.
102. Motohashi and Muramatsu 2011.
103. Motohashi 2003.
104. Interview with Hidehiro Yokoo, secretary-general, Intellectual Property Strategy Headquarters, Cabinet Office, Tokyo, August 8, 2016.
105. Sudo and Newman 2014.
106. Kushida 2016A.
107. Intellectual Property Strategy Headquarters 2015.
108. Hall and Soskice 2001, 38–39. Also Kitschelt 1991.
109. Anchordoguy 2005. Gallup (2010) finds that 24% of Japanese (versus 59% of Americans) agreed and 67% (versus 39% of Americans) disagreed with the statement: "You would rather take a risk and build your own business than work for someone else." Likewise, 31% responded yes (versus 55% of Americans) and 69% no (versus 43% of Americans) to the question: "Have you ever thought about starting your own business, or not?" And Gallup (2016) reports that Japan consistently scores toward the bottom of world standings for capitalist values. For example, only 59% of Japanese responded "yes" to the question "Can people in this country get ahead by working hard, or not?" (27th among OECD countries), compared to 81% for the United States (17th) and 94% for Norway (1st).
110. Ueno, Murakoso, and Hirai 2006.
111. Schaede 2008, 206, 210, 212.
112. Interview with Koji Hirao, chairman of the Board, Showa Women's University, and one of the early promoters of the venture capital industry as an executive at the Long-Term Credit Bank, Tokyo, August 10, 2013.
113. Schaede 2008, 206, 210.
114. Schaede 2008, 217–218.
115. Japan Industrial Location Center 2014; Ibata-Arens 2015.
116. Ibata-Arens 2008.
117. Japan Industrial Location Center 2014.
118. Harada and Mitsuhashi 2011.
119. Kirihata 2010.
120. Ibata-Arens 2005.
121. Ministry of Economy, Trade, and Industry 2006.
122. Nishimura and Okamuro 2011.
123. Ibata-Arens 2005, 111.
124. Schaede 2008, 37.
125. Eberhart, Eesley, and Eisenhardt 2014.
126. Black and Gilson 1998.
127. Rose and Ito 2005.
128. Rtischev and Cole 2003.
129. Interviews with METI officials, Tokyo, May 2014.
130. Eberhart and Eesley 2017.
131. Shishido 2014B.
132. Lechevalier (2014, 119–137) reaches a similar conclusion; Kushida (2016B) is somewhat more optimistic.
133. Shishido 2014B.
134. Interview with Kazuyuki Imazato, deputy director, Industry Revitalization Division, METI, Tokyo, August 8, 2016.
135. Schaede 2008, 220–221.
136. 2016 data from Organisation for Economic Co-operation and Development 2017A.
137. Organisation for Economic Co-operation and Development 2017A.
138. 2015 data from Ministry of Economy, Trade, and Industry 2017 and United States Census Bureau 2017.
139. See Ornston 2013 on the Nordic countries; and Vogel 2013, 368–369, on South Korea.
140. This section builds on Vogel 2013.
141. United Nations Conference on Trade and Development 2017.
142. Cole 2006.

143. Breznitz and Zysman, eds. 2013.
144. Cole 2006, 105–126; Cole and Fushimi 2011, 41–69.
145. Arora, Branstetter, and Drev 2010.
146. Kushida 2011, 279–307.
147. *The Oriental Economist* (May 2015), 5–6.
148. Ministry of Economy, Trade, and Industry 2014B, 5, 7.
149. Kushida 2012, 14–19.
150. Ministry of Internal Affairs and Communications 2010.
151. International Telecommunications Union (2017).
152. Shoji 2009.
153. Kushida 2016A.
154. Interview with Kazuhiro Haraguchi, minister of Internal Affairs and Communications (MIC), Tokyo, June 3, 2010; interviews with METI and MIC officials, Tokyo, June 2010.
155. Ministry of Economy, Trade, and Industry 2010.
156. Interviews with METI officials, August 2016.
157. Organisation for Economic Co-operation and Development 2017B.
158. Ministry of Internal Affairs and Communications 2017B, 345.

Chapter 5

1. In fact, most work within the subfields of institutional economics, economic sociology, and comparative political economy challenges this dichotomy in one way or another. See Barma and Vogel (2008, 1–9) for an overview; also Polanyi 1944; Zysman 1983; Kuttner 1996; Fligstein 2001; McMillan 2002; Martinez 2009; Reback 2009; Eisner 2011; Lynn 2010; Harcourt 2011; Prasad 2012; Mazzucato 2014; Reich 2015; Singer 2015; and many others.
2. George (2013, 21–2) demonstrates that the language of "free markets" has become more prevalent over the past century. Specifically, he finds that the term "free" increasingly precedes the term "market" in the *New York Times* from the 1900–1929 to the 1930–1979 to the 1980–2009 periods, while it appears less frequently before "nation," "government," or "democracy."
3. Leading scholars who stress the institutional foundations of markets nonetheless deploy the language of "intervention." Moss 2002, 9: "A great many interventions have been necessary precisely because these sorts of failures are pervasive in a free-market economy like ours." Nooteboom 2014, 20: "Competition is imperfect in many ways and requires a variety of government intervention." Rodrick 2015, 76: "If government can be a force for good and intervene effectively, at least occasionally, then some kind of industrial policy should be favored." Roth 2015, 230: "As we start to understand better how markets and marketplaces work, we realize we *can* intervene in them, redesign them, fix them when they're broken, and start new ones where they will be useful."
4. Prasad 2012, 44.
5. George 2013, 37–40.
6. Lindblom 1977, 152–157.
7. Azfar and Cadwell, eds. 2003.
8. Callaghan (2015) employs this term.
9. Campbell, Hollingsworth and Lindberg, eds. 1991; Nelson, ed. 2005.
10. Soskice 1999.
11. Crouch and Streeck 1997.
12. Boyer and Saillard, eds. 2002.
13. Landy and Levin 2007, 5–6.
14. Hacker and Pierson 2010, 56.
15. The First Fundamental Theorem of Welfare Economics, first elaborated by Kenneth Arrow and Gerard Debreu in the early 1950s (Rodrick 2015, 47–51).
16. Quoted in Turner 2012, 62.
17. Rodrick 2015, 97.
18. Nelson, ed. 2005, 16.

19. Turner (2012, 42) puts it this way, with reference to financial market governance: "[The] neo-classical approach does tend to dictate a particular regulatory philosophy, in which policy makers ideally seek to identify the specific market imperfections preventing the attainment of complete and efficient markets."

20. Wolf 1988; Winston 2006.

21. Harcourt 2011, 26.

22. White 1981.

23. Granovetter 1985.

24. Fligstein 2001.

25. Kahneman and Tversky, 1979; Thaler and Mullainathan, 2008; Akerlof and Shiller, 2015.

26. Roth 2015.

27. Rodrick 2007; Stiglitz 2014.

28. See Granovetter 1985.

29. North (1990) presents an even more open-ended, less functionalist, perspective on institutional change than North (1981).

30. North 1977, 709.

31. Granovetter 1985.

32. Hall and Soskice 2001. See Thelen 1999 on the "historical institutionalist" school.

33. Oye 1985; Axelrod and Keohane 1985; Yarbrough and Yarbrough 1987.

34. Rogowski 1989; Alt et al. 1996; Frieden and Rogowski 1996; Hiscox 2002.

35. Woll 2008.

36. Woll 2008, 18–19.

37. Huntington 1952; Bernstein 1955; Stigler 1971. See Carpenter and Moss 2013, 6–11, and Novak 2013, 26–32, on the evolution of "capture" theories.

38. Keeler 1984.

39. Peltzman 1989.

40. Carpenter and Moss (2013, 16–18) move beyond the theory of regulation by recognizing that capture can drive deregulation as well as regulation; they call this "corrosive capture." Likewise, Orbach (2015) stresses how government *inaction* can facilitate private-sector rent extraction. The *New York Times* and *ProPublica* find strong evidence of "deregulatory" capture in the Trump administration, with 34 of 85 known members of deregulation teams having potential conflicts of interest (*New York Times*, August 8, 2017, A14).

41. Yarbrough and Yarbrough (1987), for example, build on standard economic trade theory in assuming that liberalization increases the gains from trade. Likewise, Noll and Owen (1983) depict industry groups primarily as defenders of regulation—and not advocates of deregulation—and consumers as the beneficiaries from deregulation.

42. In Japan, for example, the majority of consumers and consumer groups supported agricultural protection, so political leaders who advocated it may have been appealing to diffuse interests as well as concentrated ones (Vogel 1999). Likewise, Ministry of Finance officials believed that their postwar financial regulatory regime not only protected financial institutions, but also bolstered the economy as a whole by preventing bank failures and facilitating the allocation of credit to growth sectors (Vogel 1996, 167–172).

43. Gamble 1988; Vogel 1996; Landy, Levin, and Shapiro, eds. 2007; Eisner 2011.

44. Gourevitch and Shinn 2005; Cioffi 2010; Culpepper 2011.

45. Vogel 1996, 15; Balleisen and Moss, eds. 2010; Carpenter and Moss, eds. 2013.

46. Crouch and Streeck 1997, 15.

47. Thelen (2014) provides an important corrective.

48. Vogel (1999) illustrates how even reasonable assumptions, such as the assumption that consumers will favor policies that promote greater choice and lower prices, can lead to faulty political analysis.

49. Gourevitch and Shinn 2005.

50. Braithwaite (2008, 27) puts this poignantly: "Not only have markets, states, and state regulation become more formidable, so has non-state regulation by civil society, business, business associations, professions and international organizations. . . . This means political science, conceived narrowly as a discipline specialized in the study of public governance to the

exclusion of corporate governance, NGO governance, and the governance of transnational networks, makes less sense than it once did."

51. Vogel (2006, 11–21) proposes one way to link the two into a model of institutional change.

52. Gourevitch 1996.

53. Fligstein 2001.

54. This section builds on Vogel 2007, 39–40.

55. Scholars of international relations have begun to focus more on private-sector governance, especially with regard to standards (Cutler, Haufler, and Porter, eds. 1999; Hall and Biersteker, eds. 2003; D. Vogel 2008; Büthe and Mattli 2011).

56. Kodak argued this point in its World Trade Organization case against Fuji Film, contending that MITI worked with Fuji to establish exclusive dealer networks that effectively shut out foreign suppliers.

57. Likewise, Hacker (2005) describes how US "policy drift" has led to substantial changes in the pension regime in the absence of major policy change.

58. Block and Somers 2014, 73–97.

59. Polanyi 1944, 71.

60. Polanyi 1944, 3.

61. Polanyi 1944, 46–55.

62. Krippner (2001, 780–782) argues that this tension in Polanyi's language does not constitute a contradiction because Polanyi clearly asserts that the market is never fully disembedded from society, and that even nineteenth-century markets were social institutions, reflecting politics, culture, and ideology.

63. Block and Somers 2014, 73–97.

64. Hall and Soskice (2001, 63) put it this way: "[The] importance of common knowledge to successful strategic interaction implies some asymmetry in the development potential of these systems. Because they have little experience of such coordination to underpin the requisite common knowledge, LMEs will find it difficult to develop non-market coordination of the sort common in CMEs, even when the relevant institutions can be put into place. Because market relations do not demand the same levels of common knowledge, however, there is no such constraint on CMEs deregulating to become more like LMEs."

65. In the subfield of comparative political economy more broadly, scholars tend to view the liberal market model as a default and deviations from this model as the puzzle that requires explanation. If we look at real-world history, however, the puzzle should be the other way around: Why have some places at some times moved toward forms of governance that empower markets?

66. Sako 2007, 403–404.

67. Smith 1976, Volume 1, 17.

68. Weber 1958; Polanyi 1944. Also see Graeber 2011, especially 89–126.

69. One could view this in terms of a particular version of modernization theory; that is, market behavior requires a process of socialization, the institutionalization of market norms. Therefore it would be harder to institutionalize the market system than it would be to preserve more traditional attitudes. One might contend that capitalist ideology is so powerful in our age that market-like behavior is in fact the default, even though it is not "natural" in the sense of being innate in the absence of this socialization.

70. Friedman 1962, 7–21; also Friedman and Friedman 1980, 1–7.

71. Hayek (1944, 32–42, 72–87) also fits within the market liberal camp, yet he has a more sophisticated position than Friedman on how governments sustain markets.

72. As Lakoff (2006, 149–155) notes, market liberals also tend to view freedom in terms of the freedom for corporations to operate in the marketplace. Yet corporations are themselves the products of government action, as we saw in Chapter 2. Governmental authority allows corporations to exercise authority over individuals. So it is not at all clear that greater freedom for corporations means greater freedom for society as a whole.

73. Harcourt 2011 (18–19) notes that Nicolas Delamare justified market regulation as a means to promote free commerce by constraining avaricious and conniving merchants in his *Traité de la Police* in 1710.

74. Taylor 2013; Pettit 1996 and 2006. Also see Carpenter 2010, 184–185.

75. Polanyi 1944, 257.

76. Freeman (2007, 8–13) critiques the way the Fraser Institute codes labor regulation.

77. Heritage Foundation 2016.

78. Gwartney, Lawson, and Hall 2016.

79. World Bank 2017. Carpenter and Moss (2013, 10) note that the authors of the Doing Business Project launched it with the express intent to promote "deregulation" that would ease barriers to the creation of new businesses. Hoshi and Kashyap (2012) use this index to assess Japan's progress on deregulation that might contribute to productivity increases. Yet by relying on this index they focus too much on regulations that impede productivity and too little on regulations that contribute to it.

80. Organisation for Economic Co-operation and Development 2015.

81. Mankiw, *New York Times* (March 23, 2014), B4.

82. For the United States: Russell Hanser (2008, 646), an attorney who has worked at the FCC, argues that intermodal competition will minimize or eliminate the need for government-mandated access to other providers' networks, so further government stewardship of the communications market may not be necessary. Also see MacAvoy 2007, 142–145. For Japan: interviews with MIC officials, May 2014.

83. *New York Times* (January 22, 2015, B3, and February 25, 2015, A1).

84. Rubinfeld 1998.

85. These corporate strategies are covered in greater detail in Vogel 2006, 115–204.

86. Kagono (2014), for example, argues that Japanese financial and accounting reforms have undermined management-labor relations, corporate culture, and international competitiveness.

87. Véron, Autret, and Galichon 2006, 160.

88. Fligstein and Roehrkasse 2016.

89. Stiglitz (2016) and Baker (2016), among others, have recommended reforms along these lines.

90. McMillan (2002), Rajan and Zingales (2003), and Shiller (2012) offer examples of sophisticated market liberal positions.

91. McMillan 2002, 226.

92. In the United States, for example, some of the sectors most powerfully shaped by marketcraft have grown the most from 1980 to 2016: professional and business services 4.7% to 12.4% of total output; real estate and rental and leasing 6.9% to 13.3%; educational services, health care, and social assistance 3.8% to 8.5%; finance and insurance 4.1% to 7.3%; and information 3.3% to 4.8% (Department of Commerce, Bureau of Economic Analysis, 2017).

93. Many studies (e.g., Atkinson and Stewart 2013) assess the IT revolution's contribution to productivity and economic growth; Atkinson and Castro, eds. (2008) argue that it has bestowed social benefits as well, including improved education, health care, environmental protection, and public safety.

94. Rajan and Zingales (2003, 25–125) and Shiller (2012) provide positive assessments of the financial sector's overall contribution to public welfare. Stiglitz (2014) finds that the periods of greatest financial innovation correlate with slower economic growth, higher economic volatility, and a drain of young talent from the real economy into finance.

95. Hsu 2015.

96. Nickell 1996; Creedy and Dixon 1999; Griffith, Harrison, and Simpson 2006; Schivardi and Viviano 2011; Petersen 2013; Buccirossi et al. 2013.

97. O'Neill and Helman 2007.

98. Maskus and McDaniel 1999; Kim et al. 2012.

99. Merges and Nelson 1990; Heller and Eisenberg 1998.

100. Samuelson 2007, 2013.

REFERENCES

Akerlof, George A., and Robert J. Shiller. 2015. *Phishing for Phools: The Economics of Manipulation and Deception*. Princeton, NJ: Princeton University Press.

Alt, James, Jeffrey Frieden, Michael Gilligan, Dani Rodrik, and Ronald Rogowski. 1996. "The Political Economy of International Trade: Enduring Puzzles and an Agenda for Inquiry." *Comparative Political Studies* 29: 689–717.

American Chamber of Commerce in Japan. 2008. "Improve Shareholder Voting Access and Disclosure to Enhance Corporate Governance and Boost the Credibility of Japan's Public Markets." Tokyo: American Chamber of Commerce in Japan.

Ammori, Marvin. 2014. "The Case for Net Neutrality." *Foreign Affairs* 93/4: 62–73.

Anchordoguy, Marie. 2005. *Reprogramming Japan: The High Tech Crisis under Communitarian Capitalism*. Ithaca, NY: Cornell University Press.

Antitrust Source. 2012. "Interview with Howard Shelanksi, Director, Fair Trade Commission Bureau of Economics." *The Antitrust Source*, December: 1–13.

Aoki, Masahiko. 1988. *Information, Incentives, and Bargaining in the Japanese Economy*. New York: Cambridge University Press.

Aoki, Masahiko. 1994. "The Japanese Firm as a System of Attributes: A Survey and Research Agenda." In *The Japanese Firm: Sources of Competitive Strength*, edited by Masahiko Aoki and Ronald Dore, 11–40. Oxford: Oxford University Press.

Arora, Ashish, Lee G. Branstetter, and Matej Drev. 2010. "Going Soft: How the Rise of Software-Based Innovation Led to the Decline of Japan's IT Industry and the Resurgence of Silicon Valley." National Bureau of Economic Research Working Paper 16156, July.

Asian Corporate Governance Association. 2008. "ACGA White Paper on Corporate Governance in Japan." Hong Kong: Asian Corporate Governance Association.

Atkinson, Robert D., and Daniel D. Castro. 2008. "Digital Quality of Life: Understanding the Personal and Social Benefits of the Information Technology Revolution." Washington, DC: The Information Technology & Innovation Foundation.

Atkinson, Robert D., and Luke A. Stewart. 2013. "Just the Facts: The Economic Benefits of Information and Communications Technology." Washington, DC: The Information Technology & Innovation Foundation.

Axelrod, Robert, and Robert Keohane. 1985. "Achieving Cooperation under Anarchy: Strategies and Institutions." *World Politics* 38: 226–254.

Azfar, Omar, and Charles A. Cadwell, eds. 2003. *Market-Augmenting Government: The Institutional Foundations of Prosperity*. Ann Arbor: University of Michigan Press.

Baily, Martin Neil, and Aaron David Klein. 2014. "The Impact of the Dodd-Frank Act on Financial Stability and Economic Growth." Presentation at the University of Michigan Center on Finance, Law and Policy, Financial Reform Conference, October 24.

Bakan, Joel. 2004. *The Corporation: The Pathological Pursuit of Profit and Power.* New York: Free Press.

Baker, Dean. 2004. "Bush's House of Cards." *The Nation,* August 9, https://www.thenation.com/article/bushs-house-cards/.

Baker, Dean. 2016. *Rigged: How Globalization and the Rules of the Modern Economy Were Structured to Make the Rich Richer.* Washington, DC: Center for Economic and Policy Research.

Balleisen, Edward J., and David A. Moss, eds. 2010. *Government and Markets: Toward a New Theory of Regulation.* New York: Cambridge University Press.

Bar, François. 2001. "The Construction of Marketplace Architecture." In *Tracking a Transformation: E-commerce and the Terms of Competition in Industries,* edited by The BRIE-IGCC E-conomy Project Task Force on the Internet, 7–28. Washington, DC: Brookings Institution Press.

Barma, Naazneen H., and Steven K. Vogel. 2008. "Introduction." In *The Political Economy Reader: Markets as Institutions,* edited by N. Barma and S. Vogel, 1–18. New York: Routledge.

Baumol, William J., Alan S. Blinder, and Edward N. Wolff. 2003. *Downsizing in America: Reality, Causes, and Consequences.* New York: Russell Sage Foundation.

Bebchuk, Lucian A., and Jesse Fried. 2004. *Pay without Performance: The Unfulfilled Promise of Executive Compensation.* Cambridge, MA: Harvard University Press.

Belloc, Filippo. 2012. "Corporate Governance and Innovation: A Survey." *Journal of Economic Surveys* 26: 835–864.

Benes, Nicholas. 2016. "Japanese Corporate Governance at the Tipping Point." Tokyo: The Board Director Training Institute of Japan.

Bergman, Mats A., Malcolm B. Coate, Maria Jakobsson, and Shawn W. Ulrick. 2010. "Atlantic Divide or Gulf Stream Convergence: Merger Policies in the European Union and the United States." Manuscript.

Bernstein, Marver H. 1955. *Regulating Business by Independent Commission.* Westport, CT: Greenwood Press.

Bevir, Mark. 2013. *A Theory of Governance.* Berkeley and Los Angeles: University of California Press.

Bhagat, Sanjai, and Bernard Black. 2002. "The Non-Correlation between Board Independence and Long-Term Firm Performance." *Journal of Corporation Law* 27: 231–273.

Biggart, Nicole W., ed. 2002. *Readings in Economic Sociology.* Oxford: Blackwell.

Black, Bernard S. 2001. "The Legal and Institutional Preconditions for Strong Securities Markets." *UCLA Law Review* 48: 781–855.

Black, Bernard S., and Ronald J. Gilson. 1998. "Venture Capital and the Structure of Capital Markets: Banks versus Stock Markets." *Journal of Financial Economics* 47: 243–277.

Block, Fred. 2007. "Understanding the Diverging Trajectories of the United States and Western Europe: A Neo-Polanyian Analysis." *Politics & Society* 35: 3–33.

Block, Fred, and Margaret R. Somers. 2014. *The Power of Market Fundamentalism: Karl Polanyi's Critique.* Cambridge, MA: Harvard University Press.

Bork, Robert. 1978. *The Antitrust Paradox: A Policy at War with Itself.* New York: Basic Books.

Borrus, Michael. 1988. *Competing for Control: America's Stake in Microelectronics.* New York: Harper and Row.

Borrus, Michael, and John Zysman. 1997. "Globalization with Borders: The Rise of Wintelism as the Future of Industrial Competition." *Industry and Innovation* 4: 141–166.

Boyer, Robert, and Yves Saillard, eds. 2002. *Régulation Theory: The State of the Art.* Translated by Carolyn Shread. New York: Routledge.

Bradshaw, Mark T., and Richard G. Sloan. 2002. "GAAP versus the Street: An Empirical Assessment of Two Alternative Definitions of Earnings." *Journal of Accounting Research* 40: 41–66.

Braithwaite, John. 2008. *Regulatory Capitalism: How It Works, Ideas for Making It Work Better.* Cheltenham, UK: Edward Elgar.

Breznitz, Dan, and John Zysman, eds. 2013. *The Third Globalization: Can Wealthy Nations Stay Rich in the Twenty-First Century?* New York: Oxford University Press.

Bronfenbrenner, Kate. 2009. "No Holds Barred: The Intensification of Employer Opposition to Organizing." Washington, DC: Economic Policy Institute.

Buccirossi, Paolo, Lorenzo Ciari, Tomaso Duso, Giancarlo Spagnolo, and Cristiana Vitale. 2013. "Competition Policy and Productivity Growth: An Empirical Assessment." *Review of Economics and Statistics* 95: 1324–1336.

Buchanan, John, Dominic Heesang Chai, and Simon Deakin. 2012. *Hedge Fund Activism in Japan: The Limits of Shareholder Primacy.* New York: Cambridge University Press.

Budros, Art. 1997. "The New Capitalism and Organizational Rationality: The Adoption of Downsizing Programs, 1979–1994." *Social Forces* 76: 229–249.

Budros, Art. 1999. "A Conceptual Framework for Analyzing Why Organizations Downsize." *Organization Science* 10: 69–82.

Büthe, Tim, and Walter Mattli. 2011. *The New Global Rulers: The Privatization of Regulation in the World Economy.* Princeton, NJ: Princeton University Press.

Callaghan, Helen. 2015. "Who Cares about Financialization? Self-Reinforcing Feedback, Issue Salience, and Increasing Acquiescence to Market-Enabling Takeover Rules." *Socio-Economic Review* 13: 331–50.

Campbell, John L. 2010. "Neoliberalism in Crisis: Regulatory Roots of the U.S. Financial Meltdown." In *Markets on Trial: The Economic Sociology of the U.S. Financial Crisis,* edited by Michael Lounsbury and Paul M. Hirsch, 367–403. Bingley, UK: Emerald Group.

Campbell, John L., J. Rogers Hollingsworth, and Leon Lindberg, eds. 1991. *Governance of the American Economy.* New York: Cambridge University Press.

Carney, John. 2012. "The SEC Rule That Broke Wall Street." *CNBC,* March 21, https://www.cnbc.com/id/46808453.

Carpenter, Daniel. 2010. "Confidence Games: How Does Regulation Constitute Markets?" In *Governments and Markets: Toward a New Theory of Regulation,* edited by Edward J. Balleisen and David A. Moss, 164–190. New York: Cambridge University Press.

Carpenter, Daniel, and David A. Moss. 2013. "Introduction." In *Preventing Regulatory Capture: Special Interest Influence and How to Limit It,* edited by D. Carpenter and D. Moss, 1–22. New York: Cambridge University Press.

Carpenter, Daniel, and David A. Moss, eds. 2013. *Preventing Regulatory Capture: Special Interest Influence and How to Limit It.* New York: Cambridge University Press.

Cassidy, John. 2013. "Ronald Coase and the Misuse of Economics." *The New Yorker,* September 3, https://www.newyorker.com/news/john-cassidy/ronald-coase-and-the-misuse-of-economics.

Chaudhry, Kiren. 1993. "The Myths of the Market and the Common History of Late Developers." *Politics and Society* 21: 245–274.

Ciepley, David. 2013. "Beyond Public and Private: Toward a Political Theory of the Corporation." *American Political Science Review* 107: 139–158.

Cioffi, John W. 2004. "The State of the Corporation: State Power, Politics, Policymaking and Corporate Governance in the United States, Germany, and France." In *Transatlantic Policymaking in an Age of Austerity,* edited by Martin Shapiro and Martin Levin, 253–297. Washington, DC: Georgetown University Press.

Cioffi, John W. 2010. *Public Law and Private Power: Corporate Governance Reform in the Age of Finance Capitalism.* Ithaca, NY: Cornell University Press.

Coase, Ronald. 1960. "The Problem of Social Cost." *Journal of Law and Economics* 3: 1–44.

Cohen, Jeffrey. 2000. *Politics and Economic Policy in the United States.* New York: Houghton Mifflin.

Cohen, Stephen, Bradford DeLong, and John Zysman. 2000. "Tools For Thought: What Is New and Important about the 'E-conomy.'" Berkeley Roundtable on the International Economy, Working Paper 138.

Cohen, Stephen, Andrew Schwartz, and John Zysman, eds. 1998. *The Tunnel at the End of the Light: Privatization, Business Networks, and Economic Transformation in Russia.* Copenhagen: Copenhagen Business School Press.

Cole, Robert E. 2006. "Software's Hidden Challenges." In *Recovering from Success: Innovation and Technology Management in Japan,* edited by D. Hugh Whittaker and Robert E. Cole, 105–126. Oxford: Oxford University Press.

Cole, Robert E., and Shinya Fushimi. 2011. "The Japanese Enterprise Software Industry." In *Have Japanese Firms Changed? The Lost Decade*, edited by Hiroaki Miyoshi and Yoshifumi Nakata, 41–69. New York: Palgrave Macmillan.

Commodity Futures Trading Commission. 1998. "Concept Release on Over-the-Counter Derivatives," May 6. Washington, DC: Commodity Futures Trading Commission.

Coriat, Benjamin, and Olivier Weinstein. 2012. "Patent Regimes, Firms and the Commodification of Knowledge." *Socio-Economic Review* 10: 267–292.

Council of Economic Advisers. 2016A. "The Patent Litigation Landscape: Recent Research and Developments." Issue Brief. Washington, DC: Council of Economic Advisers.

Council of Economic Advisers. 2016B. "Benefits of Competition and Indicators of Market Power," Issue Brief. Washington, DC: Council of Economic Advisers.

Crawford, Susan. 2013. *Captive Audience: The Telecom Industry and Monopoly Power in the New Gilded Age*. New Haven, CT: Yale University Press.

Creedy, John, and Robert Dixon. 1999. "The Distributional Effects of Monopoly." *Australian Economic Papers* 38: 223–237.

Crouch, Colin, and Wolfgang Streeck. 1997. "Introduction: The Future of Capitalist Diversity." In *Political Economy of Modern Capitalism*, edited by C. Crouch and W. Streeck, 1–18. London: Sage Publications.

Culpepper, Pepper D. 2011. *Quiet Politics and Business Power: Corporate Control in Europe and Japan*. New York: Cambridge University Press.

Cutler, A. Claire, Virginia Haufler, and Tony Porter, eds. 1999. *Private Authority and International Affairs*. Albany: State University of New York Press.

Dark, Taylor E., III. 2008–2009. "Prospects for Labor Law Reform." *Perspectives on Work* 12: 23–26.

Dau-Schmidt, Kenneth G., Joseph C. Gallo, Joseph L. Craycraft, and Charles J. Parker. 2000. "Department of Justice Antitrust Enforcement, 1955–1997: An Empirical Study." Maurer School of Law, Indiana University, Digital Repository, Paper 215.

Deakin, Simon and Frank Wilkinson. 1998. "Labour Law and Economic Theory: A Reappraisal." ESRC Centre for Business Research, University of Cambridge, Working Paper No. 92.

Demsetz, Harold. 1974. "Two Systems of Belief about Monopoly." In *Industrial Concentration: The New Learning*, edited by Harvey J. Goldschmid, H. Michael Mann, and J. Fred Weston, 164–184. Boston: Little, Brown.

Department of Commerce, Bureau of Economic Analysis. 2017. "GDP-By-Industry Data." https://www.bea.gov/industry/gdpbyind_data.htm.

Department of Labor, Bureau of Labor Statistics. 2017. https://www.bls.gov/lpc/#tables.

Dobbin, Frank, ed. 2004. *The New Economic Sociology: A Reader*. Princeton, NJ: Princeton University Press.

Dore, Ronald. 1987. *Taking Japan Seriously: A Confucian Perspective on Leading Economic Issues*. London: Athlone Press.

Easterbrook, Frank H. 1984. "The Limits of Antitrust." *Texas Law Review* 63: 1–40.

Eberhart, Robert, Charles E. Eesley, and Kathleen M. Eisenhardt. 2014. "Failure Is an Option: Failure Barriers and New Firm Performance." Rock Center for Corporate Governance, Stanford University, Working Paper No. 111.

Eberhart, Robert, and Charles E. Eesley. 2017. "Supportive Intermediaries: Junior IPO Markets and Entrepreneurship." https://papers.ssrn.com/sol3/papers.cfm?abstract_id=2183292.

Eckstein, Harry. 1975. "Case Studies and Theory in Political Science." In *Handbook of Political Science: Scope and Theory*, edited by Fred I. Greenstein and Nelson W. Polsby, vol. 7, 94–137. Reading, MA: Addison-Wesley.

Eichengreen, Barry. 2015. *Hall of Mirrors: The Great Depression, the Great Recession, and the Uses— and Misuses—of History*. New York: Oxford University Press.

Eisner, Marc Allen. 2010. "Markets in the Shadow of the State: An Appraisal of Deregulation and Implications for Future Research." In *Governments and Markets: Toward a New Theory of Regulation*, edited by Edward J. Balleisen and David A. Moss, 512–537. New York: Cambridge University Press.

Eisner, Marc Allen. 2011. *The American Political Economy: Institutional Evolution of the Market and State*. New York: Routledge.

Epstein, Richard. 1984. "In Defense of the Contract at Will." *University of Chicago Law Review* 51: 947–982.

Evans, Peter. 1995. *Embedded Autonomy: States and Industrial Transformation*. Princeton, NJ: Princeton University Press.

Fannion, Robert. 2014. "Goldilocks and the Three Corporate Forms: Bank Finance and the Creation of the German Economy, 1870–92." Manuscript.

Financial Services Agency. 2014. "Principles for Responsible Investors: Japan's Stewardship Code." Tokyo: Financial Services Agency.

Financial Services Agency. 2017. "List of Institutional Investors Signing Up to 'Principles for Responsible Institutional Investors' (Japan's Stewardship Code)." Tokyo: Financial Services Agency.

Fligstein, Neil. 1990. *The Transformation of Corporate Control*. Cambridge, MA: Harvard University Press.

Fligstein, Neil. 2001. *The Architecture of Markets: An Economic Sociology of Twenty-First Century Capitalist Societies*. Princeton, NJ: Princeton University Press.

Fligstein, Neil, and Alexander Roehrkasse. 2016. "The Causes of Fraud in the Financial Crisis of 2007 to 2009: Evidence from the Mortgage-Backed Securities Industry." *American Sociological Review* 81: 617–643.

Forbes, Steve. 2012. "Foreword." In *Wealth and Poverty: A New Edition for the Twenty-First Century*, by George Gilder, ix–xii. Washington, DC: Regnery Publishing.

Freeman, Richard B. 2007. *America Works: Critical Thoughts on the Exceptional U.S. Labor Market*. New York: Russell Sage.

Freyer, Tony A. 2006. *Antitrust and Global Capitalism 1930–2004*. New York: Cambridge University Press.

Freyer, Tony A. 2010. "Deregulation Theories in a Litigious Society: American Antitrust and Tort." In *Governments and Markets: Toward a New Theory of Regulation*, edited by Edward J. Balleisen and David A. Moss, 482–511. New York: Cambridge University Press.

Frieden, Jeffrey A., and Ronald Rogowski. 1996. "The Impact of the International Economy on National Policies: An Analytical Overview." In *Internationalization and Domestic Politics*, edited by Robert O. Keohane and Helen Milner, 25–47. Cambridge: Cambridge University Press.

Friedman, Milton. 1962. *Capitalism and Freedom*. Chicago: University of Chicago Press.

Friedman, Milton, and Rose Friedman. 1980. *Free to Choose: A Personal Statement*. San Diego: Harcourt.

Friedman, Thomas. 1999. *The Lexus and the Olive Tree: Understanding Globalization*. New York: Anchor Books.

Frydman, Carola, and Dirk Jenter. 2010. "CEO Compensation." National Bureau of Economic Research, Working Paper No. 16585.

Fujimoto, Takahiro. 2007. *Competing to Be Really, Really Good: The Behind-the-Scenes Drama of Capability-Building Competition in the Automobile Industry*, translated by Brian Miller. Tokyo: LTCB International Library Trust.

Gallup. 2010. Gallup World Poll. http://analytics.gallup.com/213704/world-poll.aspx.

Gallup. 2016. Gallup World Poll. http://analytics.gallup.com/213704/world-poll.aspx.

Gamble, Andrew. 1988. *The Free Economy and the Strong State: The Politics of Thatcherism*. Basingstoke, UK: Macmillan Education.

George, David. 2013. *The Rhetoric of the Right: Language Change and the Spread of the Market*. London and New York: Routledge.

Gerlach, Michael L. 1992. *Alliance Capitalism: The Social Organization of Japanese Business*. Berkeley and Los Angeles: University of California Press.

Global Regulation Database. 2017. https://www.global-regulation.com/.

Golden, Miriam A., Michael Wallerstein, and Peter Lange. 1999. "Postwar Trade-Union Organization and Industrial Relations in Twelve Countries." In *Continuity and Change in*

Contemporary Capitalism, edited by Herbert Kitschelt, Peter Lange, Gary Marks, and John D. Stephens, 194–230. Cambridge: Cambridge University Press.

Gourevitch, Peter. 1996. "The Macropolitics of Microinstitutional Differences in the Analysis of Comparative Capitalism." In *National Diversity and Global Capitalism*, edited by Suzanne Berger and Ronald Dore, 239–259. Ithaca, NY: Cornell University Press.

Gourevitch, Peter A., and James Shinn. 2005. *Political Power and Corporate Control.* Princeton, NJ: Princeton University Press.

Graeber, David. 2011. *Debt: The First 5,000 Years.* Brooklyn, NY: Melville House.

Granovetter, Mark. 1985. "Economic Action and Social Structure: The Problem of Embeddedness." *American Journal of Sociology* 91: 481–510.

Granstrand, Ove. 2006. "Innovation and Intellectual Property Rights." In *The Oxford Handbook of Innovation*, edited by Jan Fagerberg. Oxford: Oxford University Press. http://www.oxfordhandbooks.com/view/10.1093/oxfordhb/9780199286805.001.0001/oxfordhb-9780199286805.

Greenspan, Alan. 2007. *The Age of Turbulence: Adventures in a New World.* New York: Penguin Press.

Greenspan, Alan. 2008. "Testimony to the Committee of Government Oversight and Reform of the United States House of Representatives," October 23, https://www.gpo.gov/fdsys/pkg/CHRG-110hhrg55764/html/CHRG-110hhrg55764.htm.

Griffith, Rachel, Rupert Harrison, and Helen Simpson. 2006. "The Link between Product Market Reform, Innovation and EU Macroeconomic Performance." European Commission, European Economy Paper 243.

Grimes, William W. 2002. *Unmaking the Japanese Miracle: Macroeconomic Politics, 1985–2000.* Ithaca, NY: Cornell University Press.

Guala, Francesco. 2001. "Building Economic Machines: The FCC Auctions." *Studies in History and Philosophy of Science* 32: 453–477.

Gwartney, James, Robert Lawson, and Joshua Hall. 2016. *Economic Freedom of the World: 2016 Annual Report.* Vancouver: Fraser Institute.

Hacker, Jacob S. 2005. "Policy Drift: The Hidden Politics of U.S. Welfare State Retrenchment." In *Beyond Continuity: Institutional Change in Advanced Political Economies*, edited by Wolfgang Streeck and Kathleen Thelen, 40–82. Oxford: Oxford University Press.

Hacker, Jacob S. 2006. *The Great Risk Shift: The Assault on American Jobs, Families, Health Care, and Retirement and How You Can Fight Back.* New York: Oxford University Press.

Hacker, Jacob S., and Paul Pierson. 2010. *Winner-Take-All Politics: How Washington Made the Rich Richer and Turned Its Back on the Middle Class.* New York: Simon & Schuster.

Hall, Peter, and David Soskice. 2001. "An Introduction to Varieties of Capitalism." In *Varieties of Capitalism: The Institutional Foundations of Comparative Advantage*, edited by Hall and Soskice, 1–68. New York: Oxford University Press.

Hall, Peter, and David Soskice, eds. 2001. *Varieties of Capitalism: The Institutional Foundations of Comparative Advantage.* New York: Oxford University Press.

Hall, Rodney, and Thomas Biersteker, eds. 2003. *The Emergency of Private Authority in Global Governance.* Cambridge: Cambridge University Press.

Hamada, Koichi. 1996. "Protection of Intellectual Property Rights in Japan." Washington, DC: Council on Foreign Relations.

Hanser, Russell. 2008. "The Politics of Competition," book review article. *Federal Communications Law Journal* 60: 627–649.

Harada, Nobuyuki, and Hitoshi Mitsuhashi. 2011. "Academic Spin-Offs in Japan: Institutional Revolution and Early Outcomes." In *Comparative Entrepreneurship Initiatives: Studies in China, Japan and the USA*, edited by Chikako Usui, 138–163. London: Palgrave Macmillan.

Hardie, Iain, David Howarth, Sylvia Maxfield, and Amy Verdun. 2013. "Banks and the False Dichotomy in the Comparative Political Economy of Finance." *World Politics* 65: 691–728.

Harcourt, Bernard E. 2011. *The Illusion of Free Markets: Punishment and the Myth of Natural Order.* Cambridge, MA: Harvard University Press.

Hayek, Friedrich. 1944. *The Road to Serfdom.* Chicago: University of Chicago Press.

Heller, Michael A., and Rebecca S. Eisenberg. 1998. "Can Patents Deter Innovation? The Anticommons in Biomedical Research." *Science* 280: 698–701.

Heritage Foundation. 2016. *2016 Index of Economic Freedom: Promoting Economic Opportunity and Prosperity.* Washington, DC: Heritage Foundation.

Hermalin, Benjamin E., and Michael S. Weisbach. 2003. "Boards of Directors as an Endogenously Determined Institution: A Survey of the Economic Literature." *Federal Reserve Bank of New York Economic Policy Review* 9: 7–26.

Hirschman, Albert. 1970. *Exit, Voice and Loyalty: Responses to Decline in Firms, Organizations, and States.* Cambridge, MA: Harvard University Press.

Hirschman, Albert. 1992. *Rival Views of Market Society and Other Recent Essays.* Cambridge, MA: Harvard University Press.

Hiscox, Michael. 2002. *International Trade and Political Conflict: Commerce, Coalitions, and Mobility.* Princeton, NJ: Princeton University Press.

Hodgson, Geoffrey M. 2015. *Conceptualizing Capitalism: Institutions, Evolution, Future.* Chicago: University of Chicago Press.

Hoshi, Takeo, and Anil Kashyap. 2011. "Policy Options for Japan's Revival." National Institute for Research Advancement (NIRA) Report, January.

Hoshi, Takeo, and Anil Kashyap. 2012. "Why Did Japan Stop Growing?" National Institute for Research Advancement (NIRA) Report, June.

Hovenkamp, Herbert. 2005. *The Antitrust Enterprise: Principle and Execution.* Cambridge, MA: Harvard University Press.

Hsu, Shi-Ling. 2015. "The Rise and Rise of the One Percent: Considering Legal Causes of Wealth Inequality." *Emory Law Journal Online* 64: 2043–2072.

Huntington, Samuel P. 1952. "The Marasmus of the ICC: The Commission, the Railroads, and the Public Interest." *Yale Law Journal* 61: 467–509.

Ibata-Arens, Kathryn. 2005. *Innovation and Entrepreneurship in Japan: Politics, Organizations, and High Technology Firms.* New York: Cambridge University Press.

Ibata-Arens, Kathryn. 2008. "The Kyoto Model of Innovation and Entrepreneurship: Regional Innovation Systems and Cluster Culture." *Prometheus: Critical Studies in Innovation* 26: 89–109.

Ibata-Arens, Kathryn. 2015. "Japan's New Business Incubation Revolution." In *Handbook of East Asian Entrepreneurship,* edited by Tony Fu-Lai Yu and Ho-Don Yan, 145–156. New York: Routledge.

IBISWorld. 2017. "Domestic Arilines in the US." IBISWorld Industry Report 48111b. 2017. http://clients1.ibisworld.com/reports/us/industry/default.aspx?entid=1125.

Intellectual Property Strategy Headquarters. 2015. "'Chiteki zaisan suishin keikaku 2015' no gaiyou ni tsuite" [Outline of "Intellectual Property Strategic Program 2015"]. Tokyo: Intellectual Property Strategy Headquarters.

International Telecommunications Union. 2017. *ICT Facts and Figures 2017.* http://www.itu.int/en/ITU-D/Statistics/Pages/stat/default.aspx.

Jackson, Gregory. 2005. "Stakeholders under Pressure: Corporate Governance and Labor Management in Germany and Japan." *Corporate Governance: An International Review* 13: 419–428.

Japan Industrial Location Center. 2014. "2013 Local Economy Industrial Revitalization Survey Report." Tokyo.

Jensen, Michael C., and Kevin J. Murphy. 1990. "Performance Pay and Top Management Incentives." *The Journal of Political Economy* 98: 225–264.

Johnson, Chalmers. 1982. *MITI and the Japanese Miracle.* Stanford, CA: Stanford University Press.

Johnson, Simon, and James Kwak. 2010. *13 Bankers: The Wall Street Takeover and the Next Financial Meltdown.* New York: Pantheon Books.

Kagan, Robert A. 2001. *Adversarial Legalism: The American Way of Law.* Cambridge, MA: Harvard University Press.

Kagan, Robert A. 2010. "Fragmented Political Structures and Fragmented Law." *Jus Politicum* 4: 1–17.

Kagono Tadao. 2014. *Keiei wa dare no mono ka* [Who Controls Management?]. Tokyo: Nihon Keizai Shimbun.

Kahn, Alfred E. 2002. "The Deregulatory Tar Baby: The Precarious Balance between Regulation and Deregulation, 1970–2000 and Henceforward." *Journal of Regulatory Economics* 21: 35–56.

Kahneman, Daniel, and Amos Tversky 1979. "Prospect Theory: An Analysis of Decision under Risk." *Econometrica* 47: 263–91.

Kambayashi, Ryo, and Takao Kato. 2012. "Trends in Long-term Employment and Job Security in Japan and the United States: The Last Twenty-Five Years." Center on Japanese Economy and Business, Columbia University, Working Paper 302.

Kani, Masayo, and Kazuyuki Motohashi. 2011. "Does Pro-Patent Policy Spur Innovation? A Case of Software Industry in Japan." Paper presented at the Technology Management Conference (ITMC), San Jose, CA.

Katz, Richard. 2003. *Japanese Phoenix: The Long Road to Economic Revival.* Armonk, NY: M. E. Sharpe.

Keeler, Theodore E. 1984. "Theories of Regulation and the Deregulation Movement." *Public Choice* 44: 103–145.

Kelleher, Dennis, Stephen Hall, and Katelynn Bradley. 2012. "The Cost of the Wall Street-Caused Financial Collapse and Ongoing Economic Crisis Is More Than $12.8 Trillion." Washington, DC: Better Markets.

Kemp, Brodi. 2006. "Copyright's Digital Reformulation." In *How Revolutionary Was the Digital Revolution? National Responses, Market Transitions, and Global Technology,* edited by John Zysman and Abraham Newman, 379–390. Stanford, CA: Stanford Business Books.

Kenney, Martin. 2003. "The Growth and Development of the Internet in the United States." In *The Global Internet Economy,* edited by Bruce Kogut, 69–108. Cambridge, MA: MIT Press.

Kenney, Martin, and John Zysman. 2016. "The Rise of the Platform Economy." *Issues in Science and Technology* 32/3: 61–69.

Kim, Yee Kyoung, Keun Lee, Walter Park, and Kineung Choo. 2012. "Appropriate Intellectual Property Protection and Economic Growth in Countries at Different Levels of Development." *Research Policy* 41: 358–375.

King, Desmond, and Stewart Wood. 1999. "The Political Economy of Neoliberalism: Britain and the United States in the 1980s." In *Continuity and Change in Contemporary Capitalism,* edited by Herbert Kitschelt et al., 371–397. Cambridge: Cambridge University Press.

Kinney, Clay. 2001. "All Change for Japanese Accounting." *The Treasurer,* February, 58–60.

Kirihata, Tetsuya. 2010. "Current Situations and Issues in the Management of Japanese University Spinoffs." Graduate School of Economics, Kyoto University, Working Paper 114.

Kitschelt, Herbert. 1991. "Industrial Governance Structures, Innovation Strategies, and the Case of Japan: Sectoral or Cross-National Comparative Analysis?" *International Organization* 45: 453–493.

Krippner, Greta R. 2001. "The Elusive Market: Embeddedness and the Paradigm of Economic Sociology." *Theory and Society* 30: 775–810.

Krippner, Greta R. *Capitalizing on Crisis: The Political Origins of the Rise of Finance.* Cambridge, MA: Harvard University Press, 2011.

Kushida, Kenji E. 2011. "Leading without Followers: How Politics and Market Dynamics Trapped Innovations in Japan's Domestic 'Galapagos' Telecommunications Sector." *Journal of Industry, Competition, and Trade* 11: 279–307.

Kushida, Kenji E. 2012. "Entrepreneurship in Japan's ICT Sector: Opportunities and Protection for Japan's Telecommunications Regulatory Regime Shift." *Social Science Japan Journal* 15: 3–30.

Kushida, Kenji E. 2016A. "Governing ICT Networks Versus Governing the Information Economy: How Japan Discovered the Dilemma of Winning in the ICT Infrastructure

Race." In *Information Governance in Japan*, edited by Kenji E. Kushida, Yuko Kasuya, and Eiji Kawabata. Stanford, CA: Silicon Valley New Japan Project E-book Series.

Kushida, Kenji E. 2016B. "Japan's Startup Ecosystem: From Brave New World to Part of Syncretic 'New Japan.'" *Asian Research Policy* 7: 67–77.

Kuttner, Robert. 1996. *Everything for Sale: The Virtues and Limits of Markets*. Chicago: University of Chicago Press.

Kwak, James. 2014. "Cultural Capture and the Financial Crisis." In *Preventing Regulatory Capture: Special Interest Influence and How to Limit It*, edited by Daniel Carpenter and David A. Moss, 71–98. New York: Cambridge University Press.

Kwoka, John. 2015. *Mergers, Merger Control, and Remedies: A Retrospective Analysis of U.S. Policy*. Cambridge, MA: MIT Press.

Lakoff, George. 2006. *Whose Freedom? The Battle over America's Most Important Idea*. New York: Farrar, Straus & Giroux.

Landes, William M., and Richard A. Posner. 1981. "Market Power in Antitrust Cases: Concept and Measurement." *Harvard Law Review* 94: 937–996.

Landy, Marc K., and Martin A. Levin. 2007. "Creating Competitive Markets: The Politics of Market Design." In *Creating Competitive Markets: The Politics of Regulatory Reform*, edited by Mark K. Landy, Martin A. Levin, and Martin Shapiro, 1–22. Washington, DC: Brookings Institution Press.

Landy, Marc K., Martin A. Levin, and Martin Shapiro, eds. 2007. *Creating Competitive Markets: The Politics of Regulatory Reform*. Washington, DC: Brookings Institution Press.

Lavelle, Kathryn C. 2013. *Money and Banks in the American Political System*. New York: Cambridge University Press.

Lazonick, William. 2013. "The Fragility of the U.S. Economy: The Financialized Corporation and the Disappearing Middle Class." In *The Third Globalization: Can Wealthy Nations Stay Rich in the Twenty-First Century?*, edited by Dan Breznitz and John Zysman, 232–276. New York: Oxford University Press.

Lazonick, William. 2014. "Profits without Prosperity: Stock Buybacks Manipulate the Market and Leave Most Americans Worse Off." *Harvard Business Review*, September, 2–11.

Lazonick, William, and Mary O'Sullivan. 2000. "Maximizing Shareholder Value: A New Ideology for Corporate Governance." *Economy and Society* 29: 13–35.

Lechevalier, Sebastien. 2014. "Is Convergence towards the Silicon Valley Model the Only Way for the Japanese Innovation System?" In *The Great Transformation of Japanese Capitalism*, edited by Sebastien Lechavalier, 119–137. London: Routledge.

Lehne, Richard. 2001. *Government and Business: American Political Economy in Comparative Perspective*. New York: Chatham House.

Levitt, Arthur. 1998. "Testimony of Chairman Arthur Levitt Before the Senate Committee on Agriculture, Nutrition, and Forestry, Concerning the Regulation of the Over-the-Counter Derivatives Market and Hybrid Instruments," July 30, https://www.sec.gov/news/testimony/testarchive/1998/tsty0998.htm.

Levitt, Martin Jay, with Terry Conrow. 1993. *Confessions of a Union Buster*. New York: Crown.

Levy, Jonah, Mari Miura, and Gene Park. 2006. "Exiting *Étatisme*? New Directions in State Policy in France and Japan." In *The State after Statism*, edited by Jonah Levy, 92–146. Cambridge, MA: Harvard University Press.

Lincoln, James R., and Michael L. Gerlach. 2004. *Japan's Network Economy: Structure, Persistence, and Change*. New York: Cambridge University Press.

Lindblom, Charles E. 1977. *Politics and Markets: The World's Political-Economic Systems*. New York: Basic Books.

Lippoldt, Douglas. 2009. "Innovation and IPR Protection in the Digital Era: The Case of High Income Countries 1990–2005." *Journal of Innovation Economics & Management* 4: 171–191.

Litt, David G., Jonathan R. Macey, Geoffrey P. Miller, and Edward L. Rubin. 1990. "Politics, Bureaucracies, and Financial Markets: Bank Entry into Commercial Paper Underwriting in the United States and Japan." *University of Pennsylvania Law Review* 139: 369–453.

Littlechild, Stephen. 1983. *Regulation of British Telecommunications Profitability*. London: Department of Industry.

Logan, John. 2002. "Consultants, Lawyers and the Union Free Movement in the USA since the 1970s." *Industrial Relations Journal* 33: 197–214.

Lynn, Barry C. 2010. *Cornered: The New Monopoly Capitalism and the Economics of Destruction*. Hoboken, NJ: John Wiley & Sons.

MacAvoy, Paul W. 2007. *The Unsustainable Costs of Partial Deregulation*. New Haven, CT: Yale University Press.

Macey, Jonathan R. 2007. "Regulation in Banking: A Mechanism for Forcing Market Solutions." In *Creating Competitive Markets: The Politics of Regulatory Reform*, edited by Mark K. Landy, Martin A. Levin, and Martin Shapiro, 43–59. Washington, DC: Brookings Institution Press.

Martinez, Mark A. 2009. *The Myth of the Free Market: The Role of the State in a Capitalist Economy*. Sterling, VA: Kumarian Press.

Maskus, Keith, and Christine McDaniel. 1999. "Impacts of the Japanese Patent System on Productivity Growth." *Japan and the World Economy* 11: 557–574.

Mazzucato, Mariana. 2014. *The Entrepreneurial State: Debunking Public vs. Private Sector Myths*. London: Anthem Press.

McCloskey, Deirdre. 1998. "Other Things Equal: The So-Called Coase Theorem." *Eastern Economic Journal* 24: 367–371.

McKenzie, Donald. 2007. "The Political Economy of Carbon Trading." *The London Review of Books*, April 5, 29–31.

McKinley, William, Jun Zhao, and Kathleen Garrett Rust. 2000. "A Sociocognitive Interpretation of Organizational Downsizing." *Academy of Management Review* 25: 227–243.

McMillan, John. 2002. *Reinventing the Bazaar: A Natural History of Markets*. New York: W. W. Norton.

Menard, Claude, ed. 2004. *The International Library of New Institutional Economics*, 7 volumes. Cheltenham, UK: Edward Elgar.

Menard, Claude, and Mary M. Shirley, eds. 2005. *Handbook of New Institutional Economics*. Dordrecht: Springer.

Mercatus Center, George Mason University. 2017. "Mercatus RegData," https://quantgov.org/regdata/.

Merges, Robert P., and Richard R. Nelson. 1990. "On the Complex Economics of Patent Scope." *Columbia Law Review* 90: 839–916.

Ministry of Economy, Trade, and Industry. 2005. "Kigyou kachi kabunushi kyoudou no rieki no kakuho matawa koujou no tame no baishuu boueisaku ni kansuru shishin" [Guidelines for Takeover Defenses to Preserve and Enhance Corporate Value and Shareholder's Common Interests]. Tokyo: Ministry of Economy, Trade, and Industry.

Ministry of Economy, Trade, and Industry. 2006. "Second Term Medium-Range Industrial Cluster Plan." Tokyo: Ministry of Economy, Trade, and Industry.

Ministry of Economy, Trade, and Industry. 2008. "Kinji no shokankyou no henka o fumaeta baishuu boueisaku no arikata" [The Role of Takeover Defense Measures in Light of Changes in the Environment]. Tokyo: Ministry of Economy, Trade, and Industry.

Ministry of Economy, Trade, and Industry. 2010. "Jouhou keizai kakushin senryaku (gaiyou)" [Information Economy Renovation Strategy (Summary)]. Tokyo: Ministry of Economy, Trade, and Industry.

Ministry of Economy, Trade, and Industry. 2014A. "Nihon no 'kasegu chikara' soushutsu ken-kyuukai" [Study Group to Promote Japan's Profitability], May 20. Tokyo: Ministry of Economy, Trade, and Industry.

Ministry of Economy, Trade, and Industry. 2014B. "Nihon no miryoku o ikashita aratana kachi souzou sangyou no soushutsu ni mukete" [Generating New Value Creation Industries that Capitalize on Japan's Strengths]. Tokyo: Ministry of Economy, Trade, and Industry.

Ministry of Economy, Trade, and Industry. 2015. "Junsui mochikabugaisha jittai chousa" [Survey of Pure Holding Companies]. Tokyo: Ministry of Economy, Trade, and Industry.

Ministry of Economy, Trade, and Industry. 2017. *White Paper on Small Enterprises in Japan*. Tokyo: Ministry of Economy, Trade, and Industry.

Ministry of Health, Labor, and Welfare. 2016. "Seiki koyou to hiseiki koyou roudousha no suii" [Changes in Regular and Non-Regular Workers]. Tokyo: Ministry of Health, Labor and Welfare.

Ministry of Internal Affairs and Communications. 2010. "Wagakuni no ICT kokusai kyousouryoku no genjoutou ni suite" [Japan's International Competitiveness in ICT]. Tokyo: Ministry of Health, Labor, and Welfare.

Ministry of Internal Affairs and Communications, Administrative Evaluation Bureau. 2016. "Kyoninkatou no touitsuteki haaku no kekka ni tsuite" [An Overall Assessment of Government Regulations]. Tokyo: Ministry of Internal Affairs and Communications.

Ministry of Internal Affairs and Communications. 2017A. Roudouryoku chousa [Labor Force Survey]. http://www.stat.go.jp/data/roudou/index.htm.

Ministry of Internal Affairs and Communications. 2017B. *Jouhou tsuushin hakusho* [Information and Communications White Paper]. Tokyo: Ministry of Internal Affairs and Communications.

Mishel, Lawrence, and Alyssa Davis. 2015. "Top CEOS Make 300 Times More Than Typical Workers: Pay Growth Surpasses Stock Gains and Wage Growth of Top 0.1 Percent." Economic Policy Institute, Issue Brief #399, June 21.

Miura, Mari. 2012. *Welfare Through Work: Conservative Ideas, Partisan Dynamics, and Social Protection in Japan*. Ithaca, NY: Cornell University Press.

Moss, David A. 2002. *When All Else Fails: Government as the Ultimate Risk Manager*. Cambridge, MA: Harvard University Press.

Motohashi, Kazuyuki. 2003. "Japan's Patent System and Business Innovation: Reassessing Pro-Patent Policies." The Research Institute of Economy, Trade and Industry Discussion Paper Series 03-E-020. Tokyo: Ministry of Economy, Trade, and Industry.

Motohashi, Kazuyuki, and Shingo Muramatsu. 2011. "Examining the University Industry Collaboration Policy in Japan: Patent Analysis." Research Institute of Economy, Trade and Industry (RIETI), Discussion Paper Series 11-E-008. Tokyo: Ministry of Economy, Trade, and Industry.

Mowery, David C., and Nathan Rosenberg. 1993. "The U.S. National Innovation System." In *National Innovation Systems: A Comparative Analysis*, edited by Richard R. Nelson, 29–75. Oxford: Oxford University Press.

National Commission on the Causes of the Financial and Economic Crisis in the United States. 2011. *The Financial Crisis Inquiry Report*. New York: Public Affairs.

Nee, Victor, and Richard Swedberg, eds. 2005. *The Economic Sociology of Capitalism*. Princeton, NJ: Princeton University Press.

Nelson, Richard, ed. 2005. *The Limits of Market Organization*. New York: Russell Sage Foundation.

New America Foundation. 2014. "The Cost of Connectivity: Data and Analysis on Broadband Offerings in 24 Cities across the World." https://www.newamerica.org/oti/policy-papers/the-cost-of-connectivity-2014/.

Newman, Abraham, and John Zysman. 2006. "Transforming Politics in the Digital Era." In *How Revolutionary Was the Digital Revolution? National Responses, Market Transitions and Global Technology*, edited by J. Zysman and A. Newman, 391–411. Stanford, CA: Stanford University Press.

Nickell, Stephen J. 1996. "Competition and Corporate Performance." *Journal of Political Economy* 104: 724–746.

Nishimura, Junichi, and Hiroyuki Okamuro. 2011. "R&D Productivity and the Organization of Cluster Policy: An Empirical Evaluation of the Industrial Cluster Project in Japan." *Journal of Technology Transfer* 36: 117–144.

Noll, Roger G., and Bruce M. Owen. 1983. *The Political Economy of Deregulation: Interest Groups in the Regulatory Process*. Washington, DC: American Enterprise Institute.

Nooteboom, Bart. 2014. *How Markets Work and Fail, and What to Make of Them*. Cheltenham, UK: Edward Elgar.

North, Douglass C. 1977. "Markets and Other Allocation Systems in History: The Challenge of Karl Polanyi." *Journal of European Economic History* 6: 703–716.

North, Douglass C. 1981. *Structure and Change in Economic History*. New York: W. W. Norton.

North, Douglass C. 1986. "The New Institutional Economics." *Journal of Institutional and Theoretical Economics* 142: 230–237.

North, Douglass C. 1990. *Institutions, Institutional Change and Economic Performance*. Cambridge: Cambridge University Press.

Novak, William J. 2013. "A Revisionist History of Regulatory Capture." In *Preventing Regulatory Capture: Special Interest Influence and How to Limit It*, edited by Daniel Carpenter and David A. Moss, 25–48. New York: Cambridge University Press.

Office of the Federal Register. 2017. https://www.federalregister.gov/reader-aids/understanding-the-federal-register/federal-register-statistics.

Okimoto, Daniel. 1989. *Between MITI and the Market: Japanese Industrial Policy for High Technology*. Stanford, CA: Stanford University Press.

O'Neill, Richard. 2014. "Toward Better, More Efficient Capacity Market Design." Presentation to the Harvard Electricity Policy Group, Cambridge, MA, February 22.

O'Neill, Richard, and Udi Helman. 2007. "Regulatory Reform of the U.S. Wholesale Electricity Markets." In *Creating Competitive Markets: The Politics of Regulatory Reform*, edited by Mark K. Landy, Martin A. Levin, and Martin Shapiro, 128–156. Washington, DC: Brookings Institution Press.

Orbach, Barak. 2015. "A State of Inaction: Regulatory Preferences, Rent, and Income Inequality." *Theoretical Inquiries in Law* 16: 45–68.

Organisation for Economic Co-operation and Development. 2015. *Product Market Regulation Statistics*. http://www.oecd-ilibrary.org/economics/data/oecd-product-market-regulation-statistics_pmr-data-en.

Organisation for Economic Co-operation and Development. 2017A. *Entrepreneurship at a Glance 2017*. http://www.oecd-ilibrary.org/employment/entrepreneurship-at-a-glance-2017_entrepreneur_aag-2017-en.

Organisation for Economic Co-operation and Development. 2017B. Broadband Portal. http://www.oecd.org/sti/broadband/oecdbroadbandportal.htm.

Ornston, Darius. 2013. "How the Nordic Nations Stay Rich: Governing Sectoral Shifts in Denmark, Finland, and Sweden." In *The Third Globalization: Can Wealthy Nations Stay Rich in the Twenty-First Century?*, edited by Dan Breznitz and John Zysman, 300–322. New York: Oxford University Press.

O'Sullivan, Mary A. 2000. *Contests for Corporate Control: Corporate Governance and Economic Performance in the United States and Germany*. Cambridge: Cambridge University Press.

Oye, Kenneth. 1985. "Explaining Cooperation under Anarchy: Hypotheses and Strategies. *World Politics* 38: 1–24.

Palmer, Andrew. 2015. *Smart Money: How High-Stakes Financial Innovation is Reshaping Our World—for the Better*. New York: Basic Books.

Park, Gene. 2011. *Spending without Taxation: FILP and the Politics of Public Finance in Japan*. Stanford, CA: Stanford University Press.

Peltzman, Sam. 1989. "The Economic Theory of Regulation after a Decade of Deregulation." In *Brookings Papers: Microeconomics 1989*, 1–59. Washington, DC: Brookings Institution Press.

Pempel, T. J. 1978. "Japanese Foreign Economic Policy: the Domestic Bases for International Behavior." In *Between Power and Plenty: Foreign Economic Policies of Advanced Industrial States*, edited by Peter J. Katzenstein, 139–190. Madison: University of Wisconsin Press.

Pempel, T. J., and Keiichi Tsunekawa. 1979. "Corporatism without Labor? The Japanese Anomaly." In *Trends toward Corporatist Intermediation*, edited by Philippe C. Schmitter and Gerhard Lehmbruch, 231–270. London: Sage.

Petersen. Neils. 2013. "Antitrust Law and the Promotion of Democracy and Economic Growth." *Journal of Competition Law & Economics* 9: 593–636.

Pettit, Philip. 1996. "Freedom as Antipower." *Ethics* 106: 576–604.

Pettit, Philip. 2006. "Freedom in the Market." *Politics, Philosophy, and Economics* 5: 131–149.

Philippon, Thomas. 2012. "Finance versus Wal-Mart: Why Are Financial Services so Expensive?" In *Rethinking the Financial Crisis*, edited by Alan S. Blinder, Andrew W. Lo, and Robert M. Solow, 235–246. New York: Russell Sage.

Philippon, Thomas. 2015. "Has the US Finance Industry Become Less Efficient? On the Theory and Measurement of Financial Intermediation." *American Economic Review* 105: 1408–1438.

Pistor, Katharina. 2013. "A Legal Theory of Finance." *Journal of Comparative Economics* 41: 315–330.

Polanyi, Karl. 1944. *The Great Transformation: The Political and Economic Origins of Our Time*. Boston: Beacon Press.

Posner, Richard. 1979. "The Chicago School of Antitrust Analysis." *University of Pennsylvania Law Review* 127: 925–948.

Posner, Richard. 1984. "Some Economics of Labor Law." *University of Chicago Law Review* 51: 988–1005.

Prasad, Monica. 2012. *The Land of Too Much: American Abundance and the Paradox of Poverty*. Cambridge, MA: Harvard University Press.

Rader, Randall, Colleen Chien, and David Hricik. 2013. "Make Patent Trolls Pay in Court." *New York Times*, June 5, A21.

Rajan, Raghuram G. 2005. "Has Financial Development Made the World Riskier?" Paper presented at Federal Reserve Bank of Kansas City Symposium, Jackson Hole, Wyoming, August 27.

Rajan, Raghuram G., and Luigi Zingales. 2003. *Saving Capitalism from the Capitalists*. Princeton, NJ: Princeton University Press.

Ramanna, Karthik. 2015. *Political Standards: Corporate Interest, Ideology, and Leadership in the Shaping of Accounting Rules for the Market Economy*. Chicago: University of Chicago Press.

Reback, Gary. 2009. *Free the Market: Why Only Government Can Keep the Marketplace Competitive*. New York: Penguin Group.

Regulatory Studies Center, George Washington University. 2016. "Reg Stats." https://regulatorystudies.columbian.gwu.edu/reg-stats.

Reich, Robert B. 2015. *Saving Capitalism: For the Many, Not the Few*. New York: Alfred A. Knopf.

Reinhart, Carmen M., and Kenneth S. Rogoff. 2009. *This Time Is Different: Eight Centuries of Financial Folly*. Princeton, NJ: Princeton University Press.

Renda, Andrea, et al. 2007. "Making Antitrust Damages Actions More Effective in the EU: Welfare Impact and Potential Scenarios." Report for the European Commission. Brussels, Rome, and Rotterdam: European Commission.

Rodrick, Dani. 2007. *One Economics, Many Recipes: Globalization, Institutions, and Economic Growth*. Princeton, NJ: Princeton University Press.

Rodrick, Dani. 2015. *Economics Rules: The Rights and Wrongs of the Dismal Science*. New York: W.W. Norton.

Rogowski, Ronald. 1989. *Commerce and Coalitions: How Trade Affects Domestic Political Alignments*. Princeton, NJ: Princeton University Press.

Rose, Elizabeth, and Kiyohiko Ito. 2005. "Widening the Family Circle: Spin-Offs in the Japanese Service Sector." *Long Range Planning* 38: 9–26.

Rosenbloom, Joshua L., and William A. Sundstrom. 2009. "Labor Market Regimes in U.S. Economic History." National Bureau of Economic Research Working Paper No. 15055, June.

Roth, Alvin E. 2015. *Who Gets What—and Why*. Boston: Houghton Mifflin Harcourt.

Roubini, Nouriel. 2008. "The Rising Risk of a Systemic Financial Meltdown: The Twelve Steps to Financial Disaster." *EconoMonitor*, February 5, http://www.economonitor.com/nouriel/2008/page/18/.

Rtischev, Dimitry, and Robert Cole. 2003. "Social and Structural Barriers to the IT Revolution in High Tech Industry." In *Roadblocks on the Information Highway: The IT Revolution in Japanese Education*, edited by Jane Bachnik, 127–153. New York: Lexington Books.

Rubinfeld, Daniel L. 1998, "Antitrust Enforcement in Dynamic Network Industries." *The Antitrust Bulletin* 43: 859–882.

Sakakibara, Mariko, and Lee Branstetter. 2001. "Do Stronger Patents Induce More Innovation? Evidence from the 1988 Japanese Patent Law Reforms." *Rand Journal of Economics* 32: 77–100.

Saito, Atsushi. 2010. "Executive Compensation & Corporate Governance." Tokyo: Tokyo Stock Exchange.

Sako, Mari. 2007. "Organizational Diversity and Institutional Change: Evidence from Financial and Labor Markets in Japan." In *Corporate Governance in Japan: Institutional Change and Organizational Diversity*, edited by Masahiko Aoki, Gregory Jackson, and Hideaki Miyajima, 399–426. Oxford: Oxford University Press.

Samuels, Richard. 1987. *The Business of the Japanese State: Energy Markets in Comparative and Historical Perspective*. Ithaca, NY: Cornell University Press.

Samuelson, Pamela. 2007. "Preliminary Thoughts on Copyright Reform." *Utah Law Review* 2007: 551–571.

Samuelson, Pamela. 2013. "Book Review: Is Copyright Reform Possible?" *Harvard Law Review* 126: 740–779.

Saxenian, Annalee. 1994. *Regional Advantage: Culture and Competition in Silicon Valley and Route 128*. Cambridge, MA: Harvard University Press.

Schaede, Ulrike. 2000. *Cooperative Capitalism: Self-Regulation, Trade Associations, and the Antimonopoly Law in Japan*. Oxford: Oxford University Press.

Schaede, Ulrike. 2008. *Choose and Focus: Japanese Business Strategies for the 21st Century*. Ithaca, NY: Cornell University Press.

Scheffler, Richard M., Daniel R. Arnold, Brent D. Fulton, and Sherry A. Glied. 2016. "Differing Impacts of Market Concentration on Affordable Care Act Marketplace Premiums." *Health Affairs* 35: 880–888.

Scheffler, Richard M., and Sherry Glied. 2016. "How to Contain Health Care Costs." *New York Times*, May 3, A21.

Schivardi, Fabiano, and Eliana Viviano. 2011. "Entry Barriers in Retail Trade." *The Economic Journal* 121: 145–170.

Scott Morton, Fiona M., and Carl Shapiro. 2014. "Strategic Patent Acquisitions." *Antitrust Law Journal* 2: 463–499.

Securities and Exchange Commission. 2009. "Report and Recommendations Pursuant to Section 133 of the Emergency Economic Stabilization Act of 2008: Study on Mark-to-Market Accounting," December 30. Washington, D.C.: Securities and Exchange Commission.

Shapiro, Carl. 2000. "Navigating the Patent Thicket: Cross Licenses, Patent Pools, and Standard Setting." *Innovation Policy and the Economy* 1: 119–150.

Shiller, Robert J. 2007. "Bubble Trouble." *Project Syndicate*, September 17, https://www.project-syndicate.org/commentary/bubble-trouble?barrier=accessreg.

Shiller, Robert. 2012. *Finance and the Good Society*. Princeton, NJ: Princeton University Press.

Shishido, Zenichi. 2014A. "Introduction: The Incentive Bargain of the Firm and Enterprise Law: A Nexus of Contracts, Markets, and Laws." In *Enterprise Law: Contracts, Markets, and Laws in the US and Japan*, edited by Zenichi Shishido, 1–49. Cheltenham, UK: Edward Elgar.

Shishido, Zenichi. 2014B. "Does Law Matter to Financial Capitalism? The Case of Japanese Entrepreneurs." *Fordham International Law Journal* 37: 1087–1127.

Shoji, Yuki. 2009. "Evaluation of the Competition Policy to Encourage MVNO System in Japan." Ninth Annual International Symposium on Applications and the Internet, Bellevue, WA, July 20–24.

Singer, Joseph William. 2015. *No Freedom without Regulation: The Hidden Lessons of the Subprime Crisis*. New Haven, CT: Yale University Press.

Smelser, Neil J., and Richard Swedberg, eds. 2005. *The Handbook of Economic Sociology*, 2nd ed. Princeton, NJ: Princeton University Press.

Smith, Adam. 1976. *An Inquiry into the Nature and Causes of the Wealth of Nations*, edited by Edwin Cannan. Chicago: University of Chicago Press.

Soskice, David. 1999. "Divergent Production Regimes: Coordinated and Uncoordinated Market Economies in the 1980s and 1990s." In *Continuity and Change in Contemporary Capitalism*, edited by Herbert Kitschelt, Peter Lange, Gary Marks, and John D. Stephens, 101–134. Cambridge: Cambridge University Press.

Spencer Stuart. 2017. *2016 Spencer Stuart Board Index: A Perspective on U.S. Boards*. https://www.spencerstuart.com/~/media/pdf%20files/research%20and%20insight%20pdfs/spencer-stuart-us-board-index-2016_july2017.pdf?la=en.

Statista. 2017. https://www.statista.com/statistics/268237/global-market-share-held-by-operating-systems-since-2009/.

Stern, Jon. 2003. "What the Littlechild Report Actually Said." In *The UK Model of Utility Regulation: A 20th Anniversary Collection to Mark the "Littlechild Report" Retrospect and Prospect*, edited by Ian Bartle, 7–30. Bath, UK: University of Bath, Centre for the Study of Regulated Industries.

Stigler, George. 1964. "A Theory of Oligopoly." *Journal of Political Economy* 72: 44–61.

Stigler, George. 1971. "The Theory of Economic Regulation." *Bell Journal of Economics and Management Science* 2: 3–21.

Stiglitz, Joseph E. 2002. *Globalization and Its Discontents*. New York: W. W. Norton.

Stiglitz, Joseph E. 2010. *Freefall: America, Free Markets, and the Sinking of the World Economy*. New York: W. W. Norton.

Stiglitz, Joseph E. 2014. "Tapping the Brakes: Are Less Active Markets Safer and Better for the Economy?" Presentation at the Federal Reserve Bank of Atlanta Financial Markets Conference, Atlanta, Georgia, April 15.

Stiglitz, Joseph. 2015. *The Great Divide: Unequal Societies and What We Can Do about Them*. New York: W. W. Norton.

Stiglitz, Joseph. 2016. *Rewriting the Rules of the American Economy: An Agenda for Growth and Shared Prosperity*. New York: W. W. Norton.

Streeck, Wolfgang. 2009. *Re-Forming Capitalism: Institutional Change in the German Political Economy*. New York: Oxford University Press.

Sudo, Miya, and Simon Newman. 2014. "Japanese Copyright Law Reform: Introduction of the Mysterious Anglo-American Fair Use Doctrine or an EU Style Divine Intervention via Competition Law? *Intellectual Property Quarterly* 18: 40–70.

Takenaka, Toshiko. 2009. "Success or Failure? Japan's National Strategy on Intellectual Property and Evaluation of Its Impact from the Comparative Law Perspective." *Washington University Global Studies Law Review* 8: 379–398.

Tanzi, Vito. 2011. *Government versus Markets: The Changing Economic Role of the State*. Cambridge: Cambridge University Press.

Taylor, Robert S. 2013. "Market Freedom as Antipower." *American Political Science Review* 107: 593–602.

Thaler, Richard H., and Sendhil Mullainathan. 2008. "Behavioral Economics." In *Concise Encyclopedia of Economics*, 2nd ed., edited by David R. Henderson. Library of Economics and Liberty. http://www.econlib.org/library/Enc/BehavioralEconomics.html.

Thelen, Kathleen. 1999. "Historical Institutionalism in Comparative Politics." *Annual Review of Political Science* 2: 369–404. Indianapolis: Library of Economics and Liberty.

Thelen, Kathleen. 2014. *Varieties of Liberalization and the New Politics of Social Solidarity*. Cambridge: Cambridge University Press.

Tiberghien, Yves. 2007. *Entrepreneurial States: Reforming Corporate Governance in France, Japan, and Korea*. Ithaca, NY: Cornell University Press.

Tokyo Stock Exchange. 2016A. "2015 nendo kabushiki bunpu joukyou chousa kekka no gaiyou" [An Overview of the 2015 Stock Allocation Survey Results]. Tokyo: Tokyo Stock Exchange.

Tokyo Stock Exchange. 2016B. "How Listed Companies Have Addressed Japan's Corporate Governance Code." Tokyo: Tokyo Stock Exchange.

Tokyo Stock Exchange. 2017. *Kooporeeto gabanansu hakusho* [White Paper on Corporate Governance]. Tokyo: Tokyo Stock Exchange.

Toya, Tetsuro. 2003. *Kinyuu bigguban no seijikeizaigaku* [The Political Economy of the Japanese Financial Big Bang]. Tokyo: Toyo Keizai Shimposha.

Turner, Adair. 2012. *Economics after the Crisis: Objectives and Means.* Cambridge, MA: MIT Press.

Tyson, Laura D'Andrea, and John Zysman. 1989. "Preface: The Argument Outlined." In *Politics and Productivity: The Real Story of Why Japan Works*, edited by Chalmers Johnson, Tyson, and Zysman, xiii–xxi. Cambridge, MA: Ballinger.

Ueno, Hiroshi, Takashi Murakoso, and Takumi Hirai. 2006. "Supplier System and Innovation Policy in Japan." In *Small Firms and Innovation Policy in Japan*, edited by Cornelia Storz, 137–150. London: Routledge.

United Nations Conference on Trade and Development. 2017. UNCTADStat. http://unctadstat. unctad.org/wds/TableViewer/tableView.aspx?ReportId=15849.

United States Census Bureau. 2017. Business Dynamics Statistics. https://www.census.gov/ces/dataproducts/bds/data_estab2015.html.

Useem, Michael. 1996. *Investor Capitalism: How Money Managers are Changing the Face of Corporate America.* New York: Basic Books/HarperCollins.

Véron, Nicolas, Mattieu Autret, and Alfred Galichon. 2006. *Smoke & Mirrors, Inc.: Accounting for Capitalism*, translated by George Holoch. Ithaca, NY: Cornell University Press.

Vietor, Richard H. K. 1994. *Contrived Competition: Regulation and Deregulation in America.* Cambridge, MA: Harvard University Press.

Vogel, David. 1989. *Fluctuating Fortunes: The Political Power of Business in America.* New York: Basic Books.

Vogel, David. 1995. *Trading Up: Consumer and Environmental Regulation in a Global Economy.* Cambridge, MA: Harvard University Press.

Vogel, David. 2008. "Private Global Business Regulation." *Annual Review of Political Science* 11: 261–282.

Vogel, Steven K. 1994. "The Bureaucratic Approach to the Financial Revolution: Japan's Ministry of Finance and Financial System Reform." *Governance* 3: 219–243.

Vogel, Steven K. 1996. *Freer Markets, More Rules: Regulatory Reform in Advanced Industrial Countries.* Ithaca, NY: Cornell University Press.

Vogel, Steven K. 1997. "International Games with National Rules: How Regulation Shapes Competition in 'Global' Markets." *Journal of Public Policy* 17: 169–193.

Vogel, Steven K. 1999. "When Interests Are Not Preferences: The Cautionary Tale of Japanese Consumers." *Comparative Politics* 31: 187–207.

Vogel, Steven K. 2001. "The Crisis of German and Japanese Capitalism: Stalled on the Road to the Liberal Market Model?" *Comparative Political Studies* 34: 1103–1133.

Vogel, Steven K. 2006. *Japan Remodeled: How Government and Industry Are Reforming Japanese Capitalism.* Ithaca, NY: Cornell University Press.

Vogel, Steven K. 2007. "Why Freer Markets Need More Rules." In *Creating Competitive Markets: The Politics of Regulatory Reform*, edited by Mark K. Landy, Martin A. Levin, and Martin Shapiro, 25–42. Washington, DC: Brookings Institution Press.

Vogel, Steven K. 2013. "Japan's Information Technology Challenge." In *The Third Globalization: Can Wealthy Nations Stay Rich in the Twenty-First Century?*, edited by Dan Breznitz and John Zysman, 350–372. New York: Oxford University Press.

Von Mises, Ludwig. 2011. *A Critique of Interventionism.* Auburn, AL: Ludwig von Mises Institute.

Wallison, Peter J. 2011. "Financial Crisis Inquiry Commission Dissenting Statement." In *The Financial Crisis Inquiry Report*, by the National Commission on the Causes of the Financial and Economic Crisis in the United States, 441–450. New York: Public Affairs.

Weare, Christopher. 2003. "The California Electricity Crisis: Causes and Policy Options." San Francisco: Public Policy Institute of California.

Weber, Max. 1958. *The Protestant Ethic and the Spirit of Capitalism*, translated by Talcott Parsons. New York: Scribners.

Weber, Steven. 2005. *The Success of Open Source*. Boston: Harvard University Press.

Weber, Steven. 2006. "From Linux to Lipitor: Pharma and the Coming Reconfiguration of Intellectual Property." In *How Revolutionary Was the Digital Revolution? National Responses, Market Transitions and Global Technology*, edited by John Zysman and Abraham Newman, 217–233. Stanford, CA: Stanford University Press.

Weinstein, David E. 2001. "Historical, Structural, and Macroeconomic Perspectives on the Japanese Economic Crisis." In *Japan's New Economy: Continuity and Change in the Twenty-First Century*, edited by Magnus Blomström, Byron Gangnes, and Sumner La Croix, 29–47. Oxford: Oxford University Press.

Western, Bruce. 1995. "A Comparative Study of Working Class Disorganization: Union Decline in 18 Advanced Capitalist Countries." *American Sociological Review* 60: 179–201.

Western, Bruce, and Jake Rosenfeld. 2011. "Unions, Norms, and the Rise in U.S. Wage Inequality." *American Sociological Review* 76: 513–537.

White, Harrison C. 1981. "Where Do Markets Come From?" *American Journal of Sociology* 87: 517–547.

Williamson, Oliver E. 1968. "Economies as an Antitrust Defense: The Welfare Tradeoffs." *American Economic Review* 58: 18–36.

Williamson, Oliver E. 1985. *The Economic Institutions of Capitalism*. New York: Free Press.

Williamson, Oliver E. 1996. *The Mechanisms of Governance*. Oxford: Oxford University Press.

Williamson, Oliver E. 2000. "The New Institutional Economics: Taking Stock, Looking Ahead." *Journal of Economic Literature* 38: 595–613.

Williamson, Oliver E., and Scott E. Master, eds. 1995. *Transaction Cost Economics*, 2 volumes. Aldershot, UK: Edward Elgar.

Wilensky, Harold L. 2002. *Rich Democracies: Political Economy, Public Policy, and Performance*. Berkeley and Los Angeles: University of California Press.

Wilensky, Harold L. 2012. *American Political Economy in Global Perspective*. New York: Cambridge University Press.

Wilks, Stephen. 2010. "Competition Policy." In *The Oxford Handbook of Business and Government*, edited by David Coen, Wyn Grant, and Graham Wilson. Oxford: Oxford University Press. http://www.oxfordhandbooks.com/view/10.1093/oxfordhb/9780199214273.001.0001/oxfordhb-9780199214273.

Winston, Clifford. 2006. *Government Failure versus Market Failure: Microeconomics Policy Research and Government Performance*. Washington, DC: AEI-Brookings Joint Center for Regulatory Studies.

Witt, Michael A. 2006. *Changing Japanese Capitalism: Societal Coordination and Institutional Adjustment*. New York: Cambridge University Press.

Wolf, Charles. 1988. *Markets or Governments: Choosing between Imperfect Alternatives*. Cambridge, MA: MIT Press.

Woll, Cornelia. 2008. *Firm Interests: How Governments Shape Business Lobbying on Global Trade*. Ithaca, NY: Cornell University Press.

Womack, James P., Daniel T. Jones, and Daniel Roos. 1990. *The Machine That Changed the World*. New York: Rawson Associates.

World Bank. 2002. *World Development Report 2002: Building Institutions for Markets*. Oxford: Oxford University Press.

World Bank. 2017. *Doing Business 2017: Equal Opportunity for All*. Washington, DC: World Bank.

Yarbrough, Beth V., and Robert M. Yarbrough. 1987. "Cooperation in the Liberalization of International Trade: After Hegemony, What?" *International Organization* 41: 1–26.

Yergin, Daniel, and Joseph Stanislaw. 1998. *The Commanding Heights: The Battle between Government and the Marketplace That Is Remaking the Modern World*. New York: Simon & Schuster.

Yoo, Christopher S. 2008. "The Enduring Lessons of the Breakup of AT&T: A Twenty-Five Year Retrospective." *Federal Communications Law Journal* 61: 1–10.

Zysman, John. 1983. *Governments, Markets, and Growth: Finance and the Politics of Industrial Change.* Ithaca, NY: Cornell University Press.

Zysman, John. 2006. "Creating Value in a Digital Era; How Do Wealthy Nations Stay Wealthy?" In *How Revolutionary Was the Digital Revolution? National Responses, Market Transitions, and Global Technology,* edited by John Zysman and Abraham Newman, 23–52. Stanford: Stanford University Press.

INDEX